China has become the most relevant market for luxury goods worldwide and its effect is reshaping the industry well beyond its boundaries. At Puig we have been present in China for many years, with the objective of building our brands with a long term perspective. It has been fascinating to see at which pace consumer habits have evolved. What took decades in other areas of the world, has taken just a few years in China. These highly paced changes in consumer behavior linked to the fact that the ecosystem is absolutely unique has posed a real challenge to many Western brand owners developing their brands in this unique market. This book offers very interesting insights on the different realities of this ecosystem and the role of the different forces that interrelate in it. It has helped us get a better understanding and a new perspective to what it takes to successfully build your brands and your business in China.

*— Javier Bach, COO of Puig Beauty & Fashion*

FMCG executives all over the world need to understand how the Chinese retail and digital ecosystem is already completely redefining consumers expectations from their brands. This eye-opening and insightful book can help you prepare for the new world coming your way.

*— Patrice Bula, Executive Vice President Nestlé S.A.,*
*Head of Strategic Business Units, Marketing, Sales and*
*President Nespresso (2011–2021)*

New retail is one of the most visible examples of China's undisputed areas of leadership. This book does an excellent job of describing what it is and its various business models. More importantly through its comprehensive analyses, it unfolds all its complexity and phenomenal impact within the country and on the rest of the world.

New retail starts from consumer intimacy, is built upon excellence in supply chain, uses creativity and technology to deliver the ultimate experiential retail or "Retailtainment" as delineated and further prescribed by the authors.

We live in times of constant disruption. Through this book everyone can see how a profound transformation can be the only way forward.

*— Gianfranco Casati, CEO of Accenture Growth Markets*

In my 30 years of living and working in China, this is the first book that I have read that fully articulates and analyzes the history and key players involved in the e-commerce revolution in China. It is a must-read for anyone or any company that wants to enter the China retail market, to expand its presence in China, or to learn about global e-commerce trends.

— Mei-Wei Cheng, Former Chairman and CEO of GE (China)
and Ford Motor (China), President and CEO Siemens China, and
President and COO of AT&T China

The IMD authors understand in depth the Chinese business culture and traditions, and are able to overlay this knowledge on the western ways of doing business. The outcome is an inventory of opportunities to catch, of potential threats to assess and anticipate, and often a wake-up call to re-think strategies. China is way ahead when it comes down to e-commerce; this is a fact. As I have observed in sectors like banking, insurance or telecoms, we in the West often hide ourselves behind excuses to explain why we are behind. Different privacy concepts, stricter regulatory rules. Maybe, but what about audacity, creativity and speed of action? It's not too late to read this book, and decide whether we want to be leaders or followers.

— Michel Demaré, Chairman of IMD Business School and
Deputy Chairman of Louis Dreyfus Company

Professor Nie and her coauthors have done a great service by articulating clearly the incredible digital retail phenomenon happening in China. Our company has been trying to crack the Chinese market in a big way for 30 years by extending our business model from the West into China. Now leveraging the new retail trends, we build our Modern Agriculture Platform to help farmers grow crops in a more environmentally friendly way and to connect them directly to consumers. The ideas that this book articulates can open up great growth opportunities in China for global companies. In the future, some of these models can be applied outside China.

— J. Erik Fyrwald, CEO of Syngenta

Over the past two decades, millions of Chinese have become "modern" shoppers and consumers for the first time, the boom growth phase in the Chinese consumer economy has happened without the "legacy assets" and traditions of Western markets' retail format and platform technologies. Free of these precursors a vibrant entrepreneurial commercial culture has emerged that has scaled like nowhere earlier in economic world history, and a leading edge and completely different retail, shopper and consumer ecosystem has emerged for China. There is no longer a global standard go-to-market model for developed economies. Companies seeking to succeed in China need to build a bespoke approach in China in order to win for China in China. And whilst China continues to learn and sort out the most valuable lessons very rapidly from the rest of the world, the world needs to accelerate to learn much faster from the China experience – both to succeed in China and to evolve existing retail structures in the Western markets. I recommend reading *The Future of Global Retail* because the authors explain the revolution of new retail coming from China and how that may inspire and impact global retail leaders.

— *Jørgen Vig Knudstorp, Executive Chair, the LEGO Brand Group*

While I experience the new retail as an active consumer living in China, I must say that it is not always easy for anyone who lives in China to explain the new phenomenon and make sense of what's going on. The book does a wonderful job explaining all the "messy" complications of the new retail. As a digital native and Chinese netizen, I find the analysis of these new retail developments refreshing and insightful. It helps me see the big picture.

— *Rui Meng, China digital native/netizen*

*The Future of Global Retail: Learning from China's Retail Revolution* is a pioneering work on tracing the evolution and future of retail in China. China is the consumer story of the century and new retail is its major amplifier. Winning in new retail, and in all its growth formats is critical for all global players as this market shapes the future of consumer-led businesses in the world. The book makes for a highly engaging read, with inspiring stories of retail revolutionaries and how it all comes together. This is an extremely useful guide for all CPG executives who aspire to make sense, learn how to play and win in the most innovative, digitized and complex retail market in the world.

— *Rohit Jawa, Chairman Unilever China & EVP*
*Unilever North Asia*

Having been running a business in Asia for the last 12 years, I noticed that the more western executives are remote from China, geographically or in terms of their responsibility, the more they are scared about it. This book will help executives understand that the basic tenet running business in China is not that different from other parts of the world – you must relentlessly win your customers. The stories in this book demonstrate in a fantastic way that real customer centricity drives success. This is truly inspiring for many entrepreneurs in and out of China. The "scary" part is how these entrepreneurs in China learn so fast, experiment so quickly, and scale up so rapidly.

*– Frederic De Rougemont, CEO of USG BORAL*

This book offers a fascinating look into the Chinese retail ecosystem and its impacts on the future of global retail. The authors' masterful analysis of thousands of regional case studies provides a strategy blueprint essential for any business keen to stay ahead of the curve. Their "Beyond" Value Chain Model extrapolates local trends and ensures they are universally applicable, relevant to companies irrespective of their geography. At X5, we have had the pleasure of working with IMD through our New Retail program and have utilised many of the insights featured to transform our business for future growth. I believe it is now vital for industry leaders to pay close attention to China's road to success and learn from it. This book helps do just that.

*– Igor Shekhterman, CEO of X5 Retail Group, Russia's largest food retailer*

This book offers powerful insights. It challenges us in industries and regions outsides China to learn from these developments. As boundaries of service, product and market blur, this book compels us to ask hard questions and find dynamic solutions before it is too late.

*– Chartsiri Sophonpanich, President, Bangkok Bank Public Company*

As an active participant in the Chinese new retail revolution, I witnessed first-hand the push by capital market, the development of informational technologies, the maturation of manufacturing, and the accompanying growth of new business models. Along with it, there are of course the blood and sweat of the forgotten practitioners of new retail revolution.

Survivors of this process are winners who can more efficiently address consumers pain points and who have superior execution powers. Consumers worldwide demand better solutions to their needs. I sincerely hope that the solutions the Chinese entrepreneurs came up with, as conveyed in this book, will be more widely known and bring about changes.

*– Yihong Guan, Chairman and CEO of Jiumaojiu Group*

# THE FUTURE OF GLOBAL RETAIL

China's new retail revolution will completely transform how the world thinks about retail and digital innovation. But is the world ready yet? In this book, the authors share an insider's perspective on what is happening in China to reveal the future for global retail, and a clear framework to help you prepare.

The book presents a number of real-world cases, based on interviews and first-hand consumer experience, to decode China's retail revolution so that you can understand what is happening and why, and what it means for the rest of the world. Crucially, the book identifies five critical stages in the development of new retail that global retail executives need to grasp now: lifestyle commerce, Online-Merge-Offline retail, social retail, livestream retail and invisible retail. To help the industry get ready for this new, China-inspired paradigm in retail, the authors present a practical and simple framework – a ten-year strategic roadmap for global retail executives, which they call the "Beyond" Value Chain Model.

China's new retail is not just about fashion, cosmetics, snacks, data-driven convenient stores and commercial live streaming. At a time when the world of retail is being upended, it offers inspirational lessons in innovation, purpose and agility for global executives across the entire retail spectrum.

**Winter Nie** is a Professor of Leadership and Organizational Change at IMD Business School, Switzerland. She is the co-author of *Made in China: Secrets of China's Dynamic Entrepreneurs* (2009) and *In the Shadow of the Dragon: The Global Expansion of Chinese Companies* (2012). She started this research project in 2016.

**Mark J. Greeven** is a Chinese-speaking Dutch professor of innovation and strategy at IMD Business School and former faculty at China's leading innovation institute at Zhejiang University. He is the author of *Pioneers,*

*Hidden Champions, Changemakers, and Underdogs* (2019) and *Business Ecosystems in China* (Routledge, 2017).

**Yunfei Feng** is a researcher at IMD Business School and had many in-depth interviews and discussions with the Chinese executives. She has kept up with the most cutting-edge development in China's e-commerce and digital space. She had her own entrepreneurial venture in online business education.

**James Wang** is an economist and a Professor of Finance at City University of Hong Kong. His commentaries, written for hedge fund managers, on topics such as Sino-American relations, style and substance of the 5th-generation leaders of China, prospects of SOE reforms and other contemporary topics, were collected in the book *Early Innings of a Long Game.*

# THE FUTURE OF GLOBAL RETAIL

## Learning from China's Retail Revolution

*Winter Nie, Mark J. Greeven, Yunfei Feng and James Wang*

Routledge
Taylor & Francis Group

LONDON AND NEW YORK

First published 2022
by Routledge
2 Park Square, Milton Park, Abingdon, Oxon OX14 4RN

and by Routledge
605 Third Avenue, New York, NY 10158

*Routledge is an imprint of the Taylor & Francis Group, an informa business*

*British Library Cataloguing-in-Publication Data*
A catalogue record for this book is available from the British Library

*Library of Congress Cataloging-in-Publication Data*
A catalog record has been requested for this book

ISBN: 978-1-032-07041-4 (hbk)
ISBN: 978-1-032-07042-1 (pbk)
ISBN: 978-1-003-20507-4 (ebk)

DOI: 10.4324/9781003205074

Typeset in Joanna
by codeMantra

# CONTENTS

We are grateful to IMD and J-F Manzoni for the support.

# 1

---

# INTRODUCTION

## The new world of disruption

Carrefour, Europe's largest retailer, was among the first foreign retailers to enter China. That was in 1995, Carrefour, together with Walmart, brought the concept of one-stop shopping to the world's most populous country and expanded quickly. Enjoying "first mover" competitive advantage, it remained the fastest growing foreign retailer in China for many years, and its aggressive expansion was largely considered to be a success. By 2019, Carrefour had 233 stores, 30,000 employees and annual revenues of RMB31 billion (US$4.5 billion).[1] In the world of bricks-and-mortar retail, it seemed improbable that a competitor could achieve the same sales figures with a fraction of the workforce, and inconceivable that one individual could take on a global, corporate giant. But in today's era of "new retail", the rules of the game have changed, and one woman with her support team of 500 – just 2% of the number of Carrefour employees – did just that. Her name is Viya.

Born in 1985 to a business family in the province of Anhui, Viya became a singer and model. She travelled to Beijing and, at the age of 17, set up her

DOI: 10.4324/9781003205074-1

own small clothing shop in a wholesale market. The shop was so successful – and Viya so adept at selling – that she went on to open up a dozen clothing stores. She continued to enjoy success until an incident occurred that made her rethink her business model and start anew. A customer came into one of her shops and tried on several outfits. Instead of making her purchases at the counter, however, she turned to her phone and opened up the Taobao app (a digital shopping platform owned by Alibaba) and placed an order online so she could get a better deal. Viya was furious. It was a rude awakening. In 2012, she decided to close all her offline stores and move entirely online.

The online business proved hard, however, and the early days were, she said, "the darkest period of my life". She lost hundreds of thousands of dollars from overstocking. Although her online traffic gradually began to grow and sales volumes slowly increased, she was still losing money due to the high merchandise return rate caused by lack of quality control. She had to sell a house to pay her debts. But she persevered.

In 2016, Taobao launched a new live-streaming service, Taobao Live. They telephoned Viya and invited her on board. In one of her 2017 live-streaming events, she sold RMB70 million (US$11 million) of Haining fur clothing in just five hours and became Taobao's top seller.[2] To this day, Viya remains Taobao's number one live streamer, and it seems there is nothing she can't sell, whether it's 430,000 kilograms of rice in 1 minute, 814 houses in 20 minutes or, even more astonishingly, a rocket-launching service worth RMB40 million (US$5.7 million).

In the United States, there is a Black Friday. Not to be outdone, China created the Singles' Day. The date, November 11, was chosen because the number "1" resembles a "bare stick" – Chinese slang for an unmarried man – and "11/11" resembles a row of four single people. The event, also known as the Double 11 sale, is now the world's largest online shopping festival. Although the original idea was to celebrate singlehood, the discounts were soon extended to anyone looking for a good deal. Vendors compete against each other with aggressive discounting, and the whole nation goes into frantic shopping mode for the day.

On Singles' Day in 2019, Viya sold more than RMB3 billion (US$435 million) worth of products[3] – more than 1% of Taobao's total sales of RMB268 billion (US$38 billion). By the end of 2019, she had reached an annual revenue of RMB30 billion (US$4.35 billion)[4] – almost on a par with Carrefour. Although Carrefour was on the wane by this point, for one person to achieve US$4.35 billion in annual revenue is staggering. In 2020, Alibaba extended its Single's Day sale period to 11 days and Viya's takings increased to US$1 billion.[5]

## So how does Viya do it? Does she have a magic wand that Carrefour can borrow?

Viya is not the only one generating vast revenues. In 2019, a snack company called Three Squirrels — founded in 2012, the same year Viya moved her business online — sold RMB1 billion (US$150 million) of snack products on Singles' Day,[6] including a bewildering US$14 million worth of fruit and nut packs in just 20 minutes. In 2020, Three Squirrels ranked number one snack group across nine major e-commerce platforms, including Tmall, JD and VIP.com.

An internet-based company from its inception, Three Squirrels targeted health-conscious millennials that are used to shopping online. With a simple customer value proposition of quality products, affordability and user experience, by 2019 the business was reporting an annual revenue over RMB10 billion (US$1.4 billion).[7] It went public in July of that year and in November 2020 was valued at RMB23 billion (US$3.4 billion).[8] How can a retailer without owning a single manufacturing facility grow so fast? We all understand the value of quality products and affordability but what kind of user experience leads you to spend RMB27 (US$4) on a 185g packet of nuts? To find out, we bought a packet of Three Squirrels' California pistachios. We were pleasantly surprised to find it came with a tasting bag, wet wipes (presumably to clean our hands before and after consumption), sealing clips, disposal bags and bag openers. So does a "pleasant surprise" experience translate into sufficient repeat business? The more important question is whether there is a growth limit for a single-category online retailer?

Bianlifeng (便利蜂) opened its first store in Beijing in 2017, when convenience stores in China's largest cities were dominated by Lawson, 7-Eleven, Family Mart and Yonghui, all of which had been operating successfully for many years. Both Walmart and Carrefour had their own convenience stores as well. As a newcomer, Bianlifeng knew that the me-too strategy would not work.

The traditional convenience store model requires store managers to make hundreds of decisions every day with regard to product selection, pricing, discounts and layout. Bianlifeng, on the other hand, placed its bets on developing a "central brain" system, using smart, customer-centric algorithms and AI to make data-based decisions (for example, instantaneously alerting price-sensitive consumers of price changes), thereby maximising revenue and reducing dependence on the intuition of store managers. Can convenience stores be fully automated using AI? Can AI compete with humans? By May 2020, Bianlifeng had increased its number of stores to more than 1500, but the battle is far from over.

## Glimpsing the future of retail

New retail in China is not only about fashion, cosmetics, snacks, data-driven convenient stores and live streaming, however. Meituan (see Chapter 6) started out as a group-buying business but has evolved into a super-platform providing a wide variety of location-based services. Hema Fresh (see Chapter 7), which established its first store in 2016 in Shanghai, offers a new retail format that is a combination of physical stores, online app, eat-in food court and fresh-food deliveries. Pinduoduo (see Chapter 8), having acquired over 700 million active users within five years, pioneered a social e-commerce platform. If Hema built the fresh-food supply chain, then it was Pinduoduo that revolutionised the link between the underserved, low-income populace and multiple small and medium-sized manufacturers.

And it is not just Viya who has benefitted from livestream selling. There is another ubiquitous live-streaming phenomenon (see Chapter 9) changing the retail landscape of China. Known mostly in the Western world for her artistic short videos on YouTube, Li Ziqi (see Chapter 10) generates more than RMB1 billion (US$140 million) a year through her online Tmall store.

New retail formats are continually emerging, and disruption to the old paradigm is the new norm.

China's new retail landscape is all about innovation. In 2019, Nestlé launched its first fruit-flavoured Nescafé. Sold in three different flavours: peach, pineapple and green apple, the coffee can be brewed with iced or sparkling water. Oriented entirely towards young consumers, the Nescafé fruity iced coffee was a result of a collaboration between Nestlé and the Tmall Innovation Centre, which invited online consumers to participate in the R&D process right from the initial concept stage. The lab simulated a real online shopping environment, and the experiment mimicked real consumption scenarios. According to the Nestlé Tmall flagship store, the new product received an overwhelming response and sold 100,000 boxes on its first day.[9]

This book is not just about the practices of domestic and international companies in China. It is about emerging consumer trends and how China's new retail co-creates the trends. It is about how the companies that leverage the trends survive and thrive. It is about business model innovation and the dynamics of China's digital e-commerce space, and the power struggle among existing giants and emerging new players. It is about products, variety, prices, supply chain and logistics powered with big data and smart algorithms. It is about new retailing disrupting the old paradigm. It is about the future of China's retail market, valued at almost six trillion dollars.

## China's new dawn: lessons from China's new retail for the rest of the world

It has been almost four years since Jack Ma, the founder of Alibaba, proposed the concept of new retail in 2016. In that short time, we have witnessed rapid development, great changes and many innovations in the digital retail space. These new innovations are now gaining a global foothold, with business magazines such as *Fortune, Forbes, Economist* and *The Wall Street Journal* starting to shine a spotlight on the new retail formats emerging from China. As Mark Schneider, CEO of Nestlé, said in *Economist* in 2021, "If you want to see the future, look at China".[10]

It was also in 2016 that Nokia CEO, Stephen Elop, expressed a somewhat different sentiment when he announced Microsoft's acquisition of Nokia: "We did not do anything wrong, but somehow we lost".[11] As a business transitions from the existing to the new, what do we need to know, and what do we need to do, to stay relevant? It is hard enough for savvy Chinese "netizens" to make sense of ever-changing retail formats, let alone for those who live elsewhere. In this book, we aim to demystify the new retail revolution driven by China, explain its evolutions and discover lessons for the rest of the world. In particular, we will focus on the why, what, how and what's next of new retail, with three core objectives in mind.

### *Objective 1: decoding China's retail revolution*

— We present not just a description of the evolution of China's new retail — this has been covered in many other publications. We also propose a point of view affirmed by our ten years of research and personal experience.
— Our point of view has been formed by a systematic approach to decoding the strategic and organisational aspects of China's new retail innovators. In particular, we start eaçch chapter by looking at the consumer's pain point and then dive deep into how the innovators developed new retail concepts in response. (See Figure 1.1 and the table below for an overview of the innovators that we analysed.)

| Companies | Field | Chapter |
|---|---|---|
| Alibaba | E-commerce | Chapter 2 |
| JD | E-commerce | Chapter 2 |
| SF Express | Express delivery | Chapter 3 |
| Tencent | Social media | Chapter 5 |
| Meituan | Lifestyle e-commerce | Chapter 6 |
| Hema | Online and offline | Chapter 7 |
| PDD | Social e-commerce | Chapter 8 |
| ByteDance | Short videos | Chapter 9 |

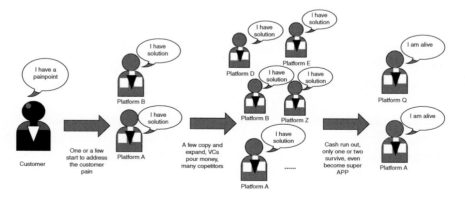

Figure 1.1  From customer pain point to solutions.

— Our analysis focuses on building an understanding of the specific organisational and strategic choices of China's retail innovators. We take a comparative lens by examining a series of competitive battles between incumbents and newcomers, foreign and domestic, and digital and non-digital players. (See the table below for an overview of the firms included.) Through analysing the battles, we diagnose how the winners differ from other competitors and why they were able to emerge as winners.

| Battle | Field | Chapter |
|---|---|---|
| Taobao vs eBay | C2C e-commerce | Chapter 2 |
| JD vs Dangdang | B2C e-commerce | Chapter 2 |
| SF Express vs Tonglu companies | Express delivery | Chapter 3 |
| QQ vs MSN | Instant messaging | Chapter 5 |
| WeChat vs Miliao | Instant messaging | Chapter 5 |
| Weibo vs other microblogs | Social media | Chapter 5 |
| Meituan vs Ele.me | Food delivery | Chapter 6 |
| Meituan vs Ctrip | OTA | Chapter 6 |
| Meituan vs Didi | Ride hailing | Chapter 6 |
| Douyin vs Kuaishou | Short videos | Chapter 9 |

This book is about how China's new retail landscape has evolved from just two online retailers — Taobao and JD — to the current environment that comprises a rich variety of formats.

Who is this book for?

## Objective 2: identify takeaways for global executives

Our key audience is the executives of global retail businesses, some of whom will have a specific interest in the Chinese market but also those who are looking at shaping the future of retail around the world. Through the case studies and our analysis and continuous discussion with global executives, we have developed a six-pronged model that enables executives to shape the future of new retail worldwide: the "Beyond" Value Chain Model. Each chapter of the book provides insights on new ways of looking at your customers, your offerings, your business model, your innovation, your supply chain and your ecosystem. In the concluding chapter, all of these insights come together in our "Beyond" model for new retail.

We believe that five categories of executives, in particular, will benefit from our insights.

1.  Executives from multinational corporations (MNCs) for which China accounts for a significant part of total revenue, who will benefit from understanding the development and competitive landscape of China's new retailing because it impacts their future growth.

China is now one of the most important markets for many Western companies. For example, in 2019, Nestlé relied on China for 8.2% of its revenues and Unilever for 16%.[12] For L'Oréal, China has become the second largest market after the United States and, in China, 50% of their sales are online.[13]

In early 2020, a Nasdaq-listed Chinese company, Luckin Coffee, achieved notoriety. Shares of Luckin Coffee crashed after American due-diligence-based investment firm, Muddy Waters, accused Luckin of fabricating the sales data of US$310 million. The scandal also dealt a fresh blow to the reputation of all Chinese stocks in the United States.

Luckin Coffee was perceived to be representative of new retail and a strong rival to Starbucks. It offered good quality, freshly ground coffee to consumers at a very low price, based on a coupon system. A cup of cappuccino originally priced at RMB28 (US$4) cost less than a dollar, and tasted just as good as Starbucks. Customers could either go to the coffee store for a takeaway or to sit and drink and chat with friends, or they could place an order online and their nearby store would deliver the coffee to their office.

Consumers appreciated Luckin Coffee. Those that found Starbucks too expensive were happy to drink Luckin at such affordable prices. Many people switched from drinking instant to freshly ground coffee, thanks to their experience at Luckin, and were reluctant to switch back. Using discount coupons, Luckin successfully cultivated customers that appreciated good coffee. However, once they had to pay the full price of US$4, the majority did not stay loyal: the price was beyond what they were willing to pay.

The failure of Luckin left an opportunity for foreign competitors. In fact, the opportunity is always there. The average annual growth rate of coffee consumption in China is 15%, in comparison with the world-wide average of 2%.[14] Not surprisingly, both KFC and Costa launched high-end instant coffee in 2020. Any newcomers, foreign or domestic, need to understand the dynamics of the sector, the mindset and behaviour of the Chinese consumer, and ever-shifting consumer preferences if they hope to succeed.

In this book, readers will not only get to know the landscape of new retailing in China but also the characteristics and buying habits of Chinese consumers. Both of them are critical to success in China.

2. Executives in the retailing sector will also benefit from this book because China's retailing evolution – or revolution – provides a glimpse of global retailing trends.

How Chinese retailers dealt with Covid-19, in particular, offers crucial lessons relevant to any retailer desperately trying to bounce back from the impact of the pandemic. One of the biggest challenges is the stagnation of offline business. Not surprisingly, more and more retailers want to transition to e-platforms.

The year 2019 was tough for retailers. A large number of well-known firms, such as fashion brand Forever 21 and luxury department store Barneys New York, declared bankruptcy. Data from CB Insights shows that in 2019 alone, 23 retail companies declared bankruptcy, compared to 17 in 2018.[15] Covid-19 exacerbated the situation and accelerated the need to be online.

Peacebird (太平鸟), a local Chinese fashion retailer with 2019 revenues of US$1 billion, had closed all its 4,600 stores by the end of January 2020, due to Covid-19.[16] Out of desperation, the company's chairman decided to develop its online business at full speed. Chinese full speed means overnight. Thousands of offline sales were converted online, and many of Peacebird's sales staff turned to live-streaming broadcasts. This dramatic overnight change, however, required a prerequisite. Peacebird had opened its Taobao online shop through the Alibaba platform as early as 2008, connecting its online and offline business channels, and this forward-thinking laid a key foundation for the overnight conversion during the epidemic.

Chinese retailers started to take the lead in the process of digitalisation, alongside the development of various new retail models. In this book, we explain what new retail, such as group buying, social media platforms and celebrity selling, means to retailers, and how they should utilise different platforms to develop an online business.

3. Executives interested in innovation, in general, and digital innovation, in particular, will gain insights from how some Chinese companies innovate in the digital space.

The most innovative retailers did not even exist ten years ago. They shot to the top rapidly by leveraging digital technology and platforms.

Their mindsets are different from traditional retailers. We demonstrate how they think.

For example, the super-app WeChat is an incredible innovation. It basically combines everything together: instant messaging, social media, e-commerce, online games, mini-programmes (whereby users can create their own mini-apps) and online payments. So far, no other single app has managed to be so comprehensive and easy to use as WeChat. Other amazing innovators include Meituan, Pinduoduo, Hema Xianshen and TikTok – each with its own breakthrough story.

4.  Any company embarking on a customer-centric strategy will benefit from finding out how customer centricity is achieved in the digital space. What we see from those emerging as winners in China's new retail is their relentless pursuit of customer centricity through business model innovation or productisation.

Those companies that survive tough competition focus on customer pain points. The whole offering is geared to finding solutions to these pain points. The customer is truly at the core of the business model.

One way to achieve customer centricity is through productisation. Productisation is not just about physical products. It translates and materialises the value proposition into a tangible and intangible experience. It takes into consideration the whole customer journey from search, interaction, payment and delivery right through to aftersales services. The optimal productisation removes any physical inconvenience that prevents potential customers from completing an order. It is so seamless that customers act on impulse quickly, without even knowing it. Optimal productisation means everything at your fingertips, with no need to toggle between different apps and no extra effort required by the customer to complete an order. Almost all the successful new retail firms operate through an all-inclusive super-app. Another way winning companies achieve customer centricity is through the use of big data. Pinduoduo pushes a product to you that you did not realise you needed, but, once you see it, you want to buy it because you don't want to miss out on such a good deal. TikTok pushes short videos to you that are so entertaining you stay glued for hours. There is no crystal ball at play here. What these firms have is big data and smart algorithms. The more you interact with them, the more accurate they become in pushing their products.

Is it ethical to create addictions based on consumer data? That is a question we need to debate.

5. Policymakers and leaders in other emerging and developing countries also stand to benefit from this book. China's trajectory in retail could help them understand the broad landscape of the sector and set the right policies and incentives to help grow their domestic market – and potentially leapfrog more sophisticated markets.

China offers an example of the developmental journey in new retail. Policymakers in developing countries such as in Southeast Asia and Africa can look at the path China has taken and learn how to grow their own digital retail. In this book, we identify the four pillars needed to build the infrastructure for new retail to take off. Any country looking to develop full scale e-commerce activity needs their governments and/or private enterprises to invest in the right infrastructure.

In China during the epidemic, even government officials took to live-streaming broadcasts on Pinduoduo, Taobao and Douyin, to help sell local agricultural products from remote rural areas. The head of Xuwen County (徐闻县), Guangdong Province, sold Xuwen pineapples; the head of Anhua County (安化县) sold locally grown black tea. These government officials embraced the live-streaming concept and used it to promote local products and, in turn, help the local economy.

Finally, all business executives and MBA and EMBA students that are interested in the cutting-edge practices of new retail will find this book helpful in keeping up with the most recent trends.

### *Objective 3: develop a future outlook for new retail*

New retail will continue to evolve, and new models and formats will emerge. In the last chapter, we will examine future trends in the retail space and discuss what they mean for companies.

## A multiple perspective

Having worked with both multinational and Chinese companies, the four authors aim to provide multiple perspectives of China's new retail, while making relevant references or appropriate comparisons to the Western world. Our combined 50-year research into Chinese companies afford us an in-depth understanding of how Chinese companies compete and how Chinese consumers evolve. The field research, with over 1,000 hours of first-hand interviews with Chinese entrepreneurs and business leaders, yields unprecedented insights. Access to a large amount of English and, in particular, Chinese original sources on these companies provides additional rich materials for piecing together a complete picture, in addition to helping referencing and cross-referencing content for accuracy. We have had many opportunities to discuss the findings with experienced executives from all over the world who come to IMD, and their line of questioning and critical feedback have helped sharpen our thinking. In a way, this book reflects their puzzles, their questions and their challenges.

Credentials aside, most important of all is our passion for the concept of new retail. We are embracing and actively participating in this new space as consumers, observers, researchers and thinkers.

## Reading guide

In this book, we provide an evolutionary perspective on new retail development and the key companies within it. We amassed a huge collection of cases based on interviews and secondary sources and, of course, first-hand consumer experience in China. Moreover, we compare, contrast and analyse. We not only show the cases but also share our insights of the "why" behind the events and the key lessons learned, and we offer recommendations based on our research and experiences.

This book has 12 chapters and can be divided into four parts. The first part includes Chapter 1, the introduction. The second part includes Chapters 2–5, which provide the four foundations for the emergence and development of new retail in China. The third part includes Chapters 6–10, which narrate the five stages of new retail. The final part includes Chapters 11 and 12, which summarise and refine the key learnings.

This book can be read as a whole or as independent chapters. You can read from the first chapter to the end, or you can also jump to the topic you are most interested in, such as Pinduoduo or celebrity selling. Each chapter is written as a standalone and can be used as an independent case study.

*Figure 1.2* Book structure.
Illustrated by Aspen Wang.

We care about both knowledge and the enjoyment of reading. We hope you have fun following the stories of the entrepreneurs and development of the companies at the heart of new retail in China.

Additional material can be found on our digital platform: chinanewretail.org.

## Notes

1  https://www.askci.com/news/chanye/20200629/1754341162727.shtml  In June 2019, Carrefour sold the majority of its business to online retailer Suning.com for $1.4 billion (https://www.ft.com/content/87530eaa-95a5-11e9-8cfb-30c211dcd229).

2  https://www.thepaper.cn/newsDetail_forward_7289248.

3  https://finance.ifeng.com/c/81IEquKmpFl, https://baijiahao.baidu.com/s?id=16831556064281329960&wfr=spider&for=pc.

4  https://www.sohu.com/a/383555130_120632139.

5    https://finance.ifeng.com/c/81IEquKmpFl, https://baijiahao.baidu.com/s?id=16831556064281329608&wfr=spider&for=pc.

6    https://www.sohu.com/a/353664358_162818.

7    Three Squirrel 2019 annual report.

8    http://stock.eastmoney.com/a/201907261189558875.html.

9    http://www.iheima.com/article-229974.html.

10   https://euro2.safelinks.protection.outlook.com/?url=https%3A%2F%2Fwww.economist.com%2Fleaders%2F2021%2F01%2F02%2Fwhy-retailers-everywhere-should-look-to-china%3Futm_campaign%3Dthe-economist-this-week%26utm_medium%3Dnewsletter%26utm_source%3Dsalesforce-marketing-cloud&data=04%7C01%7Cyunfei.feng%40oimd.org%7C8eaf0e3943314c99948d08d8afo4fafe%7Cd3113834f50947508faf7c92d551149c%7C0%7C0%7C637451783206756893%7CUnknown%7CTWFpbGZsb3d8eyJWIjoiMC4wLjAwMDAiLCJQIjoiV2luMzIiLCJBTiI6Ik1haWwiLCJXVCI6Mn0%3D%7C1000&sdata=uVkrgRFlAG2UpMlo8tU2mq4ukT4qoBHsjvaUMW41bcY%3D&reserved=0.

11   https://www.linkedin.com/pulse/nokia-ceo-cries-we-did-do-anything-wrong-somehow-lost-floreta/.

12   https://finance.sina.com.cn/stock/hkstock/hkstocknews/2020-04-28/doc-iirczymi8828744.shtml.

13   https://new.qq.com/rain/a/20200617A0NHDV00.

14   https://mp.weixin.qq.com/s/v4Qd1WvlEZ7lhQu6jQqPuA.

15   https://mp.weixin.qq.com/s/NgboUMeNHAu1K_ARXctJyw.

16   http://finance.sina.com.cn/roll/2020-04-20/doc-iircuyvh8889327.shtml.

# Part I

## FOUR PILLARS OF NEW RETAIL

# 2

## THE RISE OF CHINA'S E-COMMERCE

### A two-decade boom

The year 1999 was the last of the second millennium in the Christian Era, when much of the world was preoccupied with the supposedly menacing millennium bug. According to the Chinese zodiac, however, it was the Year of the Rabbit – a docile and harmless animal, or at least not one that suggests drama and upheaval.

In the annals of China's e-commerce, 1999 would, in fact, turn out to be a very significant year, which marked the births of a number of key internet firms that, in due course, would shape the landscape of online competition and impact the nation's lifestyle for decades to come.

In March 1999, Jack Ma founded a B2B e-commerce platform called Alibaba, in the city of Hangzhou, Žhejiang Province. In August of that year, Shao Yibo, a Harvard Business School graduate, introduced eBay's C2C model to China and established his own online trading community, Each-Net, in Shanghai. In November, Peking University graduate, Li Guoqing, followed Amazon's B2C model to found e-commerce firm, Dangdang, and started selling books online. To put things in perspective, in 1999, eBay was

DOI: 10.4324/9781003205074-3

four years old and had been listed just a year earlier; Amazon was also only four years old and had listed two years earlier. Another important Chinese player, JD, was founded by Liu Qiangdong in 1998, initially as a whole-saler for electronics products. JD did not enter into online retailing until 2003 but went on to compete aggressively with Dangdang and become the "Amazon of China".

This was both the best of times – the Chinese internet space was on the verge of explosive growth – and also the worst of times because, among other things, nobody was sure who might be among the lucky ones to survive the cutthroat competition that lay ahead. In hindsight, the paths taken by the four Chinese companies established in and around 1999 hold lessons that ought to be instructive for many. We start with the most captive character of all, Jack Ma, who is the self-appointed spokesperson for China's e-commerce revolution.

## Jack Ma: the English teacher

Jack Ma was born in 1964 in Hangzhou, a scenic city rich in culture and a popular tourist destination on China's east coast. In time, the little sleepy town would become the centre of China's e-commerce, thanks largely to him. As a teenager, Ma had a very variable academic record. His maths was very poor but his English excellent. He had to take his college entrance exam three years in a row because his maths results didn't make the grade. On the first try, he scored only one point, out of a maximum of 120.[1] (One can't help but wonder what could have been going on in his head for the two hours he sat there.) The second year, Ma vastly improved his performance – percentage-wise at least – by scoring 19 points.[2] Fortunately, he showed remarkable improvement on his third try by achieving a respectable score of 89[3] and was accepted by Hangzhou Normal University – then called Hangzhou Teacher's Institute. His outstanding English probably helped him gain a place.

In the late 1970s and early 1980s, China was beginning to open up to foreign visitors. Tourists from all over the world came to visit the famous Great Wall in Beijing and other scenic towns such as Hangzhou. To improve his English, Ma often cycled to West Lake, a favourite spot for tourists, to strike up conversations with visitors from abroad and offer free tour guiding. In 1988, he graduated from college and became an English teacher at Hangzhou Dianzi (Electronic) University. Some of his students later became joint founders of Alibaba.

In 1992, Ma and his friends established the Hope Translation Agency and through this he met many local businesses that traded overseas. In early 1995, the Hangzhou Municipal Government needed someone to send to the United States for liaison purposes and they called upon Ma. During his trip to America, Ma learned about the internet. With the help of his American friends, he built a promotional webpage for the Hope Translation Agency and left an email address on the website. A few hours later, he received five emails. It was at that moment that he decided he had to set up an internet business in China. The same year, he resigned from his prestigious role at the university – considered a particularly bold move – to become an internet entrepreneur.

Ma's initial business was China Yellow Pages, which made English home-pages for business websites. However, things didn't go entirely smoothly and, in 1997, he accepted an invitation from the Ministry of Foreign Trade and Economic Cooperation to join the China International E-commerce Centre. Within a little over a year, Ma and his team built a series of websites such as the Online Chinese Commodity Trade Market, the Online China Technology Export Fair and China Merchants. However, working for the government was too restrictive to satisfy Ma's ambitions.

## B2B: the establishment of Alibaba

In January 1999, Ma and his team returned to Hangzhou and raised RMB500,000 (US$60,389[4]) to establish a B2B e-commerce company aimed at serving small- and medium-sized enterprises (SMEs): Alibaba. Its mission was to help China's small exporters, manufacturers and entrepreneurs reach global buyers.

In March of the same year, Alibaba's website was launched. By May, the registered members of Alibaba exceeded 20,000. In October, Goldman Sachs invested US$5 million.[5] In January 2000, Softbank invested US$20 million.[6] Ma started to expand globally. Aside from Chinese and English websites, Alibaba also launched Korean and Japanese versions. In March 2000, however, the internet bubble began to burst. Ma adjusted his strategy just in time: he would aim to succeed in China first, before going global.

By December 2001, Alibaba's registered members exceeded one million, and the business began to be profitable.[7] In February 2002, in the midst of a harsh atmosphere across the entire internet sector, the Japan Asian Investment Company invested US$5 million.[8] It was interesting that among the early investors of Alibaba, two were from Japan. They helped to shape the early contours of China's e-commerce sector, which would eventually surpass that of Japan.

## C2C: Alibaba competes against eBay

The year 2003 was destined to be an eventful year for China's e-commerce, partly due to the outbreak of the SARS epidemic. In 2003, JD began to venture online – which we will discuss later. In March of that year, Ma selected ten employees from Alibaba and gathered them in his house, in secret. In May, they launched Taobao.

At first, even employees inside Alibaba didn't know that Taobao was part of Alibaba. The B2B business was growing fast, so why would Alibaba suddenly enter the C2C space? There are different versions of the story. One has it that, in early 2003, Ma met with Masayoshi Son of Softbank, in Japan. The renowned investor discussed C2C and eBay with Ma. Both thought eBay and Alibaba were too similar, so Ma took Son's advice and decided to go down the C2C route, with Taobao.

Taobao is far from the earliest C2C website in China. When it was founded, Shao Yibo's EachNet was already four years old. In contrast to Ma, Shao was a something of genius at maths. He won the gold medal in the first national "Hua Luogeng Golden Cup Contest" Junior Mathematics Competition at the age of 11. At high school, he was offered a full scholarship to Harvard University, at the age of 17. When EachNet was founded, it attracted US$6.5 million[9] of venture capital investment, and in 2000 it received another US$20.5 million.[10] The rapid development of EachNet attracted the attention of eBay, which was angling to enter China. In 2002 and 2003, eBay acquired 100% of EachNet's share for a total of US$180 million.[11] EachNet became eBay's wholly owned subsidiary in China.

At that time, EachNet already occupied more than 70% of the Chinese C2C market, while Taobao accounted for less than 10%.[12] Backed by eBay, EachNet had money, resources and talents that Taobao could hardly match. And they let it be known that they intended to put an end to any C2C e-commerce war in China within 18 months. How could Taobao, a newcomer, compete against such a powerful organisation?

Taobao conducted in-depth research on eBay's EachNet and found out that the latter was basically replicating the model of eBay in America. It made money by charging sellers commissions for each transaction, which meant the entire system was designed from the seller's angle. And to prevent buyers and sellers making direct deals off-platform, eBay EachNet prohibited direct communication between them.

To beat eBay EachNet, Taobao knew it needed to think outside the box. One option was to take the opposite route of eBay. Taobao launched its tit-for-tat strategies (Figure 2.1).

In contrast to eBay EachNet, Taobao designed their system more from the buyer's perspective, rather than the seller's. Traditionally, there were just two kinds of places to shop in China; one the street market (in some countries it is called bazaar, or hawker centre, similar to the farm market in Western countries), where people bought fresh vegetables, meat and fish; the other the supermarket, which sold all kinds of daily suppliers. Street markets were often noisy and untidy, whereas supermarkets were clean and orderly. Nevertheless, people still enjoyed the down-to-earth atmosphere of the market stalls and the fun of haggling. So Taobao re-created a street market online by designing the pages bright red, with lots of images, listing the products at random. They made the website come alive, to make people feel like they were in a real market.

In addition, Tabao recognised that most buyers like window shopping, so it listed search results that refreshed continuously to display a variety of products. It also understood that buyers don't normally trust sellers, so it encouraged the two parties to communicate directly, with no money to be transferred to the seller until the goods had been received. Finally, Taobao knew that buyers bought from sellers that had good brand recognition, so it created an evaluation system for sellers. All these seemingly inconspicuous strategies allowed Taobao to nibble away at eBay EachNet's market share.

Further, to integrate into eBay's global technology platform, in 2004 eBay EachNet moved its server from China to the United States. This caused instability in the performance of the system and it lost a large number of users to Taobao. Although eBay EachNet made attempts to block Taobao,

| | eBay EachNet | Taobao | Remarks |
|---|---|---|---|
| Charging Model | Charge the seller | Free of charge | China's C2C e-commerce market was still in its infancy and it needed to attract more merchants and customers; it did not make sense to charge fees then |
| System Design | Clear and refreshing, like a shopping mall | Colourful and messy, like a street market | Westerners like big shopping malls, Chinese people like street markets |
| Communication | Prohibited buyers and sellers from communicating directly to ensure that commissions were not lost | Launched Taobao Wangwang to facilitate direct communication and price bargaining between buyers and sellers, narrowing the distance between strangers | At that time, the trust mechanism was not well developed in China's business environment, and sellers on Taobao in particular could not rely on brand endorsement. Trust was the main problem with online shopping, and people felt unsafe to buy things directly from strangers |
| Payment | Direct money transfer from buyer to seller | Launched Alipay, where buyer pays money to Alipay rather than to seller. Money is not transferred to seller until buyer receives the goods and confirmed they are OK | Same as above |
| Search | Search function displays exactly what the buyer wants | Display different types of products repeatedly and in variations | Westerners buy with clear goals and place orders directly; Chinese people like window-shopping, and then buy something that attracts them |
| Evaluation System | Percentage system | Pyramid-type hierarchy (star, diamond, crown), multi-dimensional evaluation, buyer can upload pictures | Buyers not only prefer sellers with high evaluation score, but also prefer those with good sales history; Taobao's evaluation system later became an industry standard |

*Figure* 2.1  Taobao's strategies.

by signing agreements with some of China's first-tier portals such as Sina, Sohu and NetEase, it could not stop the upward trend of its new rival.

Three years later, in 2006, Taobao's registered users reached 22.5 million, surpassing eBay EachNet and becoming the largest C2C website in China.[13] In December, eBay withdrew from China and TOM acquired EachNet.

Let's figure out what contributed to Taobao's success, taking into consideration that eBay was so much bigger in size and stronger financially. Essentially, Taobao resolved the following three dilemmas, with decisions that were grounded in the reality of the Chinese market:

1. **Localisation vs global integration**

   Taobao adopted a series of strategies that were geared towards the demands of the local Chinese market. These included making Taobao free to use and launching instant-messaging system, Wangwang, and online payments system, Alipay. When EachNet was bought by eBay, the focus was directed towards global integration, at the expense of localisation. Although eBay EachNet began to lower their prices in 2005, it was already too late.

   Localisation is important, but it is very difficult to implement. eBay made the same mistake in India, where it acquired Baazee, India's leading e-commerce company, and tried to integrate its model that had been so successful in America. Within a few years, Baazee had dropped from the leader board of the Indian market.

   Alibaba, on the other hand, has been very cautious in its global expansion. It tends to select overseas markets where they can best transfer the experience gained in similar situations in China. Typically, these are other emerging markets, rather than America or Europe. Second, it often chooses to partner with strong, local players rather than set up its own direct subsidiaries. Third, it does not try to impose its own model on local units or partners. On the contrary, Alibaba values the local experience of each partner and cherry-picks the areas where they can help it to develop new competencies.

   For example, after the great success of Ant Financial (formerly Alipay) in China, the Alipay system was successfully replicated in markets overseas, starting with India. With a population of over one billion people and smartphone use increasing rapidly, India's payments market had vast, untapped potential. So in February 2015, Ant Financial entered a strategic partnership with Paytm, an Indian "unicorn" company specialising in mobile payments. Besides investing in Paytm, Ant Financial shared its experience with QR codes. This was crucial for overcoming challenges in transacting payments in a country where hundreds of millions of people had a mobile phone but no bank account. After Paytm introduced QR codes into its mobile payment app, the company increased its number of users from 30 million to 220 million by April 2017, and surpassed PayPal to become the world's third largest e-wallet, behind only Alipay and Ten-pay.[14]

2. **First mover advantage vs agile competitors**

As the earliest C2C e-commerce platform in China, eBay EachNet obviously had "first mover" advantage. As the industry leader, it had advantages in brand recognition, popularity, customer resources and experience. But the challenge was that its competitors were extremely agile. eBay Eachnet needed to re-evaluate the strategies that made them successful in the past (the company had been very successful in China before Taobao burst onto the scene). When Taobao began to launch its practical, localised strategies, one after another, eBay Each-Net was slow to recognise that its previous winning formula didn't work anymore. And when it made a decision to stick to its successful American model, the die was cast.

In 2003, the number of internet users in China was less than 80 million, and the number of people who had online shopping experience was under 30 million.[15] Most people only used the internet to check emails and read the news. eBay EachNet had a few million registered users but this was a drop in the ocean compared to the population size of China. eBay EachNet was still in the initial stage of the market development and was far from a time when it could start harvesting rewards. Taobao saw this. The free-of-charge strategy was not just to grab users from eBay EachNet; it also aimed at a much bigger target. Whereas Taobao's ambitions were clear, eBay failed to reassess the new competitive landscape against its old strategy.

3. **Chicken vs egg**

An e-commerce platform is a bilateral market with the typical "which comes first, the chicken or the egg" problem. More buyers beget more sellers; and the more sellers, the more buyers. When each party's existence depends on the other party, the platform must solve the chicken and egg problem and decide which party to attract first. Taobao attracted sellers with its free-to-use strategy and kept buyers on the platform through a series of tools that were adapted to Chinese consumer behaviours, such as Wangwang and Alipay, thus gradually attracting both chickens and eggs to its platform. eBay EachNet's charging strategy was obviously not as attractive to sellers, and the system not designed to cater to Chinese consumers, leaving neither side happy.

The same chicken and egg problem also exists in the field of car sharing. Passengers want to be able to catch a ride anytime, anywhere. As long as there is a sufficient number of cars on the platform, there will be more and more passengers. To address the problem of meeting passenger demand, app-based ride-hailing firm, Didi, initially attracted a large number of drivers by giving them subsidies and recommendation fees, which resulted in a rapid increase in the number of passengers.

## B2C: the rise of Dangdang

The third significant internet firm that emerged in 1999 was the first B2C e-commerce platform to be established in China: Dangdang. Dangdang essentially copied the business model of Amazon and sold books online and in its early stages won the favour of investment institutions. Dangdang received its first venture capital investment in 2000, a Tiger Fund investment in 2004 and a third round of investment of US$27 million in 2006.[16] In 2010, Dangdang debuted on the New York Stock Exchange.

On the surface, the first ten years of Dangdang went smoothly – almost too good to be true. Who would have thought that behind the facade of calmness a storm would be brewing? 2010 would turn out to be the peak year for Dangdang.

Amazon, Dangdang's benchmark, began to expand its businesses into a greater diversity of products, such as clothing, beauty, electronics and jewellery, while its book sales continued to grow. Amazon transformed itself from online bookstore to online supermarket. Dangdang, however, never got beyond selling books.

Another company, JD, which was a much later entrant into Amazon's space than Dangdang, developed from electronic e-commerce to a full-category platform. In due course it became an e-commerce giant competing with Alibaba.

So who, or what, is JD, and why did it become a competitor of Dangdang?

## JD: the Chinese "Amazon" for electronics products

Liu Qiangdong was born in Suqian, a city 500 kilometres north of Hangzhou, in 1974. Growing up in a poor region of China, Liu was a good student and he secured a place in the prestigious Renmin University of China, majoring in sociology. In 1998, Liu quit his job in a Japanese firm and began to sell CD-Rs in Zhongguancun, Beijing. His company was called Jingdong (JD). JD's business grew fast and, by 2001, it had monopolised almost 60% of the CD-R market in China.[17] However, Liu felt the constraints of being a wholesaler: on the one hand, he had a brand with great bargaining power upstream but, on the other hand, he did not have access to the end users downstream. He did not own the final customers.

In 2001, JD transformed from wholesaler to retailer, determined to become the Suning or Gome (the giants of home appliance retail) of the IT industry. By 2003, it had 12 shops. But no internet presence.[18]

In 2003, the SARS epidemic broke out. For Liu, this was perhaps the worst time for his business. Customers disappeared, the price of electronic products plummeted, and he still needed to pay rent and wages. To survive, Liu had no choice but to start selling goods online. He and his employees tried to post information on major websites to promote their products. Unexpectedly, they had six transactions on the first day.

Once the SARS crisis had subsided, JD's offline business returned and continued to increase. Perhaps most ordinary business owners would have returned to the familiarity of a resurgent offline business and continued to make money, but Liu is no ordinary person. There is an old saying in China, "If you don't cannibalize yourself, someone else will". However, that is far easier said than done and very few people are willing to take the leap into something new, especially if the current business is still doing well.

Liu, having tasted the sweetness of e-commerce, immediately decided to close down his brick-and-mortar stores and move his whole business online. In 2004, JD's online platform was launched. Taobao, which had gone live the previous year, was receiving quite a lot of criticism around counterfeit products. So JD announced that it would sell only authentic, licensed products. In 2005, JD began to sell a full inventory of digital goods. In 2007, it received the first round of investment of US$10 million from Capitaltoday. In 2008, it raised another round of investment worth US$21 million.[19]

# Beyond digital products: why selling books online matters

With ample financial backing, JD continued its product expansion. Entering the online book market in 2010 was its crucial step. Consumers usually only buy digital products once a year, but they tend to buy books several times a year. When JD began to sell books, it went head-to-head with Dangdang, the leading online book seller at that time. The seeds of the book-selling war were planted.

JD started out small in the books business. Dangdang wanted to cut the supply to JD and get JD out of the market altogether, so it asked the publishers to choose between the two: Dangdang or JD. To do business with Dangdang, publishers had to stop providing books to JD. JD decided to fight back. When Dangdang went public, in November 2010, Liu openly challenged Li Guoqing, its CEO, on Weibo ("Chinese Twitter"): "Every book JD sells will be 20% cheaper than its competitor (Dangdang)!"[20]

Actually the tactic Dangdang used to prevent JD entering the online book market is commonly used in e-commerce competition. On April 10, 2021, the state Administration of Market Supervision imposed administrative penalties of RMB18.2 billion on Alibaba's monopolistic behaviour in the online retail platform service in China.

People would later describe the war between JD and Dangdang as: "barefooted peasants are not afraid of those wearing fashion-designer shoes", with JD in the role of peasant. JD's core business and its major source of profits was digital products. Books accounted for only a very small proportion. It used the profits from its digital products to make up for the losses from books. Dangdang, on the other hand, relied heavily on its book sales and was wary about a fight with JD. JD's strategy was blunt: "Self-destruct 200 in order to kill 1,000 enemies".

In April 2011, JD raised US$1.5 billion[21] from its fifth round PE financing, while Dangdang raised US$272 million in its IPO in 2010.[22] Liu boasted: "(JD) will not make any profit on books for the next five years."[23] Li, however, had no appetite for long-term price wars, and by 2012, JD was clearly ahead in the battle; about 30%–40% of book sales were from new customers.[24] By selling books – even at a loss – JD had lowered the threshold of its website for new users and taken a crucial step towards creating a full-category platform.

## JD moves into yet another category: home appliances

Dangdang's market share declined, and it gradually dropped out of the first tier of Chinese e-commerce platforms. In 2016, Dangdang delisted from the stock market.

It seemed Liu had enjoyed the price war. Next in his sights were Suning and Gome, China's duopoly of home appliance chain stores. Whereas books are a relatively straightforward proposition – a typically low-priced, standardised product that people are used to buying online – home appliances are very different. And Gome and Suning controlled China's home appliance chain market. Their stores were close to their consumers. Home appliances are high-value goods and people generally like to try them before buying. But Liu was determined to expand into the home appliance space and had no fear of fighting another battle.

He announced the start of his war on Weibo: "JD will make zero profit from home appliances in the next three years" and "they will be 10% less expensive than Gome and Suning".[25] In the ensuing quarters, JD's sales increased, and the business saw rapid growth.

A key reason behind JD's daring price wars with Dangdang, Gome and Suning was its logistics system.

## Key to future success: homegrown logistics

One of the most strategic decisions Liu made was to build an in-house logistics system, in 2007, which included warehousing, distribution facilities and a fully self-operated distribution team. This decision, which received little support, would become a magic weapon later on. In 2007, a lot of JD's business operated on cash-on-delivery, and more than 70% of customer complaints came from service and deliveries.[26] The use of third-party logistics companies could not solve all the problems. Once JD had built its own logistics system, the service quality improved greatly and delivery speed was faster. In the areas covered by its own system, JD had a 100% guaranteed next-day delivery and half of all deliveries were made the same day. Returns (one of the most painful parts of e-commerce) were made easy too: buyers could return unwanted goods the next day – or even the same day.

Another benefit of its self-built logistics system – and that was of particular help during the price war – is lower costs. Also, a more efficient logistics system helped JD attract loyalty: people do not like to be kept waiting for their purchases and many customers chose JD because of its excellent delivery service.

In April 2017, JD Logistics was spun off and became a wholly owned subsidiary of JD. In addition to serving JD, the logistics company was now also able to serve other customers. By the end of 2019, JD Logistics' national distribution infrastructure had more than 700 warehouses, nearly 10,000 distribution stations, covered almost all regions of the country and served 99% of the entire population of China.[27] We will elaborate more on logistics in Chapter 3.

Three takeaways from JD's expansion and price war are as follows:

1. **Categories on the platform vs consumer "stickiness" (customer retention and engagement)**

    When JD expanded its product offerings, Liu envisioned that consumers might prefer buying multiple items on one platform, rather than buying books on Dangdang, electronic products on JD and clothes on Taobao. Single-category platforms eventually lose to full or multiple-category ones. Amazon illustrated this point in its own development. The top three Chinese e-commerce companies, Taobao, JD and Pinduoduo are all multi-category platforms. The platforms that failed to expand their categories of product, such as Dangdang and VIP.com, eventually stagnated and got left behind – even though they had enjoyed initial short-term success. In 2016, JD reached an in-depth strategic cooperation agreement with retail giant, WalMart, which consolidated its positioning as a full-category platform.

2. **Competition vs "moat" (core competitiveness)**

    On the surface, JD's "moat" (which keeps out competitors) appears to be its logistics system but, essentially, their moat is user experience. While Taobao's success lay in solving the trust problem of online shopping, JD focused on the supply chain, improving delivery speed, quality and after-sales service. Both Taobao and JD relieved consumers' pain points. JD, arguably, has reinterpreted the online consumer shopping experience in China. With its own logistics system, it can track and manage the consumer experience from pre-shopping (inventory checking) to post-shopping (delivery) to after-sales (return and exchange), thus raising the quality of the entire e-commerce service standard to a new level. And as e-commerce increases, economies of scale together with economies of scope will lower the overall cost further. Taobao also realised the importance of logistics to consumer experience. In 2013, it played a prominent role in establishing Cainiao, the logistics affiliate of the Alibaba Group. Although different to the self-built model of JD, Cainiao's aim was to enhance consumer experience.

Without a moat, any firm would be vulnerable in the face of competition. Although Dangdang was the earliest B2C e-commerce company in China, it failed to build its own moat, and it did not enjoy a stable relationship with its suppliers. When JD launched a price war, Dangdang's response was haphazard and not well thought-out. If consumers could buy books and other merchandises on JD, at lower prices, with more efficient logistics and better services, why would they shop at Dangdang?

**3.  Price war vs business model upgrade**

A price war is a war of marketing, with the explicit purpose of capturing traffic and customers. Price wars can be brutal to businesses and are only suitable if they can be ended quickly. If a price war does not crush the competition in the short term, the result is invariably a lose-lose situation. In Liu's price wars, he first used social media to attract public attention and then attacked his opponent's main business with his noncritical product lines. Each price war helped JD gain online traffic. But what was it that made him so confident? The war with Dangdang was a triumph of a multi-category over single-category model, and the war with Gome and Suning was between online and offline. Despite Liu's strong belief that the future of home appliances was online, he needed to persuade consumers the same, so to support his battle against the two strong incumbents, he used subsidies. This is a common tactic in China. When Didi launched its online taxi services, it too poured subsidies onto both passengers and drivers, to build up the business. Liu had the confidence to fight his price wars because he knew that the new model he was creating – through the strategic use of subsidies – would be more efficient and much better than the old bricks-and-mortar model that he was disrupting, and he believed that a multiple-category model would be more effective than a single-category model.

## B2C: JD and Alibaba's first round in retail competition

While JD was doing well in B2C, Alibaba, the undisputed leader in C2C, was not sitting idle either. No one knows exactly why Taobao decided to go B2C. It could be that, although Taobao was doing well, it was not yet able to make much money from C2C. In the B2C space, they could potentially increase profits by incorporating popular brand names. After all, Alibaba already had enough customers on its platform; why not connect them to business?

In 2008, Jack Ma announced the establishment of Taobao Mall and officially entered B2C, as expected. In the light of Taobao's low-end positioning, however, many well-known brands were initially reluctant to sell their goods on Taobao Mall. The breakthrough came when Ma travelled from Hangzhou to Shanghai to meet Tadashi Yanai, president of Uniqlo. In April 2009, Uniqlo became the first foreign apparel brand on Taobao Mall and soon achieved a sales performance of RMB10 million (US$1.5 million) per month.[28] Next, Lenovo, Jack Jones, Li Ning and other brands came on board. In 2012, Taobao Mall officially changed its name to Tmall.

Thanks to lively competition and the rise and fall of the internet giants, China's e-commerce sector developed rapidly. Between 2007 and 2013, the annual growth rate averaged 50% (in some years, it even exceeded 100%). In 2013, the transaction volume of China's online retail market reached RMB1.9 trillion (US$312 billion), surpassing the United States to become the single largest market in the world.[29]

In September 2014, Alibaba listed in the United States – the largest IPO in American history. Alibaba's market value exceeded US$200 billion.[30] On May 22, 2014, JD also successfully listed on the NASDAQ, with a market value of nearly US$30 billion.[31] In 2019, Tmall accounted for 53.5% of China's B2C e-commerce market and JD accounted for 27.8%. Together, the two behemoths took more than 80% of the largest e-commerce market in the world.[32] The natural conclusion at this point would be that the Chinese market is now set: two dominant players in a highly concentrated market. However, nothing is what it seems in China and certainly nothing remains stable for very long. For instance, players such as Vip.com or Xiaohongshu, NetEase and many others have started to enter vertical, specialised platforms.

Tencent, another internet giant, is unlikely to sit still and watch Alibaba and JD dividing the spoils between them. In September 2005, Tencent launched the C2C platform Paipai, but it was not successful. By then, Chinese internet users had already cultivated habits: they went to QQ for games and socialising, and Taobao to buy something. Later, Alipay tried to compete with WeChat on the latter's home turf but also failed. In 2014, Tencent gave up setting up an e-commerce platform by itself and instead reached a strategic cooperation agreement with JD, just ahead of JD's listing. Tencent acquired a 15% stake in March 2014 by paying cash and handing over its e-commerce businesses Paipai, QQ Wanggou and a stake in Yixun. This marked the start of JD handing out large equity stakes to other players. In June 2016, WalMart sold JD its Chinese e-commerce business, Yihaodian, in exchange for a 5.9% equity stake valued at US$1.5 billion, which later increased to over 12% (Figure 2.2).[33]

*Figure* 2.2  China's e-commerce.
Illustrated by Aspen Wang.

## Concluding remarks

In this chapter, we've laid down the first foundational pillar of new retail in China: the massive development of e-commerce that started in the late 1990s. Here we summarise a couple of the key takeaways and connect these to considerations for global executives and decision-makers.

1. The rise of Chinese e-commerce was driven by a handful of internet entrepreneurs, such as Jack Ma and Liu Qiangdong. They are the founders of their own companies and have complete control over their businesses. This means that they can decide the level of risks they are willing to take without needing board approval. Ma was able to make the decision that Taobao did not need to make a profit for the first ten years. Liu was willing to subsidise both consumers and home appliance manufacturers in order to compete with Suning and Gome. Both of them understand the importance of subsidies in exchange for online traffic in the start-up stage. For global companies to make this decision, executives have to overcome many hurdles and may risk their career reputations. Ma and Liu are playing a long-haul game. Jeff Bezos is as well.

    We normally ask questions of profit and loss but perhaps a more important question is: what is your risk tolerance and how much are you willing to lose?

2. In contrast to what many observers think of China, e-commerce has been a fairly level playing field for domestic and international companies. The wars between eBay and Taobao, or Dangdang and JD, showcase the hyper competitiveness in the market.

    This should give rise to the question: how are you differentiating yourselves in this highly competitive market?

3. Chinese e-commerce is very dynamic. New players enter, old players are replaced. Sometimes old players reinvent themselves. What's more, e-commerce developed quickly beyond the traditional categories of product, such as books.

    The practical question to ask, is: in what industry or sector of e-commerce are you competing? In our opinion, executives would do better to ask: is there such a thing called an industry boundary in the e-commerce space? The answer to this question will impact how you think of your business in the long term.

E-commerce is without doubt the foundation of new retail. The platforms that connect buyers and sellers in a myriad of ways create the necessary touchpoints for new retail concepts to leverage. The e-commerce boom also brought forth express delivery revolution. Express delivery — part of the logistics — has been critical to the success of e-commerce. Together with the ongoing logistics transformation in China, express delivery lays foundation for new retail.

## Notes

1  Shuxia Liu. Jack Ma马云传 (Chinese Edition). Harbin Publishing House.
2  Shuxia Liu. Jack Ma马云传(Chinese Edition). Harbin Publishing House.
3  Shuxia Liu. Jack Ma马云传 (Chinese Edition). Harbin Publishing House.
4  Converted at concurrent exchange rate, unless otherwise specified.
5  https://www.alibabagroup.com/cn/about/history?year=1999.
6  https://www.alibabagroup.com/cn/about/history?year=2000.
7  https://www.alibabagroup.com/cn/about/history?year=2001.
8  Shuxia Liu. Jack Ma (Chinese Edition). Harbin Publishing House.
9  http://www.people.com.cn/wsrmlt/jbzl/2000/05/tanhy/0403.html.
10 http://www.techwalker.com/2000/1013/13759.shtml.
11 http://www.people.com.cn/GB/it/1067/1913012.html.
12 http://www.100ec.cn/detail--6184688.html.
13 Minghua Tang China Private Economy (中国民营经济40年) Shandong People Publishing House.
14 https://www.antfin.com/newsDetail.html?id=590a99df70cfc66a14177b6a.
15 https://tech.sina.com.cn/i/w/2004-02-05/1601288529.shtml .
16 http://t.dangdang.com/oursHistory .
17 Xingdong Fang. My Entrepreneurial History (Chinese Edition).
18 Xingdong Fang. My Entrepreneurial History (Chinese Edition).
19 https://newseed.pedaily.cn/data/invest/26683.
20 https://tech.sina.com.cn/csj/2018-09-10/doc-ihivtsym1048264.shtml.
21 https://newseed.pedaily.cn/data/invest/27327.
22 http://stock.10jqka.com.cn/20101222/c521533692.shtml.
23 http://tech.163.com/11/0317/15/6VC09BEG000915BF.html.
24 https://www.sohu.com/a/390499854_116132.
25 Liu Qiangdong Weibo, 2012-8-14.
26 Xingdong Fang. My Entrepreneurial History (Chinese Edition).

27  JD 2019 annual report.
28  http://news.sina.com.cn/c/2009-11-10/032116580033s.shtml.
29  http://www.199it.com/archives/200124.html.
30  https://xueqiu.com/1175857472/136197874?refer=status.
31  https://m.huxiu.com/article/34305.html.
32  http://www.100ec.cn/detail--6539162.html.
33  https://www.sohu.com/a/125648388_115514.

# 3

## THE UBIQUITOUS EXPRESS DELIVERY

### The hidden power of retail

One of the legends about the Chinese zodiac is that the Jade Emperor chose which animals should be included depending on how useful they were for humans. Cows are good for ploughing the land, dogs help protect homes, dragons can make rain, and so on. Roosters, on the other hand, like to fight and are not of obvious use. To be included in the zodiac, therefore, the Rooster King came up with the idea of using his golden voice to wake people up in the morning. Like clockwork, every day at dawn, the Rooster King would rise early and call everyone to start a new day of work. Even though the rooster made the cut and was selected as one of the twelve animals of the zodiac, they are still not really held in high regard. Most idioms in the Chinese language refer to roosters in less than celebrated terms. For example, something that is insignificant is referred to as "chicken hairs and garlic peels (鸡毛蒜皮)".

The year 1993 happened to be the Year of the Rooster. It saw the emergence of a new type of occupation, a new profession – albeit an unsung one – which came to flourish throughout China. By 2019, there

DOI: 10.4324/9781003205074-4

were almost five million people employed in the role,[1] accounting for nearly 0.6% of China's working-age (16–59) population.[2] Each day, they rise early, like the rooster, and travel across the cities to deliver parcels. Some might consider their work to be a bit like "chicken hairs and garlic peels" in that it seems somewhat menial. But couriers are indispensable to Chinese society, where e-commerce permeates all aspects of life. Even during the 2020 Covid pandemic, they didn't stop working. They provided food and daily necessities for people who had to stay at home, thus forming a lifeline. The Chinese fondly call them "courier boys" or "courier brother" (快递小哥).

## The evolution of the express delivery landscape

In 1993, Chen Ping, who had just returned from finishing his studies in Japan, founded ZJS Express in Beijing; Nie Tengfei from Tonglu in Zhejiang Province founded STO Express in Hangzhou; and Wang Wei, a Hong Kong native, founded SF Express in Guangdong.

Why 1993? It is no coincidence. In 1992, former paramount leader Deng Xiaoping made a grand tour of southern China, in which he reinforced the implementation of the country's "reforms and opening up" programme. Coming three years after the 1989 Tiananmen Square incident, this was a significant message. With assurances from Deng, China's private enterprises began to spring up like mushrooms, leading to a sharp increase in the demand for express deliveries of various types of contracts, documents, bills and other small items.

The four major express delivery giants, namely, UPS (United Parcel), FedEx (United States Federal Express), DHL (German DHL) and TNT (Dutch Express), entered the Chinese market in the 1980s. Due to policy restrictions, however, they could offer only international services. In 2010, DHL, FedEx and UPS all finally obtained licenses to operate domestically – albeit items other than letters.[3] However, by then the competition that had built up amongst local delivery firms had become so fierce, the foreign companies kept their primary focus on international business. In 2019, foreign express delivery companies accounted for just 0.4% of China's express delivery market, and their business revenue accounted for 4.9%.[4]

In 1980, China Post, a state-owned enterprise, had also launched an express delivery service (EMS). However, due to the restrictions of being a state-owned institution, it was difficult to keep up with the super-fast growth of market demand. This provided opportunities for entrepreneurs in the private sector.

## Wang Wei and SF Express

Wang Wei, founder of SF Express, was born in Shanghai in 1971 and emigrated to Hong Kong with his parents when he was seven years old. After high school, rather than go on to college, he chose to become an apprentice in his uncle's factory. While on business across the border in Shunde, Guangdong Province, Wang realised how cumbersome it was to send samples to customers in Hong Kong. In the 1980s, many Hong Kong companies set up factories in Guangdong for exports to Hong Kong, which led to rising demand for the transportation of goods between the two. Quick money was made by people carrying goods from Shenzhen, a town just across the border, to Hong Kong, as luggage. It's probable that Wang was one of them – but we can't be sure. At any rate, in 1993, the 22-year-old seized on the opportunity and established SF Express in Shunde, with RMB100,000 (US$17,355[5]).

SF's early business process was relatively straightforward: after receiving an order, a courier would pick up the parcel from the sender and take it in person to Hong Kong. The business operated in an unregulated "grey area", with scant government supervision, which made it somewhat easy to get started. Even though there was no lack of competition, and SF wasn't offering any particular point of difference to other express delivery firms, business was good. After some serious thought, however, Wang decided to lower his prices by 30%, while retaining his promise for speedy deliveries.[6] This strategy attracted a new group of small and medium-sized firms and business took off. Meanwhile, Wang started to streamline the delivery process by requiring goods to be packed together before shipping. He positioned SF as the medium to high-end courier, focusing on speedy delivery of small parcels. The low-price strategy turned out to be very successful, and, by 1997, 70% of goods travelling from Shunde to Hong Kong were transported by SF.[7]

In 1996, SF Express began to extend its business model from Guangdong to the whole country. The first express delivery companies in China all turned to franchising as a way of expansion, which allowed them to establish a courier network at a very low cost and expand rapidly. SF also attempted to use franchising. However, there were some obvious disadvantages: the customer base was controlled by the franchisees, and the service quality was not uniform. Wang was keen on pursuing service quality and professionalising his business, while the franchisees just wanted to make money; there was no loyalty towards working for one particular company. To solve the problem, Wang decided to adopt a top-down, direct-management model which, not surprisingly, did not go down well with the franchisees. In the face of strong resistance, in 1999 Wang pushed ahead with the programme regardless. Things turned nasty and, at one point, it was rumoured that Wang almost got killed. He has had several bodyguards around him ever since.[8]

Over the following three years, Wang transformed SF from a franchise to a direct-management model, taking absolute control of the entire network. Complete control was crucial for SF's standardised management, brand building and overall process management. In 2002, the business established its headquarters in Futian District, Shenzhen and expanded all the way north: to Shanghai, Beijing and the far northeast. It gradually rolled out a courier network across the whole of China.

SF Express was positioned at the mid- to high-end market segment. High-value small items such as letters and documents were its core business. Customers were predominantly commercial and Wang observed they typically valued speed over price. In 2003, the SARS epidemic swept across mainland China and investors became cautious. SF, however, took advantage of the plunge in air freight rates and signed an aircraft-leasing contract with Yangtze Express. SF Express became the first private express delivery enterprise in China with an air cargo service, while other privately owned courier firms were still fighting their price wars. In 2010, SF Express bought its first own aircraft. By 2019, it had a total of 71 cargo planes and was China's largest cargo airline. The use of air transport for shipping now accounts for 18% of SF Express's total volume.[9]

Targeting mid- to high-end markets, purchasing the most advanced handheld terminals to track parcels in real time, owning a fleet of aircraft, recruiting highly educated staff, paying employees higher than its competitors, and having a full control of the operations... All contributed to SF Express's ability to maintain its record of fastest deliveries and lowest complaint rate for many years. Once SF has established their dominant market position, its prices are the highest in China. SF Express' "fast, accurate and safe" promise sets the benchmark for the industry. Its average income per order is about RMB22 (US$3.15),[10] much higher than the national average of about RMB12 (US$1.72).[11]

## The Tonglu companies and e-commerce

When discussing China's express delivery industry, there is one particular place that requires a mention: Tonglu, in Zhejiang Province. Known as the "hometown of express delivery", five of the founders of the top ten private express delivery companies in China hail from Tonglu: STO Express, ZTO Express, YTO Express, HTO Express (later became Best Express) and Yunda Express. The key employees of these five companies are also mainly from Tonglu.

Clusters of companies in one industry all in the same region is an interesting phenomenon that is probably unique to China, as is company founders of one industry all hailing from the same place. Aside from the Tonglu delivery companies, other notable clusters include Xinhua, in the province of Hunan: most of the printing and copy shops all across China are owned by people from Xinhua. And take leather shoes: 70% are produced by people from Wenzhou, also in Zhejiang Province.[12] In the health sector, 80% of private hospitals are owned and operated by people from Putian, Fujian Province,[13] while Yiyang, in Hunan, has become the "hometown of badminton", having produced at least five world badminton champions.[14]

What lies behind this curious phenomenon? In the early days of China's "Reform and Opening-up" programme, at the start of the 1980s, the dissemination of information about industry knowhow and market access was often restricted to a small circle of friends and families. What's more, people from the same neighbourhood tended to share not only information but also access to capital and key personnel. Once someone was successful in executing a certain business model, others from the same region would tend to mimic it. This was especially true for labour-intensive and low-threshold manufacturing or service industries.

At the time of SF Express' founding, international trade in the Yangtze River Delta region (which includes Shanghai municipality, Jiangsu Province and Zhejiang Province) was flourishing. One problem, though, was that goods exported from Hangzhou needed to declare duties to customs in Shanghai and customs declarations had to be completed within a certain period of time (often 24 hours). Although state-owned EMS provided a customs declaration service, it took three days at best. However, there was one particular train schedule that left Hangzhou around 9pm, arriving at Shanghai at 4am the next day. Although it was a slow train, stopping at all the stations, it was cheap. A round-trip train ticket cost RMB30 (US$5.2). If a client paid RMB100 (US$17.3) for the customs declaration service, then the gross margin before deducting labour and other costs was RMB70 (U$12.1). Upon such a profit was founded Nie Tengfei's STO Express, in Hangzhou, in 1993.

STO Express developed rapidly and Nie's wife, Chen Xiaoying, his brother, Nie Tengyun and his brother-in-law, Chen Dejun, all joined the company. Sadly, Nie Tengfei was killed in a car accident in 1998, and Chen Xiaoying and Chen Dejun took over STO Express. In 1999, Nie Tengfei's brother, Nie Tengyun, established Yunda Express. The accountant of STO Express, Zhang Xiaojuan — also a classmate of Chen Dejun — persuaded her husband, Yu Weijiao, who was in the timber business, to switch his career to express delivery, and YTO Express was established in 2000. Lai Haisong, Yu Weijiao's classmate, seeing so many people around him starting express delivery firms, decided to establish ZTO Express in 2002. In 2005, Xu Jianrong, also a Tonglu native, gave up his meat-processing business, acquired HTO Express and officially entered the express delivery industry too.

People call STO, ZTO, YTO, HTO (Best Express) and Yunda as the "four TOs and one Da" (四通一达). Relatives followed relatives, friends followed friends, classmates followed classmates and many people from Tonglu founded delivery firms. Most came with limited education but, together, they took half of the market, just in time for the boom in e-commerce sweeping across mainland China (Figure 3.1).

Figure 3.1  The relationships between the Tonglu companies.

## The diverging business models of the Tonglu companies and SF

The "four TOs and one Da" operated differently from SF Express. They advertised low prices and relied on franchisees to expand rapidly. Many of the franchisees provided services for more than one express delivery company, and there was intense competition among them. There were many complaints about delivery speeds and the number of missing, lost or damaged packages was relatively high. While not as competitive as SF in the high-end commercial market, which valued speed and reliability, the Tonglu players took advantage of the wave of expansion that flowed from the rising e-commerce tide. The people that bought their daily necessities online, such as toothpaste and shampoo for a couple of dollars, or items of clothing for US$10, cared more about the cost of delivery than the speed.

Alibaba's Taobao business, which launched in 2003, was growing exponentially, and Jack Ma began to seek collaboration with express delivery companies. At first, he reached out to state-owned China Post, but their prices were too high for Taobao. Yu Weijiao, founder of YTO Express, seized the opportunity. To cooperate with Taobao, Yu cut his prices even lower. The price of inter-province delivery with YTO was around RMB18

(US\$2.23), which was eventually reduced to RMB12 (US\$1.49), and the within-province rate was lowered from RMB15 (US\$1.86) to RMB8 (US\$0.99).[15] In 2006, Ma signed a cooperation agreement with Yu. The other "four TOs and one Da" soon followed. With the explosive growth of e-commerce, the development of the express delivery industry entered the fast lane. By 2008, one-third of China's express delivery business came from online shopping. By 2018, this had jumped to 78%.[16]

In the face of the booming e-commerce market and stiff competition from the Tonglu quintet, SF Express responded in 2013 with a price-matching discount of 40% on standard goods. By the following year, SF's revenue from e-commerce had increased, but at the expense of overall gross profit margins. In 2018, SF Express launched a new brand, "SXJD Freight" – a franchise model.

The year 2016 was an IPO year for China's express delivery companies. In October 2016, YTO Express went public with a market cap of RMB98 billion (US\$14 billion).[17] In the same month, ZTO Express listed on New York Stock Exchange with a market cap of over RMB90 billion (US\$13.4 billion).[18] At the end of December, STO Express listed with a market cap of RMB30 billion (US\$4.32 billion)[19] and Yunda listed in January 2017 with a market cap of RMB48.6 billion (US\$7.09 billion).[20] In February 2017, SF listed with a market cap of RMB230 billion (US\$33.4 billion) (Figure 3.2).[21]

ZJS Express, one of the three forerunners of the express delivery business, had enjoyed a promising start but faded later on. Poor governance structure probably played a role, with founder Chen Ping departing the firm only to return … several times. Eventually, ZJS Express fell out of the top tier of the sector.[22]

Driven by e-commerce, China's express delivery industry developed at pace. By 2014, total volume had reached 14 billion parcels, surpassing the United States and becoming the world's largest.[23] In 2018, China accounted

| Year of IPO | 2016 | 2016 | 2016 | 2017 | 2017 |
|---|---|---|---|---|---|
| Company | YTO | ZTO | STO | Yunda | SF |
| Market cap (billion \$) | 14 | 13.4 | 4.32 | 7.09 | 33.4 |

Figure 3.2 Express delivery companies IPO.

for more than half of the global express parcel market.[24] The scale also brought down the cost. The average unit price of express delivery dropped from RMB28.5 (US$3.75) a piece in 2007 to RMB11.8 (US$1.69) a piece in 2019. Although SF Express still charges higher, at RMB21.93 (US$3.14), their prices have also started to fall.[25]

## In-house logistics

Rather than rely on external firms, some e-commerce platforms created their own logistics systems, which brought a lot of advantages.

JD was one of them – as noted in Chapter 2. When a customer shops with JD, the system automatically processes the order and matches it to the warehouse with the appropriate inventory. It automatically generates the bar codes and shipping labels that allow the packing staff to match the items to the correct order. After picking, packing and sorting, the order is shipped to a delivery or pickup station in the customer's city. If it contains products from different warehouses, the products are combined and delivered to the customer as a single package. Once the order has been shipped, the system automatically updates the inventory level for each product, ensuring that additional inventory will be ordered as needed. For goods with stock at the corresponding regional fulfilment centre or front distribution centre, orders received by 11am are delivered on the same day and orders received by 11pm are delivered by 3pm the following day. Before placing an order, the customer can see when they will receive the product and can track the shipping status through mobile apps at each step. Such a seamless process is almost impossible for other platforms that rely on third-party delivery.

JD's nationwide fulfilment infrastructure is the largest among all e-commerce companies in China.[26] By the end of 2019, JD had established regional fulfilment centres in seven major cities, front distribution centres that stock high-demand products in 28 cities and over 700 warehouses in 89 cities. JD's fulfilment facilities covered almost all districts across China.[27]

While the fixed cost of building such a huge infrastructure is extremely high, the marginal cost to serving one additional new customer is minimal, as long as the system has not reached capacity. In April 2017, JD Logistics separated from JD to become its own independent entity, providing comprehensive supply chain solutions such as warehousing, transportation, delivery and after-sales service, to third parties. In February 2018, JD Logistics raised approximately US$2.5 billion from outside investors.[28] In 2019, the revenue from logistics and its other services reached US$3,372 million, which was about four times that of 2017, and comprised 4.1% of JD's total revenue.[29]

JD is not the only e-commerce platform that created its own fulfilment infrastructures. Suning and VIP.com also built their own logistics facilities. Suning's transformed into an independent third-party logistics company in 2012, while VIP dropped its logistics arm in late 2019 in favour of a strategic cooperation with SF, due to high costs.[30] Scale effect is of crucial importance to survival in the logistics industry.

When e-commerce platforms such as JD opening up their logistics infrastructures to provide services to third-party customers, they compete directly with SF and other independent express delivery companies. In 2019, JD Logistics bagged more than 40% of the total revenue from third-party clients.[31]

## Smart logistics network: Cainiao – delivery plus technology

Unlike JD, Taobao relied on third-party fulfilment firms. Almost 80% of Taobao's deliveries were carried out by the five Tonglu companies. As Taobao became more dependent on the five firms, the problems of slow speed and low-quality services became apparent, particularly during the first Singles Day sale in 2009, when the delivery companies were not prepared for the surge of volume. Some goods were not delivered until the end of the year – over six weeks after the sale day – and some food products were spoiled. Consumers complained. In 2013, Alibaba – Taobao's parent company – took the lead in setting up the Cainiao Network Technology Company, in which the "four TOs and one Da" invested, taking 1% of the shares.

Rather than create a logistics firm, however, with its own couriers and fleet of vehicles,[32] Ma was insistent that the Cainiao Network be a data-driven company.[33] The idea behind Cainiao was to build a "backbone network" of intelligent logistics and to improve the speed, efficiency and quality of the express delivery industry through the use of big data. Its goal was to achieve "24-hour delivery within China and 72 hours worldwide".[34]

Cainiao's first move was to unify the bill format of all the express delivery firms. Different formats were used by different companies, which meant sellers had to access each system separately, which added to costs. In addition, there were many paper bills that were not connected to the system, meaning information had to be entered manually, which also kept costs high. The paper bills also made it impossible for the delivery industry to digitalise. In May 2014, Cainiao launched a standardised electronic bill platform, which connected the systems of various delivery companies and merchants, so that all the information required during the whole process of collection, transfer and distribution was standardised. In December 2015, Cainiao started to offer cloud-based enterprise resource planning (ERP) systems to logistics companies, which allowed their full operating systems to be integrated into the Cainiao Cloud. Yunda Express, Best Express, STO Express and TTK Express all adopted Cainiao's cloud solutions. While providing services to the delivery companies via Cainiao, Alibaba also invested in them. By the end of 2019, Alibaba had become one of the major shareholders of the five Tonglu delivery firms.

Although it didn't own its own vehicles or employ its own couriers, Cainiao did build its own warehouses, with the logic being to shorten the supply chain. In a traditional e-commerce supply chain, a commodity is sent from the supplier's warehouse to the logistics provider's distribution centre, where it passes through various levels of the provider's logistics network until eventually it arrives on the consumer's doorstep. This lengthy supply chain, together with the fact the warehouses were not unified, led to slow deliveries, low efficiency and low service quality. By mid-2018, Cainiao had finished building a nationwide warehouse network, which covered over 30 million square metres.[35] Some of the warehouses were self-built, while others were constructed in collaboration with firms such as COSCO Logistics and EMS.

In 2015, Cainiao began to establish partnerships with local supermarkets, convenience stores and small, independent shops, using these as pick-up and delivery locations and thus improving "the last 100 metres" of service delivery. These were called Cainiao Post (菜鸟驿站) and, by the end of 2019, they extended to over 40,000 local shops.[36]

In December 2013, Alibaba also invested HKD180 million (US$23 million[37]) in RRS Logistics (日日顺), a subsidiary of Haier Electronics, which provided the delivery of household electronic appliances, installation and service nationwide.[38]

While logistical efficiency was the key aim of Cainiao, the company also focused on sustainability. In June 2016, the Cainiao Green Alliance was formed, in association with 32 partners. The alliance promised to make half of all packaging materials renewable by 2020, by using 100% bio-degradable packing materials.[39] In March 2017, it set up a green logistics foundation with the China Environmental Protection Foundation (CEPF), the Alibaba Foundation and six Chinese logistics companies, with a plan to invest RMB300 million (US$43 million) into the research of best practices throughout the logistics and supply chain, looking particularly for innova-tions in packaging, clean energy for delivery vehicles and using big data to optimise resources.[40]

Within a few years, the intelligent logistics backbone network created by Cainiao began to have an effect. Domestically, thousands of logistics companies became connected to the network, cutting the average time of express delivery from more than four days to two-and-a-half.[41] Same-day or next-day delivery became standard in over 1600 counties. From elec-tronic bills to intelligent order distribution, and from logistics "eyes" cam-eras to intelligent voice assistants,[42] platform-level technologies became the high-powered engines of the development of China's gargantuan logistics industry. Worldwide, Cainiao has more than 80 global logistics partners and 231 cross-border logistics warehouses, covering 224 countries and re-gions. In Spain, the Netherlands, France and throughout Southeast Asia, customers enjoy 72-hour delivery.[43] This, however, is not the end of the story. In 2018, Cainiao announced a five-year investment of RMB100 bil-lion (US$14.57 billion) in a national "smart logistics backbone network" (Figure 3.3).[44]

In 2019, the number of express delivery items in China exceeded 60 billion, which is equivalent to more than 40 items per person. One year later, in 2020 the number reached to 80 billion. These impres-sive numbers can be attributed not only to the rapid development of e-commerce and an accompanying logistics network, but also to the mas-sive investment in infrastructure. While China's railways mainly take care of passenger transportation, it is the expressways that carry freight. There are now 150,000 kilometres of highways across the country (highways enable speeds of 60–120 kilometres per hour), which is the longest high-way mileage in the world, and 40,000 kilometres more than second-ranked United States.[45] At present, China's highways have been able

*Figure* 3.3  China's logistics landscape.
Illustrated by Aspen Wang.

to cover almost all cities and towns with populations over 200,000. For any developing countries aiming to develop e-commerce, it is essential for government to invest in infrastructure.

A basic road and railway infrastructure, however, does not alone guarantee that e-commerce will take off. You still need companies to provide the logistics services. Businesses like SF Express and the "four TOs and one Da" survived the competition among literally hundreds of other express delivery companies and became hugely successful, so there must be a few things they did right.

1.  With a population of 1.4 billion and a GDP second only to the United States, China is a vast country with wide regional variations in economic development. Beijing, Shanghai and most of the coastal provinces enjoy living standards approaching that of developed countries. China's interior and frontier regions, on the other hand, lag far behind. There are also obvious differences in economic development between urban and rural areas. Consequently, the market is big enough to allow for the coexistence of different operating models in the express delivery industry:

- The first is the third-party delivery model, as adopted by SF and the Tonglu firms, who provide services to e-commerce platforms, other sellers and individuals.
- The second is the vertical integration model, as adopted by JD and Suning, who own e-commerce platforms and also have their own logistics fulfilment systems.
- The third model is Alibaba's Cainiao, which is an ecosystem in itself that provides both digital and physical infrastructures connecting all the players, thus improving the efficiency of the industry as a whole.

Within the third-party model, SF relies on direct management, whereas the Tonglu five opted for franchisees. Whether you choose a franchise model or not, of vital importance is to make a strategic choice of which customer segment to target, what products/services to provide and which model to deploy. The same lesson extends to China's e-commerce platforms. Even though there are dominant players, and it seems that there is no more space to develop or expand, there is always a way to find a gap. Nothing is cast in stone in China e-commerce landscape.

2.  Managing five million couriers: the express delivery industry is typically labour-intensive. There are over five million couriers in China who deliver parcels and take-away food. This is roughly the same size as the population of Singapore. Most couriers are not well educated and have not had the opportunity to attend college. However, they are crucial part of a delivery company, as they are the contact point with customers – whether senders or receivers – and their performance directly affects customer experience. SF Express and JD Logistics follow similar practices. They hire their couriers themselves, and the couriers' income depends on how many parcels they collect or deliver. To make more money, most couriers work more than eight hours a day. Couriers who have worked at JD for more than five years can, on average, afford to buy a condo in their hometown.[46] In addition to reasonable pay, express delivery companies try to instil a sense of respect for courier profession. In April 2016, an SF courier had a slight collision with a car in Beijing. The driver of the car insulted the courier and slapped him in the face. Wang Wei, the founder and chairman of SF, was furious and – although he usually kept a low

profile – published a message in his WeChat: "I declare to all my friends: if I do not pursue justice in this matter, I am not qualified to be president of SF Express!" The courier ended up being invited to ring the bell when SF Express was listed on the Shenzhen Stock Exchange, in 2017. Couriers in China are motivated by the respect they receive, as well as their relatively good income.

3.  The important role of technology: it's not just Cainiao that uses technology to improve the operational efficiency of the logistics industry. All the leading express delivery companies are pursuing digital transformation and are investing in high-tech. In 2018 and 2019, SF's R&D accounted for 2.3% of operating income – quite remarkable considering its typical profit margins are 5%–8%.[47] In comparison, FedEx has invested 1%–2% in R&D every year since 2000.[48] As the growth rate of e-commerce has declined since 2014, the growth rate of the express delivery industry has also dropped, from more than 50% before 2017 to around 20%. Moreover, as the express delivery network system needs more manpower and China now has a shortage of labour, labour costs are increasing. The delivery companies are very clear that the competition for the next stage is on technological capabilities. SF, JD and the "four TOs and one Da" already operate their own delivery robots and drones and most of their customer service is provided by AI.

## Concluding remarks

The second foundational pillar of China's new retail revolution is the rapid and sophisticated development of the express delivery sector. Albeit in response to booming e-commerce demand, the speed of its development remains quite a feat, especially when considering China's size and diversity. It is safe to say that without the entrepreneurial rise of the logistics sector, very little of the e-commerce promise could be delivered. Indeed, the express delivery companies laid the foundation and e-commerce giants, such as JD and Alibaba's Cainiao, added intelligence, but the driving force today is still the army of hardworking delivery men.

The development of China's logistics sector is informative for global executives and decision-makers because it shows:

1. How to tackle and exploit the large market size of China.
2. How to solve the problem of managing an army of uneducated labour.
3. What role technology can play in making operations more intelligent.

With e-commerce and logistics forming the first two foundational pillars of new retail, the next chapter introduces the third pillar and one of the necessary accelerants of the retail revolution: payment solutions.

## Notes

1  Ubiquity. China Post and Express News Publishing House.
2  http://economy.caixin.com/2019-01-24/101373750.html .
3  http://finance.people.com.cn/n/2015/0101/c1004-26310867.html.
4  https://mp.weixin.qq.com/s?__biz=MzIxNjY1NzI4NQ==&mid=-2247492163&idx=1&sn=888e31409320d307e662e19b4cb14973&chksm=9 7871ea9a0f097bf77978afd2cfb41e1ef15392e18e89a2e20c1444df2d0b3a3ffb 9eb3f0a62&scene=4#wechat_redirect Post Industry Development Statistical Bulletin, 2019
5  Converted at concurrent exchange rate, unless otherwise specified.
6  Wang Wei: SF Express Going Forward. Beijing Time-Chinese Publishing House.
7  https://tech.sina.com.cn/it/2017-02-28/doc-ifyavvsh7032231.shtml.
8  Wang Wei: SF Express Going Forward. Beijing Time-Chinese Publishing House.
9  SF Express 2019 Annual Report.
10  SF Express 2019 Annual Report.
11  http://www.chyxx.com/industry/202005/863239.html
12  http://www.21xie.com/new_view.asp?id=1540.
13  https://www.cn-healthcare.com/article/20141125/content-464358.html.
14  http://hunan.sina.com.cn/news/2016-08-23/detail-ifxvcsrn8978297.shtml.
15  Ubiquity. China Post and Express News Publishing House.
16  http://www.chyxx.com/industry/201908/768632.html.
17  https://finance.sina.com.cn/360desktop/stock/s/2016-10-21/doc-ifxwz-tru6736042.shtml.
18  https://finance.sina.com.cn/stock/usstock/c/2016-10-27/us-ifxxfysn7887659.shtml.
19  https://m.chinaz.com/mip/article/636315.shtml.

20    https://baijiahao.baidu.com/s?id=1568310630162625&wfr=spider&for=pc.
21    https://finance.sina.com.cn/roll/2017-02-24/doc-ifyavwcv8744182.shtml.
22    Ubiquity. China Post and Express News Publishing House.
23    Ubiquity. China Post and Express News Publishing House.
24    http://www.chinairn.com/hyzx/20190413/14165837.shtml.
25    https://www.sohu.com/a/391455538_115503?scm=1002.590044.0.2743-a9.
26    JD 2019 annual report.
27    JD 2019 annual report.
28    JD 2019 annual report.
29    JD 2019 annual report.
30    https://www.sohu.com/a/359174447_250147.
31    https://mp.weixin.qq.com/s/ZlZR1w1d-5YJYe55oxVLmQ.
32    http://field.10jqka.com.cn/20170601/c598748412.shtml.
33    https://tech.sina.com.cn/i/2018-05-29/doc-ihcffhsu8144410.shtml.
34    https://www.cainiao.com/markets/cnwww/aboutus?spm=a21da.148512.0.
      0.25f0304530C1j.
35    https://www.cainiao.com/markets/cnwww/cn-news-detail?spm=a21da.14
      4546.0.0.1ce43045uUBAvb&id=71.
36    https://baijiahao.baidu.com/s?id=1649978611166388024&wfr=spider&
      for=pc.
37    Exchange Rate 1$=7.7352HKD.
38    https://m.huxiu.com/article/24537.html.
39    https://www.cainiao.com/markets/cnwww/aboutus-milestone-new?spm
      =a21da.7827996.0.0.5f1045couZGtGr.
40    https://tech.qq.com/a/20170318/000054.htm.
41    https://baijiahao.baidu.com/s?id=1601946360412886890&wfr=spider&-
      for=pc.
42    Ubiquity. China Post and Express News Publishing House.
43    https://tech.sina.com.cn/i/2018-05-29/doc-ihcffhsu8144410.shtml.
44    https://www.cainiao.com/markets/cnwww/aboutus-milestone-new?spm
      =a21da.148509.0.0.60e63045FxF7IS.
45    https://mp.weixin.qq.com/s/9W67TmVq2ISlIdHQctyn2A.
46    Fang Dongxing. My Entrepreneurial. Oriental Publishing House.
47    SF Express 2019 Annual Report.
48    https://www.sohu.com/a/325455113_343156.

# 4

# THIRD-PARTY PAYMENT

## Turning China into a cashless society

In October 2003, Cui Weiping (崔卫平), an avid online merchant who happened to be in Japan, reached a deal with a buyer in Xi'an, China, for a Fuji digital camera for RMB750 (US$90.6[1]).[2] At that time, Taobao had only just been established and China's online transaction volume was still very small. Use of credit cards or debit cards for online payments was rare and customers typically paid cash for their everyday purchases. Payments for online shopping relied on cash-on-delivery. And RMB750 (US$90.6) was not a small sum. The two strangers discussed at length how to make the deal but failed to find a solution. October 15, however, saw the launch of Alipay, which changed everything. Designed as a "custodian model", whereby an organisation holds funds for safekeeping, the Alipay payment process requires the buyer to transfer money to Alipay rather than directly to the seller, and the funds are forwarded on to the seller only once the buyer confirms receipt of the item. Cui's deal was the first successful transaction in the history of Alipay.[3]

DOI: 10.4324/9781003205074-5

## Alipay – a key to trust

Today, people take the Alipay model for granted. Before Alipay, however, there was no such solution for e-commerce payments anywhere in the world. When Taobao came online in May 2003, user growth was slow. There was no shortage of e-commerce sceptics and people were generally cautious about online transactions. Sellers were concerned that they wouldn't receive payment after delivering the goods, whereas buyers were not sure if they would receive the merchandise after paying for it. Taobao's founder, Jack Ma, quickly realised what was missing in the C2C system: the crucial element of trust between the participants. If Taobao was to develop further, he knew it must tackle this problem head on.

The natural place to start was eBay's payment system: PayPal. After all, eBay was the industry's standard-bearer and by far the largest competitor. PayPal was a convenient online payment system, and yet it could not solve the issue of lack of trust facing Chinese online shoppers. Taobao's team brainstormed for ideas, not only by testing out competitors' solutions but also by visiting online forums to check out user feedback. Their proactive customer research and intense internal discussion gradually led them to the idea of a custodian model.

From the perspective of product design, Alipay's payment solution was not a major innovation. PayPal had been processing online payments for years. And from as early as the 17th century, the United Kingdom had been operating a custodian service, which over the years had developed into an independent banking business (trust accounts). In a trust account, banks keep the client's entrusted funds, and make payment in accordance with what is agreed. Alipay's model is a combination of PayPal's online payment function and a bank's custodian service.

The advantages of Alipay were obvious immediately. If different sellers offer similar products, customers will naturally choose to buy from the seller that provides a no-pay guarantee if the goods are not received. As a result, more and more sellers began to adopt Alipay. The new transaction service alleviated the anxiety of shoppers, many of whom were new to e-commerce. Sellers and buyers might not trust each other, but they could all trust Alipay. Once the issue of trust had been resolved, Taobao and the whole e-commerce sector in China entered a completely new stage of development.

Figure 4.1  Alipay vs PayPal.
Illustrated by Aspen Wang.

Alipay's understanding of trust was firmly rooted in the company's DNA. Not content with solving the problem of online payments, it wanted to go further to minimise the risks for customers. In February 2015, Alipay launched a campaign under the slogan: "If anything goes wrong with your transaction, we pay (你敢付，我敢赔)". This meant that any customer that suffered a loss to online fraud while using Alipay would be compensated in full. (Figure 4.1)

## An Alipay account – beyond payment

When Alipay first launched, the payment settlement was fulfilled by the finance department of Taobao, using Excel to record the transactions. The buyer transferred money to Alipay's corporate account at ICBC (the Industrial and Commercial Bank of China) then, once they confirmed receipt of the goods, Alipay transferred the funds from its ICBC corporate account to the seller's bank account. Initially, there were few payments to process.

However, as the business grew exponentially so the workload increased significantly, and there was a new problem to solve: how to improve efficiency and reduce cost.

The company consulted with the ICBC and the two parties agreed to develop an electronic processing interface. Once live, the new system eased the workload pressure. Alipay went on to link up with the online banking systems of more than a dozen commercial banks in China. As a consequence, buyers on Taobao could jump directly onto the online banking interface to complete the payment process.

The only way to reduce costs, however, was to reduce the number of bank transfers. At the end of 2004, Alipay launched a member account system, whereby Taobao shoppers could apply for an Alipay member's account. In this way, Alipay established a virtual account system: if there were several payments to be made from to one seller, Alipay could consolidate them into one transaction. With the number of money transfers greatly reduced, so were the bank costs.

The new member's account system brought more unexpected benefits. When a member's Alipay account showed a positive balance, it led to a higher transaction frequency. And individual accounts meant that multiple financial services – beyond simple payments – could also be provided. More importantly, information such as members' shopping habits and payment history could be captured as big data, which would become a valuable asset later on.

## Express payment: the challenge

Taobao's transaction volume surged, rising from RMB8 billion (US$0.98 billion) in 2005 to RMB200 billion ($29.3 billion) in 2009.

This posed new challenges for the payment system,[4] as payment process failures were high. When shoppers made a payment, they jumped onto the online systems of various banks, which were different and cumbersome. Many potential customers were lost due to the unwieldy payment process.

Naturally, this was unacceptable to Alipay, which went back to the drawing board and conducted more research. It found that almost all banks provided a similar service to customers as the utility companies. Utility customers only needed to sign a one-time authorisation for their water and electricity bills to be deducted by the banks automatically. There was no need for them to login and go through the verification process. Alipay started to lobby the banks. In 2010, it persuaded the ICBC, CCB (China Construction Bank) and the BOC (Bank of China) to agree that its credit card customers could link up to their Alipay accounts, once they had obtained authorisation and authentication. Now, to complete an online payment, Alipay users needed only to enter a verification code sent via mobile phone, instead of having to perform a complicated verification process each time. This became known as "express payment". Express payment not only improved the payment success rate but also laid a solid foundation for the subsequent development of mobile phone payment capabilities.

In May 2011, after more than six years' experimenting with their own operations, Alipay obtained a licence from the People's Bank of China to operate third-party payments.[5]

## Mobile payment: win or perish

By 2013, smartphone users in China accounted for 43% of all mobile phone users. It seemed as if the Chinese migrated overnight from PC to mobile. Alipay, however, was not yet ready for the mobile revolution. A sense of crisis engulfed the entire company. In early 2013, it made an "all-in" bet on the mobile platform. A team of more than 300 technicians was formed and worked day and night for three months developing a mobile app. Alipay version 7.0 was launched, which was followed in 2015 by an improved version 9.0. Alipay had positioned itself as a platform offering a variety of services. Its app allowed users to connect easily with location-based services to hail a taxi, buy movie tickets, order a takeaway or find the nearest petrol station. App users could also manage money saved in Alipay to invest in a money market fund or other wealth management products.

The decision to move to mobile was prescient. By 2019, 53% of the population used a smartphone[6] and payment transactions had reached a total of RMB347 trillion (US$49.7 trillion), placing China at the top of the world mobile-payment rankings.[7] In the fourth quarter of 2019, Alipay accounted for 55.1% of China's mobile-payment market.[8] Had it missed the mobile revolution, the competitive landscape would be very different; Taobao and Alipay could have been overtaken by competitors.

## Yu'ebao: from payment solution to financial services provider

With the Alipay member account system up and running, its combined total balance grew rapidly. And yet, the ease with which the express payments worked made it less attractive for members to keep their accounts in balance. The more convenient the express payment, the less likely people were need to keep a positive balance in Alipay account. Alipay needed to maintain the excellent customer experience of its express payments system, while at the same time increasing user loyalty and stickiness (retention and engagement). One way was to pay interest. Financial services had been a part of Alipay's vision for some time, and this was a perfect starting point.

In June 2013, Alipay, in collaboration with Tian Hong Asset Management, launched Yu'ebao, the first ever internet fund. Yu'ebao allowed its users to put money deposited in Alipay into a money market fund managed by Tian Hong Asset Management. The fund offered an annual return of around 3.6%,[9] which compared very favourably with the 0.35% interest offered on current account deposits.[10] Within ten days, it attracted over one million users and by 2016, the assets base reached RMB700 billion (US$105.4 billion).[11]

Alipay continued to launch other new financial services. Users mainly invested their money in Yu'ebao to earn interest while still enjoying the flexibility of a current account. But, in addition, they could also buy wealth management products such as mutual funds, precious metals and even insurance policies. In April 2015, the consumer credit service, Ant Credit Pay (蚂蚁花呗), was launched. Based on their credit rating, users were granted a consumption credit amount ranging from RMB500 (US$80.3) to RMB50,000 (US$8,027) and could enjoy up to 41 days of interest-free borrowing. Many of Ant Credit Pay's customers were not covered by traditional financial institutions, and it was especially popular with the generation born after the 1980s. A loan service, Ant Borrow, also came online. According to their credit scoring, Ant Borrow users could apply for loans ranging from RMB1,000 (US$160) to RMB300,000 (US$48,166), with a maximum repayment period of 12 months.

With the advent of Yu'ebao, the challenges were no longer specifically about payment transactions but were more about leveraging user flow and transactions. On the one hand, it was important to diversify the offering and, on the other, to retain customer retention and engagement. In summary, Alipay allows consumers to spend money, manage money, earn interest on money and borrow money – all on one platform.

## Ant Financial: not just for Taobao

October 2014 saw the establishment of Ant Financial. This was Ma's long-cherished idea – for Alipay to serve other customers in addition to Taobao and to develop as an independent entity. In fact, Alipay was already separate from Taobao, having become a part of the Zhejiang Alipay Network Technology Company back in December 2004. In 2011, Yahoo challenged the rather vague transfer of ownership just before the IPO of Ma's shares. "Yahoo Inc. disclosed that China's Alibaba Group has transferred owner-ship of its online-payments company to a new entity controlled by Alibaba Chief Executive, Jack Ma".[12]

Ma and other co-founders and early employees of Alibaba hold 76% of Ant Financial's shares.[13] Currently, Alibaba does not directly own shares of Ant Financial, only indirectly via the co-founders' ownership. Alipay and Yu'ebao are both parts of Ant Financial. Ant Financial brought to market many new financial products including Ant Credit Pay for online consumer loans, Ant Dake (蚂蚁达客) for crowdfunding, Ant Fortune for wealth management and Ant Financial Cloud that provides cloud services for financial institutions. Ant Financial and its affiliate Alipay have been active investors both domestically and in nearby Asian markets such as India, South Korea, Thailand and the Philippines.

The promotional video on the homepage of Ant Financial's website portrays the lives of ordinary people. Alibaba has been serving small and medium-sized enterprises (SMEs) since its inception, and the customers of Ant Financial are the "little people" – "as small as ants" – who "neverthe-less can be tenacious and feisty".

In May 2015, the Zhejiang Banking Regulatory Commission granted Alibaba an internet banking licence. MYBank, owned by the Ant Financial Group and a couple of other companies, held one of six new banking licences granted to privately owned companies under a pilot scheme aimed at diversifying China's financial system. Ant Financial's internet financial ecosystem was maturing. MYBank offers financial services for consumers, farmers and SMEs; in particular, SMEs in the e-commerce sector. By June 2018, MYBank had served over 1,042,000 SMEs with a total loan amount of over RMB1.88 trillion (US$292 billion).[14]

To further enable the globalisation of Alibaba's e-commerce and follow the Chinese customers on their journeys overseas, Ant Financial entered the international financial markets, which led to an increase in its valuation. In

July 2015, it received "A-round" funding from eight investment institutions including China's National Social Insurance Fund and CDB Capital, giving it a super-unicorn valuation of US$45 billion. Ten months later, the valuation increased by US$$15 billion, or one-third. In April 2016, Ant Financial raised US$4.5 billion with an even larger valuation of US$60 billion.

When it listed on the Hong Kong and Shanghai stock exchanges on November 5, 2020, Ant Financial expected to make its IPO the largest in history, with a valuation of US$313 billion, and planned to raise US$34.5 billion.[15] However, on November 3, 2020, the Shanghai Stock Exchange suspended the IPO, claiming changes in the regulatory environment meant that the company had yet to meet the listing requirements at the bourse – a sign of the tense relationship between the leading fintech company and the Chinese regulators. One of the concerns raised was the risk associated with Ant Financial's high leverage ratio (Figure 4.2).

The creation of Alipay and later Ant Financial laid a solid foundation for the emergence of mobile payments and made an indelible contribution

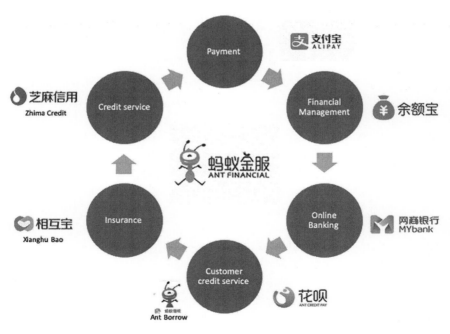

Figure 4.2 Ant Financial's offerings.

to the e-commerce sector in China. Without Alipay, the development of China's electronic payment and internet finance could have been held back by several years. Alipay solved one problem after another on its way to offering better and more integrated customer services. It grew from being merely a payment tool for Taobao into a financial unicorn offering a full range of financial services rivalling traditional banks. Alipay is so convenient that the Chinese prefer it to credit cards or even cash.

## WeChat pay and the payment war

In 2005, Tencent, parent of WeChat, also launched its payment tool, Fortune Pass (财付通). In 2013, Fortune Pass connected with WeChat to become WeChat Pay. Tencent was considered to be leader in social media but not online payments. According to an iResearch report, in 2014, Alipay commanded 82.3% of the Chinese online payment market, and Tencent was a distant second at 10.6%. Pony Ma — founder and CEO of Tencent — wanted to shake things up.

Among the many traditions related to Chinese New Year, it is customary to give out "red packets", or pocket money, to relatives and friends (particularly to children) as part of the festivities. WeChat rolled out an online version of exchanging red packets and it went viral: five million users participated in WeChat red packets on New Year's Eve of 2014 alone. In Chinese New Year 2015, 30 million users exchanged over one billion red packets. As the explosive growth continued in 2016 and 2017, WeChat's payment system gained millions of users.

Chinese New Year spawns the greatest human migration on earth. Over the course of a month, an estimated three billion trips are made by people in China. As migrant workers living in the cities went back to their family homes in the countryside, they took with them the new-found payment technology. As of Q3 in 2018, based on monthly and daily active user counts, WeChat Pay was dominant in the large and evolving Chinese online payment market.

Although Tencent gained the upper hand in the red packet war, Alipay refused to play second fiddle in the overall game of online payments. The larger "payment war" extended to all spheres of Chinese commercial life, both online and offline – each fruit stand, and hotel, at a time. The Chinese have become so used to scanning QR bar codes to pay for taxi rides, or parking, that they find it inconvenient when travelling abroad, where payments are still largely based on cash and credit cards. Street beggars use QR codes. You can't be a beggar in China without a smart phone and WeChat account.

The battle between WeChat pay and Alipay accelerated the consolidation of mobile payments into Chinese society and laid a foundation for the new retail that was to follow. Many people shun wallets nowadays as a cashless society is increasingly becoming the reality.

What are the reasons behind the success of Alipay and WeChat Pay? How were they able to solve one difficult problem after another and continue to explore new opportunities and become so monumental?

1. **From copycat to innovation**. Twenty years ago, when Chinese e-commerce was in its infancy, most entrepreneurs looked at American e-commerce models that they could replicate. They took American firms to be the blueprints. But a copycat strategy was not going to make the Chinese global leaders in e-commerce. And innovations based on finding solutions to consumer needs do not necessarily require major technological breakthroughs. Alipay solved the customer need for trust with its custodian transaction model, which is simply a modification of the transaction process rather than a significant invention. In fact, it could be viewed as a combination of PayPal and more traditional bank trust accounts. The change was modest, but it ushered in a new era of e-commerce in China and set the foundation for Alipay's future growth. Likewise, Alipay's independent account system was not a technological breakthrough, but it did help the company develop into an independent third-party payment tool, and it was an indispensable prelude to the establishment of Ant Financial.

2. **Extreme customer centricity**. Alipay's success is the outcome of solving customer service problems. In the fast-paced internet era, for corporations to mature, they need to identify and solve new problems. If there is one important principle that Alipay followed, it was "extreme customer centricity". Not content with the initial success of its trusted payment system, Alipay pushed on to launch the "if anything goes wrong with your transaction, we pay" campaign. Innovation

is a corollary of the relentless pursuit of customer centricity. Two decades ago, most Chinese companies were technologically inferior to their overseas competitors; they had to work harder to improve customer experience. What multinational companies can learn from their Chinese counterparts is to think from the customer perspective: make the products or services more user-friendly and convenient and bring as much value as possible to the customers.

3. **The inertial giants.** The emergence of Yu'ebao undoubtedly had a huge impact on China's commercial banks. The traditional banks had already thought about selling money market funds over the internet but they did not initiate these types of services for fear of disrupting their own business model whereby they gained profit on the difference between lending and borrowing rates. In other words, the customer's best interests were neglected in favour of corporate profit. This is not dissimilar to the story of Kodak. Kodak was the first to invent digital photography. But it didn't adopt it for fear of losing its vested interests in the traditional photo film business. The moral here is that someone else will disrupt your business if you are unwilling to yourself.

## Concluding remarks

Today, Chinese consumers use their mobile phones to order food, buy movie tickets, order takeaways or hail a taxi. At roadside stalls, they scan QR codes to pay the stall holder. Financial services are just a few taps away, even if they have only one yuan in their account. Alipay and WeChat Pay played a crucial role in enabling all of this.

However, we should not forget that these developments were in response to the specific challenges of online transactions and − later on − emerging opportunities that Alibaba and Tencent exploited swiftly. Figure 4.3 provides a summary. Here again, we highlight the entrepreneurial drive and pragmatic mindset of solving real problems that customers face.

In the next chapter, we introduce the last enabling pillar, social media, a true accelerant of new retail without which customer touchpoints would have been limited to the various static platforms where purchases are made.

| Challenge | Opportunity | Innovation |
|---|---|---|
| Trust in online transactions between strangers | | Alipay |
| Settlement efficiency | | Virtual account system |
| Failure of payment transfer | | Express Payment |
| Mobile payment | | Alipay mobile |
| | Positive balance in Alipay | Yu'ebao |
| | High transaction volume | Consumer credit and consumer loans |
| | Plethora of offerings | Ant Financial – the world's largest fintech |

Figure 4.3  Milestones of Alipay/Ant Financial.

## Notes

1   Converted at concurrent exchange rate, unless otherwise specified.
2   You Xi, Ant Finance: The Rise of a Technological and Financial Unicorn, CITIC Press.
3   You Xi, Ant Finance: The Rise of a Technological and Financial Unicorn, CITIC Press.
4   https://site.douban.com/186720/widget/notes/11049613/note/251005100/.
5   Mark Greeven, Wei Wei, Business ecosystems in China.
6   https://www.iimedia.cn/c1061/67391.html.
7   https://3g.163.com/news/article/FCBSLIEQ0519811T.html.
8   https://kuaibao.qq.com/s/20200401AZP0BX00?refer=spider.
9   Mark Greeven, Wei Wei, Business ecosystems in China.
10   http://www.southmoney.com/lilv/dingqicunkuanlilv/201311/36329.html.
11   You Xi, Ant Finance: The Rise of A Technological and Financial Unicorn, CITIC Press.
12   https://m.yicai.com/news/785795.html.
13   https://xueqiu.com/8508206045/138305822.
14   https://www.mybank.cn.
15   https://www.forbes.com/sites/sarahhansen/2020/10/26/ant-group-will-raise-345-billion-in-biggest-ipo-ever/?sh=65b538e76072.

# 5

# SOCIAL MEDIA PLATFORMS

## The new retail accelerator

With the establishment of e-commerce platforms, the development of payment methods and the construction of logistics networks, the three basic conditions for the evolution of new retail were in place: the information flow, the capital flow and product flow. It seemed that e-commerce was ready to race ahead. However, our research revealed that more catalysts were needed for e-commerce to grow exponentially and thrive: social media platforms.

The development of new retail has relied increasingly on social media platforms such as Weibo, WeChat and Xiaohongshu (小红书). Indeed, some of the new retail models have their origins in social media platforms, and their subsequent rapid development was dependent upon them. Social media helped cultivate certain consumer habits and consumer behaviours. For example, people now tend to check online reviews before they go to restaurants, or compare prices and ratings on different websites before buying electronic goods or cosmetics. Without social media, some of the new retail formats may not have emerged at all, or certainly not at the

DOI: 10.4324/9781003205074-6

speed they have. Social media platforms are an integral part of China's new retail landscape, and we include them as one of the foundational pillars of the new retail evolution.

While social media platforms in China are highly diverse and special-ised, in this chapter we focus on the three that best represent the social media revolution in China: WeChat, Weibo and Xiaohongshu.

## Tencent: from QQ to WeChat

### Pony Ma

The first key player in this chapter is Pony Ma. Unrelated to Jack Ma, the founder of Alibaba, Pony Ma established Tencent in 1998, a year before Alibaba was launched.[1]

Pony Ma's Chinese name is Ma Huateng (马化腾). Outside of China he may not be as well-known as Jack Ma, but he is just as ambitious. Jack Ma is a talented communicator whereas Pony Ma is more focused on the tech-nical side of consumer solutions. As the chairman and CEO of Tencent, he is still involved in product development.

Born in 1971, Pony Ma spent his childhood years in Hainan province, an island in the South China Sea. In 1984, when he was in junior high school, he moved to Shenzhen with his parents. In the early 1980s, Shenzhen was a fishing village with just 30,000 people; today it boasts a population of over 13 million and is among China's four super-first-tier cities together with Beijing, Shanghai and Guangzhou. While Ma continued his studies in Shenzhen Middle School, he met three of Tencent's future co-founders: Tony Zhang (张志东), Charles Chen (陈一丹) and Daniel Xu (许晨晔).

As a child, Ma was fascinated with astronomy. On his 14th birthday, he wanted his parents to buy him a telescope. The telescope cost over RMB700 (US$238), equivalent to about four months of his father's salary. When his parents refused to buy it for him, Ma wrote in his diary that they "stran-gled a scientist's dream".[2] His mother came across the diary and his parents relented. Ma got his telescope.

Ma took his college entrance exam in 1989. He received good results and could have gained entry into a prestigious university such as Tsinghua University in Beijing, or Shanghai's Fudan University. But, against a back-drop of political turmoil that summer (the Tiananmen Square protests),

Ma instead stayed in Shenzhen and went to the newly established Shenzhen University. It was not in the same league as Tsinghua or Fudan but, in the long run, the decision paid off.

## The "Gang of Five"

Ma's main interest was astronomy, but Shenzhen University did not have an astronomy department so he decided to major in computer science. Also studying computer science were Tony Zhang and Daniel Xu. Charles Chen studied chemistry.

In his senior year, Ma completed an internship at the Shenzhen Liming Computer Network Company, which was regarded as one of the most tech-savvy computer firms in southern China. Here, he made his first product: stock analysis software. The company paid him RMB50,000 (US$8,678) for it. The amount was equivalent to almost three year's salary for a college graduate. Ma's talent for product development had become evident.

By 1993, the four classmates had graduated and gone their separate ways. Zhang and Xu continued their postgraduate studies in Guangzhou and Nanjing, respectively, while Chen went to Shenzhen's customs bureau and Ma joined the Shenzhen Runxun Communication Development Company, as a software engineer. Runxun provided paging station services. Pagers were popular all over China, and a paging station service was a very profitable business. Runxun was listed on the Hong Kong Stock Exchange. At its peak, its annual turnover was RMB2 billion (US$347 million) and gross profit margin exceeded 30%.[3] Runxun's good fortune would not last long, however, as pagers were soon replaced by mobile phones.

Ma worked at Runxun until 1998, when he decided to start his own business. His original idea was to develop a software system that could call a pager from the internet and allow the pager to receive news and e-mails. He asked Zhang, Xu and Chen to join him. When the four classmates sat down to discuss the business plan, they realised that none of them had prior experience in sales. Ma thought of Jason Zeng (曾李青), a cheery communications graduate. Born in 1970, after graduating from Xidian University (西安电子科技大学), Zeng became marketing manager of the Long-mai Company, an outlet of the Shenzhen Telecom Data Communications Bureau. There he had persuaded a real-estate developer to invest RMB1.2

million (US$145,000) in broadband and create China's first "broadband community". With the addition of Zeng, the "Gang of Five" was ready to launch Tencent together.

The new company started with RMB500,000 (US$60,000). The Chinese name of Tencent is Teng Xun (腾讯). "Teng" is from Ma's name – Ma Huateng (马化腾); "xun" might come from "Runxun(润迅)" or from "Tongxun (通讯)" – "communication" in Chinese. Ma was in charge of strategy and product development; Zhang was responsible for technology and Zeng took care of marketing. Xu and Chen worked part-time.

Tencent was ready to go.

## The birth of OICQ

From 1998, mobile phones started to become popular, gradually replacing pagers. Tencent's internet-connecting pager business went nowhere.

Although pagers were on the way out, internet-based instant messaging services were starting to get noticed. In 1996, three Israeli college students developed ICQ ("I seek you"). ICQ users could chat, send messages and transfer files to their relatives and friends. ICQ was a hit with young people and, within a year, became the world's most popular instant messaging software.[4] By 1998, the number of users exceeded 10 million,[5] and ICQ was bought by AOL for US$407 million.

Great internet products will always attract imitators in China. Tencent was just one of them. Ma knew about ICQ when he worked for Runxun but there were already similar products in China, such as PICQ and NetSprite (网际精灵), and Tencent had no plans to do the same thing. Nevertheless, when Guangzhou Telecom invited bids to develop a Chinese instant messaging tool similar to ICQ, Tencent, needing business, took up the opportunity and submitted a plan for "OICQ". Although the bid failed, Tencent decided to go ahead and develop it anyway.

In February 1999, OICQ was launched, and Zhang's team continued to search for ways to improve the product. Ma and Zhang visited internet cafés to gain insights into user experiences and identify bugs that needed fixing. Nine months later, OICQ had over one million registered users, leaving PICQ and NetSprite far behind.

But without a profit model, OICQ quickly burned through Tencent's funds, leaving only RMB10,000 (US$1,209) in the account. There was no money to add more servers and all employees' pay had to be cut by 50%. Depressed, Ma decided to sell the company. He set the asking price at just RMB3 million (US$363,000) but no buyer came forward with an offer.[6]

Faced with a dwindling cash pool and little chance of being acquired, Zeng thought of venture capital and Tencent attracted IDG and PCCW as investors, probably encouraged by the hefty price AOL had paid for ICQ. However, although OICQ was popular, no one knew how to make money from it.

More problems were to follow. In 2000, AOL sued Tencent for IPR infringement and demanded the return of two domain names, OICQ.com and OICQ.net. Ma decided to rename OICQ as QQ. In November 2000, QQ2000 was launched and became one of the classic versions of QQ in its corporate history. From then on, the development of QQ accelerated, and the number of users soon exceeded 100 million.

Even with a surging user base, however, Tencent still could not find a profit model. Against the backdrop of the internet bubble in 2000, the company was in danger of running out of the newly invested funds from IDG and PCCW. Just as Ma was running out of ideas, MIH, an investment company headquartered in South Africa, came to the rescue.

Tencent came onto MIH's radar by accident. David Wallerstein, MIH's vice president of China operations, had noticed that every time he went to an internet café in China, everyone was using OICQ. He saw that the general managers he worked with, in lots of different companies, had their OICQ number printed on their business cards. He became curious about the popularity of OICQ and contacted Tencent.

With the help of funding from MIH, Tencent was able to continue operating.

As Nietzsche said: "That which does not kill us, makes us stronger", a maxim that applies to Tencent.

## Fighting for profit

Eager to find a working profit model, Tencent sought the help of China Mobile (which later became the dominant mobile operator in China). At the end of 2000, China Mobile launched its "Monternet" service, which provided mobile phone users with value-added services such as games, and image and music downloads. Revenue was divided between China Mobile and the third-party content providers. Tencent became one of the first three partners and finally began to make some money.

But over-reliance on income from Monternet gave Ma a strong sense of insecurity and he searched for alternative profit models. His concerns were later borne out. In 2004, China Mobile, worried about the threat to its monopoly status, closed the door to its third-party partnerships.

Tencent tried to gain revenue through advertising but with poor results. The majority of QQ users were under the age of 25 and the big advertisers, which were mainly from the car industry, real estate, or high-end cosmetics and luxury goods, were a mismatch. The company also tried to charge for QQ account applications, but this caused a huge outcry. A membership-fee model didn't work either – probably because few young Chinese consumers had credit cards, which made online payment inconvenient.

The issue of payment was a problem for all the online operators. In 2002, Tencent launched a virtual currency, "Q Coin", with one Q coin equivalent to RMB1 (US$0.12). Users could buy Q coins as part of their mobile fee, thus bypassing the need for credit cards. In 2003, the company launched a new function, the "QQ show", which mimicked South Korea's sayclub.com website. This was a virtual show, where users could use Q coins to purchase virtual clothing, accessories and scenery to design their own personalised, virtual image. It was an immediate hit with Tencent's young users and became a vital revenue stream.

Older generations of Chinese and many Western cultures didn't see the attraction of the QQ show; they couldn't understand why people would want to spend money on virtual "dressing up". For more than two thousand years Chinese culture had been influenced by Confucianism, which emphasises respect for hierarchy, restraint of desire and observance of etiquette. Open expression was traditionally avoided, for fear of being scrutinised or criticised. On the QQ show, though, young people were able to express themselves freely in a virtual world. Tencent wasn't just selling virtual props – it was selling emotional sustenance. The QQ show was one of the secrets of Tencent's early success.

On June 16, 2004, Tencent listed on the Hong Kong Stock Exchange. The first day's turnover rate was 104% and the closing price fell below the issue price.[7] The market value was HKD7.2 billion (US$0.93 billion).[8] Sixteen years later, in 2020, Tencent's market value had reached HKD5 trillion (US$689 billion), a 694-fold increase.[9] If you invested US$10,000 in Tencent stocks in 2004, it would be worth US$6.9 million today.

## Allen Zhang (张小龙) and WeChat

Competition was increasing, however. Microsoft's MSN was on its way, posing a huge threat to Tencent. Yet this threat turned out to be Pony Ma's greatest lucky draw.

In 2005, QQ accounted for 77.8% of China's instant messaging market, followed by Microsoft's MSN at 10.58%. However, among the 20 million business users, Tencent accounted for 47% and MSN for 53%.[10] One of the reasons for Tencent performing less well among business users was that many companies banned the use of QQ during working hours. It is important to note, though, that Microsoft had achieved its higher percentage without having conducted any prior local research and without promoting MSN locally. In 2005, Microsoft decided to separate out its MSN business and localise its operations.

In the face of such a strong competitor, QQ had to fight back. But it was difficult to change people's perceptions of QQ, and it was hard to attract more business users. Tencent thought of another way, through e-mail. E-mail and instant messaging tools were usually bundled together for business users. Microsoft's Hotmail was very powerful, however, the QQ mailbox was not. Tencent, already listed and funded, thought the best and fastest way of catching up would be through acquisition and fixed its sights on Foxmail.

Foxmail was a mailbox product developed by Allen Zhang in 1996. The Chinese version had more than four million users within one year, and the English version had users in more than 20 countries, making Foxmail one of the top ten domestically produced software programs in China. Allen sold Foxmail for RMB12 million (US$1.5 million) in 2000. In February 2005, it was acquired by Tencent. However, the biggest asset of this transaction was not Foxmail per se; it was Allen Zhang.

In the first few years he was at Tencent, Zhang was in charge of the mailbox business and made many attempts to improve current functions and create new functions, such as "drift bottles" (random messages from strangers – which appealed to younger generations) and "reading spaces" (containing interesting articles and novels). Many of these innovative features were later incorporated into WeChat. Although the QQ mailbox gained more users, it had not yet found a way to make a profit. Zhang felt under pressure.

MSN eventually failed in China; the reason attributed to the problems with localising multinational corporations. Tencent threw everything behind their QQ product, whereas MSN was not of Microsoft's priorities. The running joke was that in 2005, MSN's China team put forward a request to Microsoft to develop the function of offline message, and in 2008, the request was approved.[11] By then, MSN's battle with QQ was over. The head of MSN's R&D in China later joined Tencent.

## The birth of WeChat

In 2010, a software called Kik, a very simple mobile phone instant messaging system, attracted Zhang's attention. Within 15 days of going online, it was downloaded by over a million people. Two weeks later, Xiaomi released a copycat product, Miliao (米聊). Two months on, in January 2011, Zhang and his team of ten launched WeChat.

Rather than promote this new product through the traffic of QQ, however, Zhang decided that WeChat should first prove it had a "natural growth curve". The first version didn't cause much of a splash. The second version added a voice-chat function, which proved highly attractive. In July, a "view people nearby" function was launched, which meant users could find other "WeChatters" in the vicinity and add them as friends. The number of users started to surge. At one point, over 100,000 joined in a single day. Zhang saw the natural growth curve he was looking for and Tencent began to promote WeChat in force, using QQ's significant source of traffic.

In the instant messaging race, Miliao had started out fastest, but Xiaomi did not have the experience of Tencent in operating a huge number of users and its server kept crashing and Miliao fell behind in the race.

WeChat, created for mobile phones, became indispensable to Tencent in the new mobile era. By October 2018, there were over a billion users – and more than half of them clicked on the app at least ten times a day.[12]

## "A lifestyle"

Zhang's motto was "WeChat is a lifestyle"; a slogan that is at once simple and profound. But if you look at the functions the app offers: group chat, location sharing, "moments", red envelopes, "official accounts", "mini-programs" and more, it is not hard to see that WeChat is an integral part of daily life.

"Moments" was launched In April 2012 and allows users to share photos and texts, which friends can comment on and interact with. Viewing moments of friends became part of daily routines, transforming WeChat from simple instant messaging tool into a social platform.

Not long afterwards, the "Official Account" was launched. A strategic innovation, the Official Account had two features: media and e-commerce. Those who were good at writing could open a personal account (later called We-media), and those who liked someone's content could subscribe to follow them – and they could forward the articles in their own Moments. A business could also open an Official Account, to publish information and sell products or services, and users could subscribe to it, thereby making themselves a targeted customer. The public nature of the accounts gave We-medias and businesses the opportunity to connect and interact with users in a social environment. The distance between company and customer had never been closer. The WeChat Official Account is now a "must" for most companies. Any business trying to succeed in the Chinese market has to look at how they can use WeChat.

As people spend more and more time on mobile phones, more and more apps are created. Many apps are used only occasionally but users still need to download and install them on their mobile phone. Zhang was keenly aware of this problem and, in 2017, WeChat launched the "Mini-program" feature. This allowed apps to develop "mini-programs" embedded within WeChat – without any downloading or installation – and allowed users to share mini-programs with their WeChat friends. For businesses, by linking a WeChat Mini-program to their public account, they could improve customer retention and engagement and transform product content into e-commerce opportunities. Today, almost all mainstream apps have WeChat Mini-programs, including Pinduoduo and JD. With the Mini-program function, WeChat went beyond being a platform and became an all-encompassing software ecosystem.

As comprehensive as Tencent's offerings are, however, there are all kinds of user needs in the social media space, and they can't monopolise them all.

## *Weibo*

Twitter was established in 2006, as a microblog, where users could post short messages of up to 140 characters. They could also view, comment and forward information posted by others. In 2007, the number of Twitter users surged, and big names signed up, including American president, Barack Obama.

The earliest to imitate Twitter in China was Fanfou, founded by Wang Xing, who later founded Meituan. (We will talk about Meituan and Wang Xing in Chapter 6.) Fanfou was very popular in 2008 and 2009 and attracted many avant-guard "netizens". Unfortunately, all the Fanfou servers were shut down in 2009 when it fell foul of public security restrictions, which became an opportunity for Sina.

In September 2009, Sina Weibo ("weibo" means "microblogging") was launched. Sina already operated the most popular blog in China – Sina Blog. Sina was good at creating "star power" and invited show-business stars, business celebrities and big-shot media reporters to help promote Sina Weibo. It quickly became the most influential microblogging site in China. Many people have become famous on Sina Weibo by publishing content and interacting with fans. For example, Taobao shop owner Eve Zhang (张大奕) joined Sina Weibo in 2010. She ran her own Taobao clothing store and, in 2014, began to post photos and videos of her merchandise and interact with her followers, who went on to make purchases through her Taobao store. Eve Zhang's Weibo now has close to 12 million followers.[13]

Aside from Sina, Sohu, NetEase and Tencent also launched Weibos. Tencent Weibo started up in May 2010, over six months after Sina Weibo. But neither Tencent, Sohu nor NetEase was as successful as Sina. Tencent went on to develop WeChat and gave up on its Weibo war with Sina. Today, when people talk about Weibo, they mean Sina Weibo. As of December 2019, it had 516 million monthly active users (MAU) and 222 million average daily active users (DAU).[14]

The success of Weibo is not just down to the celebrity effect. Weibo fulfils people's desires for self-expression. Before the emergence of microblogging, people could only obtain information through official government media channels, either the People's Daily or CCTV. However, people are full of opinions, whether they have the relevant knowledge or not. Winter Nie, one of the authors of this book, told us about her mother, whose grandfather, father and brothers were trained as traditional Chinese medicine doctors. Though her mother had never gone to the medical school, she loved to hand out advice on illnesses and medicine. Nie's mother is not alone. Many Chinese are self-proclaimed leaders in various fields. When they hear or see something, they like to comment and put forward their opinion. Like any other society, there is always a group of amateur spectators, commentators and news reporters and Weibo is their perfect outlet.

Weibo brought about an era of socialised, online communication. Users publish, choose and disseminate information, thereby disrupting the traditional mode of top-down communication. Content that has a general appeal can be distributed speedily at very low cost. Kaifu Lee, who served as the president of Google Greater China, said: "Because of Weibo, everyone is available and should be involved, so that they can become the creators of new media!"[15]

Weibo became the birthplace of key opinion leaders (KOLs). Even internet celebrities on other platforms, such as Douyin or Kuaishou, used Weibo to interact with followers.

## Xiaohongshu

WeChat is a social platform between acquaintances. People interact with their relatives, friends and colleagues, creating a flow of information. The launch of WeChat's "Official Account" allowed WeChat to function as a communications channel.

Weibo is a social platform between strangers. The content is mainly news and entertainment gossip. The speed of information dissemination is much faster than on WeChat.

Although reading news and gossip are popular pastimes, people also need professional opinions, however, and like to interact with key opinion leaders (KOLs). Xiaohongshu's popularity is related to this area – untouched by WeChat and Weibo.

Charlwin Mao (毛文超), the founder of Xiaohongshu (小红书), was born in 1985 and is a typical member of the business elite. He graduated from Shanghai JiaoTong University (上海交通大学), one of the top five comprehensive universities in China, and joined Bain Consulting. Four years of work experience later, he went to Stanford to complete his MBA. Mao's business idea came from his own experience. When he was shopping for his parents, he searched for overseas shopping guides and drew an almost complete blank. After graduating from Stanford in 2013, he returned to Shanghai and founded Xiaohongshu, with his friend Miranda Qu. Xiaohongshu means "Little Red Book" for overseas shopping and is positioned as a verified word-of-mouth platform for overseas products.

Xiaohongshu's founding team launched its first product by finding shopping experts to write shopping strategies for eight countries, or regions, such as the United States and Japan. These provided information and advice on products, pricing, tax rebates, discounts and store comparisons. After three months on the Apple Store, Xiaohongshu had hundreds of thousands of downloads.[16] One week after Xiaohongshu went live online, Mao went to Hong Kong. He uploaded pictures of the iPhone5 he bought. The photos attracted more than 100 comments and questions, including "is purchase restricted?", "do you need to wait in a long line", "are there gold-coloured phones?", "can you swipe a credit card?" and even "can I swipe a credit card that is not in my name?" and so on.

It was clear that users wanted to purchase the products discussed on Xiaohongshu so, in 2014, it launched an e-commerce platform, mainly for cross-border purchases. In 2018, Xiaohongshu accounted for 3.7% of China's cross-border retail e-commerce. Tmall International took the number one spot with 31%.[17] Xiaohongshu's social media power had evidently not fully translated into e-commerce functionality. Consumers still used it to gain information but then switched to other platforms to make their purchases. As of July 2019, the number of Xiaohongshu users exceeded 300 million and, by October 2019, MAU exceeded 100 million.[18]

Xiaohongshu transformed from a small community focusing on discussions about overseas shopping into a lifestyle-sharing platform. The content shared includes beauty and skin care, travel, fitness, food, etc. More and more people are using Xiaohongshu and the frequency of active participation is also increasing. The brands have gradually expanded from overseas-only to overseas and domestic. The company's slogan changed from "finding good things abroad" to "recording and sharing my life (标记我的生活)". There are more than three billion pieces of pictures, texts, short videos, etc. published on Xiaohongshu every day. Xiaohongshu has the most KOLs in the field of beauty, skincare and fashion. About 90% of Xiaohongshu's users are women, of which 70% were born after 1990.[19] Users of Xiaohongshu prefer to participate in discussion and content creation. For example, after purchasing cosmetics recommended by a KOL, followers post pictures and comments, which creates more content and more relevance. This kind of interaction is more active than on the Douyin and Kuaishou sharing platforms, which we will discuss in Chapter 9, and the user retention and engagement stickiness is also stronger.

Xiaohongshu entered the domain of foreign brands and gained significant attention. Although sharing its name with the famous volume of Chairman Mao quotations, "Little Red Book" (小红书), its focus areas could hardly be different: luxury products, travel, cosmetics, fashion and beauty, among others. Xiaohongshu's top influencers range from television personalities and actresses to high-school students and stay-at-home mothers. Western luxury brands leverage Xiaohongshu's power by partnering with powerful KOLs such as Fan Bingbing and Rita Wang, two famous movie actresses. (Figure 5.1)

*Figure 5.1* Social media platforms in China.
Illustrated by Aspen Wang.

| | Type of social interaction | Limitations |
|---|---|---|
| WeChat | Social platform between acquaintances | Closed system of interaction |
| Weibo | Social platform among strangers | Gossip and fake news |
| Xiaohongshu | Social platform with KOLs | Specialised topic areas |

Among Chinese social media platforms, there are virtually no foreign companies. This is related to the policies of the Chinese government and gives Chinese companies a competitive advantage. The domestic landscape of social media, however, is no less competitive than anywhere else. In the face of fierce competition, Chinese social media have evolved from mere copycats to innovative powerhouses, driving the new retail landscape.

1. **Local advantages of internet companies.** So far, we have looked at eBay and Taobao, Amazon and JD, PayPal and Alipay, ICQ/MSN and QQ, Hotmail and the QQ mailbox. In the first two decades of internet development, Western companies enjoyed big advantages in technology. However, as the industry matured, technology gave way to products and products gave way to user experience. When it comes to user experience, regional culture, user-consumption behaviours and localisation play a key role in competition. Local advantage is more prominent in e-commerce than in manufacturing sectors. The difference between Chinese and Western social media platforms is also reflected in the profit model. Almost all American social media platforms rely on advertising for profit, while their Chinese counterparts have more choice. The virtual props of QQ, the games on WeChat and the e-commerce of Xiaohongshu are all great sources of income.

2. **"Coming late is the safest way".** "First mover advantage" is often emphasised in the Western business world. But in the case of Pony Ma, it actually worked in the opposite direction. Ma said: "Because the internet market is too new, and the development is too fast, there are many possibilities. If you dominate by yourself, there may be no way to prove that you have made the right choice". Ma later summarised his opinion as a strategy: "Coming late is the safest way".[20] From QQ to WeChat and payment solutions, Tencent almost always followed the first mover, meticulously innovating and finally surpassing them. Today, with the user base of QQ and WeChat, Tencent is more confident in innovating and exerting latecomer advantages in various fields. Ma never considered "being first" important. He competed with William

Ding for games, with Jack Ma for e-commerce, Sina for microblogs and Robin Li for search engines. People gave Ma the nickname "public enemy" because he would often take the idea from other competitors and try to win the ensuing battle. However, being public enemy does not mean he wins all the time. After all, Tencent failed to catch up with Sina on Weibo and it also gave up on its own e-commerce platform, instead investing in JD and Pinduoduo. But it established dominant positions in a number of important fields, such as QQ, WeChat and online games.

3. **Internal competition, opportunities vs efficiency.** While Allen Zhang was developing WeChat, Tencent also had several other teams working on similar tasks independently. In fact, from a business line perspective, the development of WeChat did not officially belong to Zhang's team. In Tencent there is what is called an internal "horse-racing mechanism". No matter what new projects are underway, they are not decided upon entirely by top management; business units can compete on the same project. WeChat, Arena Of Valor, QQ games, etc., are all the results of Tencent's horse-racing mechanism. After several teams have created a product, they are put online to compete with each other. Tencent then decides how much resource to allocate to promote the product based on its performance, and whichever product grows the fastest organically gets to become an independent business. The horse-racing mechanism could be seen as a waste of resources but, if there are "unmissable opportunities", a certain level of waste and trial and error are unavoidable. When we talk about ByteDance, the parent company of Douyin in Chapter 9, for example, we will see that ByteDance had several short video projects such as Douyin, Huoshan short video (火山小视频) and Xigua video (西瓜视频), all incubating at the same time, and let them compete with each other. ByteDance calls this model "bulk incubation". Whether it is called bulk incubation or horse racing, the idea is to use internal competition to get the best product to market quickly.

## Concluding remarks

China's social media platforms are clearly catalysts that helped transform traditional e-commerce into new retail. The internet landscape of social media platforms is radically different from the rest of the world due to regulatory and political considerations. As a consequence, in China, a parallel universe of social media platforms has emerged; one that is arguably more competitive and creative than anywhere else in the world. As the BBC reported,[21] Chinese social media platforms are leading the way for the future of social media. With the newly emerging middle classes equipped with ample disposable income and aspirations to embrace the new material world, China has entered an era of new retail built upon convenient online payment systems, accessible logistics networks and ubiquitous social platforms.

With the three social media platforms we explored in this chapter, the final pillar of the foundation for China's new retail revolution is in place. In the next chapters we explore the new retail approaches that build on these pillars.

## Notes

1   We have another famous "Ma", Peter Ma who created Ping An in 1988. Now Ping An is the largest insurance group in the world by market cap. "Ma" means "horse" in Chinese; so people also refer to the three founders as "the troika." Peter Ma won't be featured in our book, even though he is one of most successful entrepreneurs in China (Ping An was valued at $220 billion (RMB1,540 billion) by the end of 2019). According to 2019 Fortune China 500, Ping An was ranked first for financial performance (profitability) out of all Chinese non-state-owned enterprises (non-SOEs), which means its profitability was ranked ahead of Tencent and Alibaba. Additionally, Ping An's reach is beyond insurance and includes banking, trust and other financial services; it is also in Fintech, AI, automobile, healthcare, real-estate and smart city solutions, etc.

2   Wu Xiaobo. Tencent 1998–2016. Zhejiang University Publishing House.

3   Wu Xiaobo. Tencent 1998–2016. Zhejiang University Publishing House.

4   https://www.sohu.com/a/281851614_100038287.

5   https://www.sohu.com/a/281851614_100038287.

6   Wu Xiaobo. Tencent 1998–2016. Zhejiang University Publishing House.

7   Wu Xiaobo. Tencent 1998–2016. Zhejiang University Publishing House.

8   https://xw.qq.com/cmsid/20200307A0KWVG00.

9   https://pcedu.pconline.com.cn/1355/13557685.html.

10  Wu Xiaobo. Tencent 1998–2016. Zhejiang University Publishing House.

11  Wu Xiaobo. Tencent 1998–2016. Zhejiang University Publishing House.

12  https://zhuanlan.zhihu.com/p/55961764.

13  https://www.weibo.com/p/1003061549362863?is_all=1.

14  https://baijiahao.baidu.com/s?id=16702658296204616608&wfr=-
    spider&for=pc.

15  Li Kaifu. Weibo: Change Everything. Shanghai University of Finance And
    Economics Publishing House.

16  http://www.woshipm.com/evaluating/1931606.html.

17  http://www.woshipm.com/evaluating/1931606.html.

18  http://www.linkshop.com.cn/web/archives/2020/445126.shtml.

19  https://www.sohu.com/a/348384520_730804.

20  Wu Xiaobo. Tencent 1998–2016. Zhejiang University Publishing House.

21  https://www.bbc.com/future/article/20201117-how-china-social-media-
    apps-are-changing-technology.

# Part II

## FIVE STAGES OF NEW RETAIL

# 6

## LOCATION-BASED E-COMMERCE

### Lifestyle remade

Food has always been an integral part of Chinese culture. As Confucius said, "At the origination of all ceremonies are those relating to eating and drinking (夫礼之初，始诸饮食)". This aspect of Chinese culture permeates daily lives. For example, when people meet and say hello, their greetings are literally "Have you eaten?" When talking about the number of people in a family, they ask "How many mouths are there in the household?"

Work is often directly linked to the concept of eating. A job is referred to as a "rice bowl 饭碗" and a really good job is a "golden rice bowl金饭碗", whereas an "iron rice bowl铁饭碗" is a very stable one and "losing one's rice bowl 丢饭碗" means being sacked. The act of firing somebody is colourfully described as "frying a squid".

The Chinese love for food is not just apparent in the words they use. People wait patiently for hours at their favourite restaurants and are generally very picky about the freshness of ingredients and how dishes are prepared. A popular hotpot restaurant chain, Haidilao, provides a variety of amenities and services for customers while they wait, such as battery-charging

DOI: 10.4324/9781003205074-8

stations, drinks, chess boards, manicures and babysitting – all at no extra charge.

Eating out is a prime social activity for the Chinese. When friends meet up, it is important that they find a good restaurant ("good" does not necessarily mean expensive; first and foremost, the food has to be tasty) and colleagues exchange recommendations for restaurants and which dishes are the best. The Chinese spend a seemingly inordinate amount of time discussing food and like to show off their culinary knowledge. The family dinner table conversation often starts with food before venturing on to other subjects, like movies, holidays or school.

Thanks to the ever-expanding ranks of the middle class armed with rising disposable income, consumer aspiration in China has shifted from meeting basic needs to improving quality of life. There is more consumer demand for dining out, travelling and entertainment. A McKinsey report predicted that the size of the upper middle class will continue to expand and, by 2022, would include 54% of Chinese urban households,[1] which is over 400 million people.[2] Millennials (the generation born between 1984 and 2000) are becoming the dominant force of consumption, with an average annual growth rate of 11% – twice that of consumers over the age of 35. Millennials are more likely to seek quality products, demand high service standards and try new things.

The development of internet e-commerce has provided new ways for shopping, which has greatly facilitated people's desire to improve their lives. However, there is also a new solution for lifestyle services, such as eating out and entertainment.

## Meituan Dianping: lifestyle remade

Xiao Li, a 27-year-old IT engineer living in Beijing, was in a good mood, as he usually is on a Friday. On leaving his apartment, he grabbed one of the bikes parked near the community gate. He took out his phone and scanned a QR code to pay the RMB1.5 yuan (US$0.22[3]) rental fee. The cost of the ten-minute ride was worth it because it meant he could snatch an extra ten minutes' sleep. He worked through the morning until noon and, to save time, decided to get a takeaway for lunch. Using the Meituan app he ordered from the restaurant that offered the quickest delivery time. Half an hour later, he was enjoying his meal. By 6pm, he had left work to meet up with two high school classmates. Whenever the three of them met, they always went for Sichuan cuisine. On the Dianping app, Xiao Li picked out a Sichuan restaurant with very good reviews that was close to the subway station, and booked a table. During dinner, the three of them used the Maoyan (猫眼) app to buy discount movie tickets. After the movie, they checked out a nearby club, based on the rave reviews it had received on Dainping.

Ordering a takeaway lunch, checking out reviews of Sichuan restaurants, booking a table, buying movie tickets and finding a nearby club ... were all at Xiao Li's fingertips and he needed just one app, Meituan Dianping. Meituan Bike, Meituan Takeaway, Dianping and Maoyan all belong to the same company.

At 9:30am on September 20, 2018, Wang Xing, founder of Meituan, performed the ceremony of "striking the gong" on the floor of the Hong Kong Stock Exchange. Meituan Dianping was officially listed at an IPO price of HKD69 (US$8.8) and the opening price was HKD72.9 (US$ 9.1). Its market cap of US$51 billion surpassed those of Xiaomi (US$48 billion) and JD (US$38 billion),[4] and Meituan Dianping became China's fourth largest internet company after Alibaba (US$436 billion), Tencent (US$402 billion) and Baidu (US$77 billion).[5] In 2015, Wang Xing set a goal to build Meituan into a company with a market value over US$100 billion. China, with a population of 1.4 billion, had a huge potential for lifestyle services and Meituan set its sights on fulfilling those needs.

## Wang Xing: a born entrepreneur

At the time of its listing, Meituan had already been established for eight years and Wang Xing had been an entrepreneur for 15 years. He had shown himself to be shrewd businessman, identifying a number of commercial opportunities.

Unlike many other Chinese of the same era, Wang's childhood was not one of poverty. He was very good academically and gained a place at Tsinghua University, China's equivalent to MIT in the United States. Unusually, he was admitted without having to sit the entrance exam. After graduating, he received a scholarship to the University of Delaware, majoring in electrical engineering and computer science.

In 2003, when Wang was 25, he saw the great opportunities that the internet in China offered and decided to return home. While we often hear about Steve Jobs, Bill Gates and Mark Zuckerberg dropping out of college to go into business, given the emphasis the Chinese place on higher education, it was an extremely bold move. Wang started no fewer than ten entrepreneurial projects, the most famous of which, in 2005, was Xiaonei.com (校内网, "intra-school net") – a campus Social Network Software (SNS) similar to Facebook. Xiaonei.com attracted over 30,000 users in three months, with the first sign-ups coming mainly from top universities such as Tsinghua, Peking and Renmin. In 2006, the number of users exploded. But Wang had no funds to add more servers and he was forced to sell the company, for US$2 million.[6] Xiaonei.com was later renamed Renren.com and, in 2011, went public in the United States with a market value of over US$7 billion.[7]

In 2007, Wang founded another company, Fanfou (饭否, "have you eaten?"), which was based on Twitter and gained popularity in 2008 and 2009, before the launch of Weibo. Fanfou attracted avant-garde netizens (such as programmers) and the number of users soon exceeded one million.[8] However, in 2009, the Chinese government tightened regulations around internet content and Fanfou was shut down.[9] Other Chinese portal giants, such as Sina and Netease, started to launch their own micro-blogs, while Fanfou could only sit and watch. The Fanfou venture stalled.

## Group-buying war: the last man standing

By 2010, Wang had been a serial entrepreneur for seven years. Most of his ventures had gone nowhere but he wasn't giving up. This time, he founded Meituan, a copy of American e-commerce platform Groupon, which provided discounts based on group buying. The main profits would come from commissions. Group-buying websites normally earn 10%–50% of transactions.

Before Meituan's launch, there was already a group-buying company in China called Lashou (拉手网, "hand in hand") and many other similar firms began to spring up, including 55Tuan (窝窝团) and Nuomi (糯米网), as well as Groupon's Chinese company GaoPeng (高朋) and Manzuo (满座). By August 2011, there were more than 5,800 similar websites in China,[10] which demonstrates how Chinese entrepreneurs like to plunge in head-long when they see a new market with a low entry barrier. A lot of capital flooded the group-buying space but most companies burnt through their funds trying to attract customers.

At the end of 2010, Meituan received its A-round financing – US$12 million – from Sequoia Capital.[11] Compared to the funding received by its competitors, this was not a large amount. From 2010 to April 2011, Lashou completed three rounds of financing and received a total of US$160 million.[12] In April 2011, Dianping (点评) received C-round financing of US$100 million.[13] In July 2011, Meituan received Series B financing of only US$50 million – Alibaba being the lead investor.[14] To compete with each other, many companies spent millions on advertising. Among them, Nuomi with a RMB200 million (US$25 million) ad campaign and Dianping, which, in 2011, spent a total of RMB340–400 million (US$37–50 million) on advertising.[15]

Faced with this onslaught, Meituan took a more cautious approach. First, it adopted different promotion strategies for consumers and merchants. On the consumer side, the company purchased online advertising and, to attract merchants, it created a strong and effective on-the-ground pro-motion team. Second, the company invested heavily in its IT system so it would be user-friendly to both buyers and sellers. Third, it avoided big cities such as Beijing, Shanghai and Shenzhen, where the competition was fierce, focusing on provincial capitals and second-tier cities, where the other group-buying companies were not in force. While most Chinese en-trepreneurs are good at acting quickly and learning through doing, Wang's great strength was thinking things through. While others threw money at boosting traffic, he took a different approach.

In the second half of 2011, Lashou failed to get listed in the United States. The capital market began to question the group-buying profit models and became cautious about further investment. Many firms were short of funding, some due to overspending on advertising. By the first half of 2014, only 176 group-buying websites had survived. The mortality rate for the sector stood at 96.5%.[16]

Meituan, which remained rational and cautious throughout the adver-tising frenzy, had the most cash in its account. In May 2014, it received US$300 million C-round financing[17] and emerged as the winner of the group-buying war. In 2014, the company's annual transaction volume exceeded RMB46 billion (US$7.5 billion) and it had expanded to more than 100 cities nationwide, with a market share of over 60%.[18]

Dianping was different to the other group-buying companies. Established in 2003 in Shanghai, its main business was restaurant reviews. The revenue came from key-word searches and by 2010 it was the number one website for restaurant reviews. It diversified into group buying but struggled along with many of its competitors. However, with the advantage of having accumulated both merchant and consumer resources over the years, Dianping was among the survivors. In 2014, Tencent acquired a 20% share of Dianping for US$400 million.[19]

In October 2015, Meituan and Dianping merged, amassing an astonishing 81% market share between them. Wang became CEO of the new company, Meituan Dianping.[20] In November 2015, Tencent invested US$1 billion into the new merger.[21] Although Alibaba had been the first to invest in Meituan in 2011, it lost control of Meituan to Tencent.

Wang later commented on Meituan's success using a sentence from the book, The Art of War (孙子兵法), by Sun Tzu, one of the most famous Chinese historical books about war strategies: "Not being defeated by the enemy depends on how you do it, and whether you can defeat the enemy depends on what the enemy does.不可胜在己，可胜在敌". He further explained that "It is not that We (Meituan) beat our competitors, but they stumbled themselves".[22]

## Food delivery: competing with Ele.me

In 2008, when Wang was still running Fanfou, Zhang Xuhao, a graduate of Shanghai Jiaotong University (上海交通大学), started Ele.me. Zhang Xuhao liked playing games but found it was difficult to order a food delivery while he was in the middle of a game and he seized on it as a business opportunity. As a postgraduate student from a top-tier university in China, he could easily have found a job in a global top 500 company, but instead, he decided to set up the food-delivery company, Ele.me.

Meituan, although it had survived the group-buying war, still lacked a clear profit model. Lashou's failure made Wang acutely aware of the limitations of the group-buying model. The firm conducted an in-depth study of Ele.me and decided that the food-delivery market was huge. It made a bold prediction that the daily volume would exceed ten million.[23] In the second half of 2013, Meituan launched its food-delivery business in 30 cities simultaneously. Ele.me was active in only 12 of these cities.[24]

In May 2014, Baidu also established its food-delivery subsidiary, Baidu Waimai (百度外卖), which targeted high-end, white-collar customers. For a time, Meituan, Ele.me and Baidu Waimai were in a three-way competition. However, Meituan's market share continued to rise. In August 2017, Ele. me acquired Baidu Waimai (in October 2018, Baidu Waimai was renamed "Star.Ele.me").[25] The three-way competition was reduced to a fight between the two giants, Meituan and Ele.me. According to the *Analysis Report on the Development of China's Mobile Internet Industry in the First Half of 2018*, released by the third-party internet big data-monitoring agency Trustdata, Meituan, Ele.me and Baidu Waimai accounted for 59%, 36% and 3% of the market, respectively.[26] Meituan was clearly leading the pack with a market share exceeding the sum of Ele.me and Baidu Waimai.

How did Meituan, a late comer, beat Ele.me at its own game? At first, Meituan tried to follow a similar strategy to its more established rival but soon found that it couldn't catch up quick enough. So in 2014, it hired 1,000 new employees, gave them one month's training and sent them out to 100 different cities to expand Meituan's presence,[27] while Ele.me stayed put in the few cities in which it already operated. Baidu Waimai, the third player in the food-delivery game, appeared to lack any clear strategy. When parent company Baidu switched its focus from food delivery to AI, it sold Baidu Waimai to Ele.me.

In February 2018, the Alibaba Group acquired Ele.me for US$9.5 billion,[28] and in October, they announced the merger of Ele.me and Koubei into Alibaba Local Life Services. Koubei was founded in 2004 with a business model similar to Dianping but its development had been much slower. Alibaba invested in it in 2006 and, in 2015, Alibaba and Ant Financial jointly invested RMB6 billion (US$924 million), with the aim of transforming Koubei into a lifestyle-service platform.[29]

The new competition was Meituan/Dianping vs Ele.me/Koubei and behind these players were two giants: Tencent and Alibaba.

Meituan and Ele.me competed ferociously on all fronts. One of the most lively and eye-catching altercations was the "battle of the helmets". Meituan started off by launching a kangaroo-ear helmet for its couriers. Ele.me riders retaliated with bamboo dragonfly helmets. Meituan riders then wore cute little yellow duck helmets, while Ele.me riders took to a cool-blue, second dimension-style helmets. Then both Meituan and Ele. me riders wore Monkey King helmets... and the battle went back and forth over many rounds, incorporating couriers' jackets and attracting advertising. The helmet battle brought a lot of colour and fun to the streets and laneways of China and it also drew a lot of attention to Meituan and Ele.me.

## OTA: competing with Ctrip

Meituan also set its sights on the online travel agency (OTA) space. Early in 2012, Wang stated that Meituan would be "a location-based, e-commerce platform" meeting every facet of lifestyle needs.[30] That same year saw the launch of Maoyan, which provided an online booking service for movie tickets. Food-delivery and OTA businesses were added in 2013. Meituan was still far from becoming a super-platform for lifestyle services, but that didn't prevent Wang from pursuing his ambition.

In 2013, when Meituan entered the OTA market, there were already several listed OTA companies. The history of China's OTA industry development is also one of price wars. In May 1999, Ctrip, the first OTA company in China, was launched in Shanghai and in December 2003 it listed on the NASDAQ, with a market cap of over US$500 million.[31] By 2007, Ctrip held a dominating 56% market share in China, while that of the second-ranked eLong (艺龙) was 18%.[32] In 2010, with the emergence of mobile internet, eLong and Qunar (去哪儿) threatened to overtake Ctrip. Qunar was an online search platform for flights and price comparisons, while eLong focused on online hotel bookings. The two nibbled away at Ctrip's market share which, by 2011, had fallen to 41%.[33] In order to withstand the challenge, Ctrip initiated a price war with eLong and Qunar, which lasted several years. Each of them spent hundreds of millions of dollars in the process and the price cutting led to huge losses for all OTA companies, leaving the industry in bad shape. In May 2015, Ctrip, together with the Plateno Group and Tencent, acquired eLong's shares from Expedia. After the acquisition, Ctrip held a 37.6% stake, became the largest shareholder of eLong and controlled 89% of the online hotel booking market in China.[34] On October 26, 2015, Ctrip swapped shares with Baidu to acquire 45% of Qunar and incorporated Qunar into Ctrip, thereby using acquisition to solidify its lead position.

The timing of Meituan's entry into the OTA market was good. In 2013, Ctrip was focusing on its price war with eLong and Qunar and had no time to deal with Meituan. Besides, Ctrip mainly focused on the star-rated hotels, while Meituan set its sights on the budget hotel market. Cross-marketing worked for Meituan: when people were ordering takeaway food on the app, they came across links to hotels and tried out Meituan's hotel booking services. Eighty percent of Meituan's hotel bookings were users of its food-ordering service.[35] Trustdata's 2018 Q2 *China Online Hotel Reservation Industry Development Analysis Report* showed that in the second quarter of 2018, Meituan ranked number one in terms of room nights and accounted for 46.2% of the domestic online hotel booking market, exceeding the sum of Ctrip, Qunar and eLong put together.[36] Of course, with margins for star-rated hotels higher than for budget hotels, Ctrip remained ahead of Meituan in terms of revenue.

## Ride hailing competing with Didi

On February 14, 2017, Valentine's Day, Meituan quietly launched its ride-hailing service in Nanjing, followed by Shanghai and other cities. In response, Didi, the leader of China's online ride-hailing market, launched a food-delivery service, on April 1st – April Fool's Day. Securing a foothold in the ride-hailing market meant burning money in subsidies, however, and Meituan's financial losses continued to mount. In 2018, Meituan stated in its IPO prospectus that "we do not expect to further expand this (ride-hailing) service". In 2019, the Meituan ride-hailing app went offline. In the meantime, Didi's food delivery business also went nowhere and was shut down too.

Meituan didn't give up on investing in ride hailing, though. In 2019, the Meituan app connected with ride-hailing service providers including Shouqi (首汽约车), Cao Cao (曹操出行) and Shenzhou (神州专车). In April 2018, it acquired bike rental company Mobike for US$2.7 billion, with 65% cash and 35% Meituan shares.[37] In 2019, Mobike was connected to the Meituan app and changed its name to Meituan Bike. By 2019, new Meituan bicycles had replaced the old Mobike bicycles. The colour of the new bicycles was yellow, and they were designed to last longer and the corresponding riding fee was also increased. As a result, the gross margin in 2019 in the new bike rental business increased, mainly thanks to improvements in operational efficiencies and price increase.[38] Although the overall bike rental business continues to lose money, the deficit has narrowed.

## Delivery: beyond food and Meituan

To support the food-delivery business, Meituan established a huge distribution network, which included hundreds of thousands of delivery riders. With such an extensive network, the company clearly intended to deliver more than just food.

In July 2018, a new brand was launched, "Meituan Super-Fast Buying" (美团闪购), which was rolled out in 2,500 cities and counties across the country. It aimed to use Meituan's distribution network as a delivery service for retailers such as supermarkets, convenience stores, fresh food stores, flower shops, etc.

In 2019, just after Chinese New Year, the company launched "Meituan Online Grocery Shopping", where consumers could order fresh vegetables, fruit, meat, eggs, rice, noodles, cooking oil, seafood and other foodstuffs online. To do this, it set up "residents' service stations" in communities where there was a high population density. The stations provided storage, sorting and distribution and were called "front warehouses". They served residents within a two-kilometre radius and delivered fresh groceries within 30 minutes. By the end of 2019, Meituan had 40 front warehouses in Beijing, 15 in Shanghai and 3 in Wuhan.[39]

In May 2019, Meituan launched the new brand "Meituan Delivery", a world-leading delivery platform that extended its services to more industries and more customers. Meituan Delivery's technology platform, delivery network and value chains were opened up to ecosystem partners.

— **Technology platform:** Meituan's "super brain" — a real-time delivery system to effect systematic and super-fast order dispatch.
— **Delivery network:** almost 10,000 delivery centres and front warehouses across the country; in May 2019, the average number of active delivery riders exceeded 600,000 per day, daily delivery orders exceeded 30 million and the average delivery time was within 30 minutes.[40]
— **Value chains:** more than 3.6 million merchants across the country and more than 400 million users downstream.[41]

While the delivery network was something tangible that was visible to the public, what they couldn't see was the invisible "super brain" of big data and AI technology that was behind it. Meituan's "super brain" backs up tens of millions of orders per day. The dispatch system can perform around 2.9 billion route-planning algorithm operations per hour and calculate optimised delivery routes in an average of 0.55 milliseconds.[42] The "super brain" plans the most suitable routes and number of riders based on order density and restaurant distribution. At the same time, the system assigns order delivery according to the real-time location of the rider, the restaurant and the user, making sure the order is within the rider's delivery range. It then takes into account that the rider is likely to receive another four orders in the meantime and will integrate all the data including location of restaurants and users, the restaurant's speed to prepare meals and the corresponding street traffic conditions, to plan out the shortest route. For example, if there are several gates in a community, the system will know which gate is the nearest and fastest, whether there is an elevator in the building, how long it takes to climb stairs compared to waiting for elevators, and so on. It can automatically detect the risk of delivery delays and re-dispatch orders. Meituan also developed a smart voice headset that allows riders to take orders without using their hands.

In 2020, with the sudden emergence of the Covid-19 pandemic, Meituan's autonomous delivery vehicle began operating in Shunyi District, Beijing. Once a consumer has placed an order on the app, the intelligent delivery vehicle picks up the goods and travels driver-free to the customer, who opens the box to take out their items. There is no person-to-person contact in the whole process.

In the future, Meituan's delivery riders and autonomous delivery vehicles could serve almost every aspect of people's daily life, from meals to daily necessities.

## Not only B2C, but also B2B

As a lifestyle services platform, Meituan has hundreds of millions of consumers on one side and millions of merchants on the other, and serving merchants is equally important to the company as serving consumers. Wang believed the driver of the development of the internet industry would shift from the growth of users (the consumer side) to the merchants' improvement of value chain efficiency (the business side).[43]

Meituan already helped merchants with online marketing, through restaurant reviews and food delivery. Towards the end of 2015, the company introduced further merchant services, which came in three major parts: the restaurant management system (RMS) that improves the digital management and efficiency of merchants; the Kuai Lv (快驴进货), which helps merchants improve the efficiency of the supply chain; and the Meituan Microloan (美团小贷), which provides a solution to the cash-flow problems that businesses often face.

Kuai Lv developed rapidly from its launch in 2016. It provided merchants with the procurement and delivery of a range of goods including rice noodles, grains, cooking oil, drinks, meat, poultry, vegetables and eggs. By the end of 2019, Kuai Lv covered 22 provinces and 45 cities across China and the number of active merchants using Kuai Lv's service was around 450,000.[44]

In 2019, Meituan launched the Meituan Academy, to fulfil the knowledge needs of SME owners in industries such as food, accommodation and beauty. The academy provides thousands of online video courses on how to run a business and offers practical tips. The video courses cover a wide range of topics from marketing to operations, using real-life cases and received over 12 million views in just one year.[45]

By providing all kinds of B2B services to the store owners and merchants, Meituan effectively killed two birds with one stone: increasing merchant loyalty and therefore making it more difficult for competitors to steal them away, and also helping them to manage their businesses better and increase profits for themselves and Meituan.

## Meituan: lifestyle O2O e-commerce platform

Meituan currently provides food delivery, ride hailing, hotel bookings, movie reviews, restaurant reviews, restaurant reservations and other lifestyle services. In its 2018 IPO prospectus, the company said it was China's leading "lifestyle o2o e-commerce platform, connecting consumers and merchants with technology". Meituan's mission is to help people "eat better, live better".

Illustrated by Aspen Wang.

The year 2019 was an important year for Meituan, as it turned profitable. Its 2019 annual profit was RMB2.9 billion (US$416 million), while its 2018 losses were RMB11.1 billion (US$1.62 billion).[46] This change in fortunes was mainly due to the change of gross profit margin of the new·business from −37.9% to 11.5%.[47] In 2018, the majority of losses were Mobike's, at RMB4.55 billion (US$663 million).[48]

Meituan divides its business into three parts: "food delivery", "to shop, OTA", "new business and others". The performance of these three business lines is as follows (Figure 6.1).

According to Trustdata, Meituan's market share in food delivery reached 65.8% in the third quarter of 2019, making it the dominant player in the sector.[49] It has the world's largest, most efficient and timely delivery network.[50]

As for the second part, "To shop, OTA", the number of hotel room nights booked through Meituan in 2019 continued to exceed the sum of Ctrip, Qunar and eLong.[51] Gross margins of the OTA business were high and OTA has become something of a cash cow for Meituan.

|  | Food delivery | | To shop, OTA | | New business | |
|---|---|---|---|---|---|---|
| Revenue (RMB/%) | 54,843 | 56.2% | 22,275 | 22.8% | 20,409 | 21% |
| Revenue (US$ ) | 7,861 | | 3,193 | | 2,926 | |
| Revenue growth/2018 | 43.8% | | 40.6% | | 81.5% | |
| Gross margin | 18.7% | | 88.6% | | 11.5% | |

Figure 6.1  2019 financial performance (million).
Source: Meituan Dianping 2019 annual report.

"New business" is the fastest growing segment of the company. The number of active merchants has increased from 2 million in 2015 to 6.2 million in 2019.[52]

Today, not only in China but also internationally, there are virtually no other companies that provide such a wide range of lifestyle services as Meituan Dianping. Meituan's services include group buying – similar to Groupon; restaurant reviews – similar to Yelp; food delivery – similar to Grubhub; OTA – similar to Kayak; and ride hailing – similar to Uber. Singapore's multinational firm Grab comes quite close, in that it offers ride hailing, food delivery and payment, but its scope is not as wide-ranging.

What contributed to Meituan's success? Some reasons are China-specific. The first is the population density of metropolitan areas. Even a small city in China has an average of 800,000 to 1.2 million residents. There are more than 200 Chinese cities with a population of more than one million, while there are only ten cities in the United States with a population of above one million.[53] The second reason is labour cost. Delivery riders earn around RMB5 (US$0.7) for one delivery; 67% of riders earn less than RMB5,000 (US$700) per month and 86% are in the 20–40 years age group.[54] Delivery costs are much higher in the west. Grab might copy the Meituan model in the future, as it is already established in Southeast Asia where the population and delivery costs are similar to that of China. Meituan's successful experience could be relevant to Grab.

In its IPO prospectus, Meituan commented: "We are an innovative pioneer in the global service industry e-commerce model".[55] The new generation of Chinese internet companies represented by Meituan are surpassing the companies they were once benchmarked against.

1.  **High-frequency business.** Lifestyle services are a high-frequency
    transaction business; people need food every day, whereas they buy
    shampoo or clothes less frequently. Meituan has more consumer in-
    teractions than Alibaba. That's why the alarm was raised at Alibaba
    when Meituan made a strategic alliance with Tencent, leading Al-
    ibaba to spend US$9.5 billion – an outrageous overvaluation – to
    acquire Ele.me. Let's look at the thinking behind this acquisition. Al-
    ibaba needed to be in the high-frequency lifestyle services and Ele.
    me was one of the few options, if not the only option, left. We could
    look at US$9.5 billion in another way – to recover loss of face for
    failing to get Meituan. Meituan was able to enter the OTA race late –
    even when the market was already hyper competitive, and the win-
    ner almost decided – because it could leverage the user base from its
    high-frequency business. It seemed to be easier to move from high
    frequency to low frequency but perhaps the reverse could be true. A
    Ctrip user might order food delivery on the platform. Meituan ac-
    quired Mobike for a very high price, when it was still losing money
    itself but now that it offers bike rentals, white-collar workers are on
    its app more times a day, hiring bikes and ordering food delivery –
    both high-frequency services. So strategically it did make sense but
    what about financially?

2.  **Advantages of super-platforms.** Meituan has become a one-stop
    platform for consumers to eat, drink, play and entertain. On the one
    hand, it increased the retention rate and stickiness of users through
    its diversity of products and services; on the other, it reduced costs
    through cross-selling. People who used Meituan's group buying also
    tried its food delivery and hotel bookings, which means customer
    acquisition cost is extremely low. This organic acquisition of users is
    the key ingredient to Meituan's success. In 2018, 80% of users who
    booked hotels through Meituan were converted from the food deliv-
    ery part of its app. In 2019, the average number of transactions per
    user per year reached 27.4, an increase of 15.4% from 2018.[56] The
    proportion of marketing expenses as a percentage of revenue has de-
    creased year by year, from 177.7% in 2015 to 22.9% in 2018 and 19%
    in 2019.[57] Today, as internet traffic dividends continue to decrease,
    the scale effect of Meituan's super-platform and the advantages of its
    own traffic and cross-selling highlight its value.

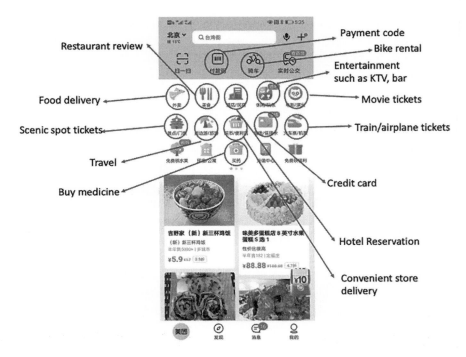

Figure 6.2  Meituan app

3.  **Even latecomers have an opportunity.** Meituan was not the first to market with any of its businesses. When the company was first established, the group-buying market leader was Lashou; when it entered the food delivery space, Ele.me was already there; when it set its sights on the OTA market, Ctrip and Qunar were very powerful existing players. Each time Meituan was able to surpass the industry leader. It accomplished this in different ways. The dominant logic for internet businesses is that the "network effect" means winner takes all. Meituan, however, seems to defy this logic. In China, there are several examples of late-comers enjoying ample opportunities. However, to take advantage of these, there are three conditions that must be met. The first is that late-comers really need to differentiate. In the group-buying war, Meituan didn't follow the trend of burning money on advertising. Instead, it adopted a powerful offline promotion team to convert merchants. It avoided the fiercely competitive first-tier cities by focusing on the second-tier cities. With food delivery, it entered markets where

Ele.me was absent. In the OTA space, it focused on the budget hotel category instead of the star-rated hotel category in which Ctrip was dominant. Meituan is very good at finding differentiated positioning, avoiding head-to-head confrontation and cutting in from areas that opponents have overlooked to erode an opponent's market share. The second condition is that they need to have sufficient cash. When everyone else was running out of money, Meituan was still solvent – the financial backing of Tencent was crucial. The third condition is that they need to have traffic or a customer base. Without these three conditions in place, latecomers have a slim chance of catching up.

Today, while most Chinese people are on Weibo, there are a few who still use Fanfou. Wang Xing is one of them. He uses Fanfou to post his ideas and thoughts on music, fiction, sports, history and personal development, for example. An influential speaker in China once commented: "What is the strongest trait of Wang Xing? The ability to think. What does Wang Xing like best? Thinking".[58] Wang spends a lot of time reading and thinking and his interests are diverse. Here is an example:

If one day there is a conference in the galaxy, and I am the only representative from the earth, what should I say to the aliens? How do I introduce the earth and human civilisation? I derived from this, what should I experience.

I want to tell the aliens what has existed on this planet and what has happened. Including the most magnificent natural scenery, the most prosperous cultural landscape, the best music, the best literature (no matter what languages), the best architecture, the best food and the core concepts of mankind.[59]

This reflects how Wang Xing thinks about the most basic relationship in the world.

## Concluding remarks: questions for executives to ask

1. How well do you know the key events in a customer journey of your key offering? What are the pain points in a typical journey?

2. How do you know which needs to satisfy and how to satisfy those needs? What approach or mechanism can you put in place to meet the needs worth solving?

3. What digital services do you offer and how do you make sense of the customer touchpoints and interactions?

4. Would you anchor your digital service, like an app, in functions or in a lifestyle journey?

5. Is your business reaping the benefits of high-frequency retail business?

6. How aware are you of the platforms in your industry and whether or not you can partner up with them?

7. What is the platform or digital service that you can learn from and benchmark against in your region and industry?

## Notes

1  https://www.mckinsey.com.cn/mapping-chinasmiddle/.
2  http://www.chyxx.com/industry/202005/866720.html.
3  Converted at concurrent exchange rate, unless otherwise specified.
4  https://tech.sina.com.cn/zt_d/meituandianpingipo/.
5  https://www.laohu8.com/stock/.
6  https://tech.sina.com.cn/csj/2018-11-19/doc-ihnvukff4523950.shtml.
7  https://finance.ifeng.com/c/7hqVWCosXnk.
8  https://www.sohu.com/a/273459330_136682.
9  https://www.ssffx.com/xinqingsuibi/10709.html.
10 http://www.sino-manager.com/106681.html.
11 http://finance.sina.com.cn/stock/zldx/2018-09-20/doc-ifxeuwwr6290990.shtml.
12 http://finance.sina.com.cn/leadership/mroll/20110510/16159819286.shtml.
13 https://tech.sina.com.cn/i/2011-04-26/14325451916.shtml.
14 http://www.sino-manager.com/106681.html.
15 https://36kr.com/p/5298517.
16 https://tech.sina.com.cn/i/2014-10-24/10029730026.shtml.
17 http://www.sino-manager.com/106681.html.
18 http://www.100ec.cn/home/detail--6221916.html.
19 https://tech.qq.com/a/20150403/030725.htm.
20 https://finance.sina.com.cn/chanjing/gsnews/20151014/074223468835.shtml.

21   http://finance.ifeng.com/a/20151103/14053637_0.shtml.

22   https://www.sohu.com/a/218528576_664480.

23   http://dy.163.com/v2/article/detail/E326G2RL0519H58O.html.

24   http://dy.163.com/v2/article/detail/E326G2RL0519H58O.html.

25   https://finance.qq.com/a/20180402/014932.htm.

26   https://www.sohu.com/a/244400394_403354.

27   https://www.sohu.com/a/225237774_350699.

28   https://finance.qq.com/a/20180402/014932.htm.

29   https://baike.baidu.com/item/口碑网/2753722?fr=aladdin.

30   https://www.sohu.com/a/238430136_100109332.

31   https://www.sohu.com/a/288517597_173488.

32   https://tech.sina.com.cn/zl/post/detail/i/2016-11-01/pid_8508859.htm.

33   https://tech.sina.com.cn/zl/post/detail/i/2016-11-01/pid_8508859.htm.

34   https://tech.sina.com.cn/zl/post/detail/i/2016-11-01/pid_8508859.htm.

35   MeiTuan Prospectus.

36   http://www.199it.com/archives/761254.html.

37   https://www.huxiu.com/article/240057.html.

38   MeiTuan 2019 Annual Report.

39   http://www.ironge.com.cn/cj/72539.html.

40   https://about.meituan.com/en/detail/92.

41   https://about.meituan.com/en/detail/92.

42   https://about.meituan.com/en/detail/92.

43   https://www.huxiu.com/article/356594.html.

44   https://www.huxiu.com/article/342016.html.

45   https://i.meituan.com/awp/hfe/block/272d02889936ff2b9f5b/94001/
     index.html?dd_func_wk=true&ehwebview=1.

46   MeiTuan 2019 Annual Report.

47   MeiTuan 2019 Annual Report.

48   MeiTuan 2018 Annual Report.

49   https://gu.qq.com/resources/shy/news/detail-v2/index.html#/index?id=-
     SN2020052522111179dee780&s=b&wxurl=qqstock%3A%2F%2FnewsV2%
     2F13%2F%2FSN2020052522111179dee780%2F%2F%2F&pagetype=share.

50   MeiTuan 2019 Annual Report.

51   https://gu.qq.com/resources/shy/news/detail-v2/index.html#/index?id=-
     SN2020052522111179dee780&s=b&wxurl=qqstock%3A%2F%2FnewsV2
     %2F13%2F%2FSN2020052522111179dee780%2F%2F%2F&pagetype=sh
     are.

52   MeiTuan 2019 Annual Report.

53   https://www.thoughtco.com/biggest-u-s-cities-4158615.

54   2019 Meituan Riders Poverty Alleviation report.

55   MeiTuan Prospectus.

56   MeiTuan 2019 Annual Report.

57   MeiTuan 2019 Annual Report.

58   https://mp.weixin.qq.com/s/3czQCMlepHCLVgqNkhueAw.

59   https://mp.weixin.qq.com/s/3czQCMlepHCLVgqNkhueAw.

# 7

# FRESH FOOD

## Merging online and offline

Since the emergence of e-commerce, Taobao, JD and others have moved all kinds of merchandise from offline to online. Meituan has successfully moved various lifestyle services from offline to online as well. Today, people seem to be able to buy everything online – clothing, electronics, daily necessities, movie tickets – which greatly facilitates and enriches life-style. But there is one area closely related to people's everyday living that is still being bought predominantly offline: fresh food.

Fresh produce, such as vegetables, fruit, meat, eggs, poultry and seafood, is indispensable to Chinese people. They might order takeaways once or twice a week, buy clothes once a month and book hotels a few times a year, but Chinese people cannot do without fresh food for more than a day or two.

In China, there are two main places to buy fresh food. One is the roofed bazaar or covered market (similar to the open-air farmers' markets in Europe), near to residential communities, which most people visit on an almost daily basis. The markets may appear somewhat chaotic, but the

DOI: 10.4324/9781003205074-9

vendors get up very early to procure the freshest produce from the whole-salers and people like the hustle and bustle. With house prices rising in so many metropolitan areas, however, fresh-food markets are disappearing fast.

The other place where people buy fresh food is the supermarket. How-ever, while there is plenty of variety in the supermarkets, they are not always located close to residential communities. Convenience stores are closer but they offer much fewer items and the average Chinese is always on the hunt for the freshest meat and fish. Will the development of e-commerce pro-vide new ways to procure fresh produce?

## Hema: online and offline

At 6:30 one afternoon, Ms. Wang, who lives in the Pudong District of Shanghai, was on her way home from her work. Once on the subway, her thoughts turned to the family dinner. She had two choices in mind.

The first was to buy something at the Hema Xiansheng Store (盒马鲜生) near to where she lived and take it home to cook. Although the Hema Xian-sheng Store was en route, it would still take 10 to 20 minutes to select her purchases and go through the check-out. Normally she would enjoy the experience of shopping in-store. Today, though, it was hot, and she was tired.

She chose the second option. On her mobile phone she opened the Hema app, where it took just a few minutes to select some vegetables and fresh shrimp and pay via Alipay. While she continued her journey home, the employees in the Hema Xiansheng store began to sort and pack her order and arrange for delivery. Half an hour later, Ms. Wang arrived home, just as the food she ordered on the Hema app was delivered. Ms. Wang places orders two to three times a week on the Hema app, mainly buying fruit, vegetables, fresh seafood and meat, with the average order worth around RMB100–200 (US$14–28[1]).

While Taobao, JD and Meituan started up by copying counterparts in America, Alibaba's Hema Xiansheng has been an original innovation since its birth. Hema Xiansheng's pronunciation in Chinese is the same as "Mr. Hippo" and Hema's logo is also a hippo. Its first physical store opened in Shanghai in January 2016 in the basement of Tower 1 Jinqiao International Commercial Plaza; a premium location. Hema's expansion accelerated from 2017 on and, by May 2020, it already had close to 200 stores across 20 cities,[2] with ambitions to open 2000 stores by 2022.[3] Since its inception, Hema has been a clear leader in fresh-food retailing and has captured a lot of attention in the new retailing era.

Let's see what's special about a Mr. Hippo store.

- **Location.** Location is by far the most important factor. In the traditional retailing era of bricks-and-mortar stores, this rule never changed. Although Hema's is an innovative model, they still have traditional, physical stores so location is super important. The stores are situated mainly in first and second-tier cities, usually in shopping malls near to large, residential, well-to-do communities. The real estate prices of these high-density areas are usually quite high. And so is the consumption level of the local residents.

Illustrated by Aspen Wang.

- **Physical Store.** Hema's offline stores typically occupy a floor space of some 5,000 square metres and combine the three functions of "fresh food supermarket, catering and in-store dining, and fulfilment centre for online shopping". While the stores look pretty much like a supermarket, they are designed more like a high-end outlet. Customers who live within a three-kilometre radius of the store can place orders online for home delivery, which is normally completed within 30 minutes. Unlike the traditional markets or supermarkets, a Hema store also functions as a warehouse and distribution hub. In addition to the shopping area where goods are displayed, there is also a sizable logistics area. Many high-frequency purchase items are stocked in the logistics area, which makes it more convenient to sort, pack and deliver. There are cold storage areas in the store to maintain freshness of certain food items. In addition, a Hema store also has a food hall. Most Hema stores designate around 15%–50% of floor space to catering and dining. The food stalls are operated by third parties and Hema not only charges them rent but also takes 20% of their revenue as commission. In addition to generating good cash flow, the food halls also help to attract and retain customers. Just as Alibaba, Hema's parent company, collects rent and commission from vendors on its online platform, it also collects rent and commission offline, through its Hema stores.

- **Products.** In addition to other daily necessities, Hema's main featured product is fresh seafood. King crab, Australian lobster, abalone and salmon are placed in a prominent display area, where they are pre-packed and price-tagged, so no weighing is required, which speeds up the shopping process. Hema Xiansheng's high-end products are generally competitively priced. For example, a live 400g Boston lobster at RMB89 (US$12.7) compared to the frozen equivalent at JD for RMB100 (US$14).[4] From 2018, Hema started to co-create new products together with local and international brands. It launched "golden 24 hours" fresh milk with New Hope Diary and "daily fresh" milk with Fonterra. By October 2019, Hema's own brand represented 10% of its sales revenue – a high percentage compared to traditional retailers, where it is generally lower than 5%.[5] Hema calls its own brand "He Brand" and aims to increase its percentage of revenue to 50%

in 2021.[6] In 2019, in order to enhance its "He Brand", Hema opened up its own agricultural base, Hema Village, to produce agricultural products. The very first Hema Village was in Sichuan Province. In May 2020, Hema set up its first Hema Village in Shanghai, which produces Cuiguan pears. This Hema Village is a "digital agricultural base" equipped with an array of high-tech solutions, including an IoT system, traceability system, drones, remote orchard surveillance robots, an integrated irrigation and fertilising system, and digital sensors. By September 2020, there were 117 Hema Villages across China.[7] There is even a Hema Village in Rwanda in Africa, which grows Hema's own chilli peppers.[8]

- **Fulfilment:** One of Hema's stand-out features is fast delivery. Most orders are delivered within 30 minutes to residents within three kilometres of the store. Customers can also appoint a specific delivery time, for example, placing an order at 3pm for delivery between 6:00 and 6:30pm. For the store to select the right goods, pack and deliver within half an hour, requires economising on every aspect of the operational process. One of the eye-catching devices in Hema stores is the ceiling conveyor belt. Once a customer places an order online, an in-store staff member packs the ordered items up in a bag and loads it onto the conveyor belt. The belt sends the bag to the logistics area. The whole process takes less than five minutes. The conveyor belt is essential to 30-minute delivery guarantees. Some high-frequency goods are stored in the logistics area, which also helps to speed up the sorting and packing process.

- **Information and payment.** The price tags attached to products in Hema stores are electronic displays, which allow the company to easily adjust prices and ensure uniform pricing online and offline. Customers can scan the barcode on the price tag to get details of the product, such as its origin, and also to check customer feedback. In terms of payment, customers have to use Hema app. Free WiFi is in every store and designated staff members help customers with downloading and using the app. While this form of online payment may not suit some customers, for Hema it not only reduces the checkout time but also enables them to collect valuable customer information.

In summary, Hema's value proposition is a combination of three things:

1) Quality fresh food – particularly seafood – at a competitive price, which customers can select to have cooked for them to dine in-store, or to take home.
2) A completely integrated smartphone-centric experience, from product information available via QR codes on product labels, to automated check-out, to payment via Alipay.
3) The option to order online for free and fast home delivery, within a three-kilometre radius of each store.

The concept looks great and certainly sounds appealing. But what about its financial performance? On Alibaba global investor day in September 2018, Hou Yi, vice president of the Alibaba Group and CEO of Hema, disclosed some operational data: online sales accounted for more than 60% of total sales; the average daily sales of a single store exceeded RMB800,000 (US$115,000); and the single-store surface efficiency (turnover/store area) of stores that had been open for more than one-and-a-half years was more than RMB50,000 (US$7,167)[9] (the same figure for traditional supermarkets was RMB15,000 (US$2,150).

## Fresh food e-commerce: varieties of models

What is the difference between fresh food and other products? Why are clothing, electrical appliances, computers, mobile phones, toys and even takeaway services all successful e-commerce products whereas the online penetration of fresh food is so low? We identified several reasons. One obvious factor is that the shelf life of fresh food is short – just a few days, compared to clothing that can last for months if not years. Compounding this, the fresh food logistics' chain is very long. From procurement at origin, to transportation, storage and distribution, the product loss rate is high throughout the whole process. Meanwhile, the cost of a cold food logistics chain is also high. Thus, for high-frequency, low-price, short-shelf-life fresh food such as vegetables, it is almost impossible to cover the logistics cost of online sales. In addition, fresh food, unlike clothes, soft drinks or potato chips, is not a standardised product. The quality of vegetables from different farms can vary and the vegetables from the same farm can also vary depending on the time they were picked. Consumers are not comfortable buying fresh produce if they can't see it first.

So how big is the market for fresh food? In 2018, the clothing market in China was around RMB2 trillion (US$294 billion[10])[11] and in 2016, the market for 3C (Computer, Communication, Consumer electronics) products was roughly RMB2 trillion (US$288 billion).[12] In 2018, China's fresh food market was estimated to be RMB5 trillion (US$729 billion).[13] Not only is the market for fresh food huge, it is also what economists call an inelastic demand (meaning people do not vary their demand depending on price). We call it a high-frequency product. For this reason alone, there are plenty of competitors in the fresh food e-commerce space and Hema was not the earliest entrant.

China's first fresh food e-commerce venture, Yiguo Fresh (易果生鲜), was established in 2005. It also later founded FruitDay (天天果园).[14] Compared to other fresh food such as vegetables and seafood, fruit is relatively easy to store and transport. Most of the original fresh food e-commerce companies started out selling fruit and they did not try and combine offline with online. Their warehouses were bigger than Hema's and covered a much larger service area. After a customer placed an order, the fruit was dispatched from the warehouse and delivered within one to two days. The fresh food e-commerce companies had to build their own cold chain (a temperature-controlled supply chain) delivery systems and logistics capabilities, as few third-party express delivery companies could handle fresh food. Although a self-built cold chain system was a very costly investment, it had the potential not only to enhance customer experience but also to create entry barriers for new competitors. Until 2014, the distribution cost of fresh food was as high as RMB40–50 (US$6.5–US$8.2) per order. With such high costs, the price of fresh food online was not cheap, and the e-commerce companies stuck to mainly organically grown or imported fruit with higher prices and higher gross margins. Even so, most of the vertical, fresh food e-commerce platforms lost money.

After 2013, the big multi-product, multi-function e-commerce platforms began to enter the fresh food business. Tmall launched Tmall Fresh, and JD launched JD Fresh. From 2013, Alibaba made four rounds of investment in Yiguo Fresh, including one of US$300 million in 2017.[15] Alibaba was mainly interested in the cold chain warehousing and distribution logistics capabilities of ExFresh (安鲜达), Yiguo Fresh's subsidiary, and using it to provide a logistics service to Tmall Fresh. JD invested in FruitDay in 2015.

However, a one- to two-day delivery did not meet customers' needs when it came to fresh food such as vegetables and seafood. Fresh-food purchases are often unplanned but require immediate delivery. There is not much customer appetite for fresh food deliveries that take a day or two.

To shorten the delivery time, a company called Missfresh (每日优鲜), which was established in 2014, explored a new model for fresh food e-commerce: the "front warehouse". Here, "front" means being close to customers and the community. The front warehouse was generally located near a densely populated community, with a floor space ranging from 100 to 400 square metres and served residents within a one- to three-kilometre radius. The front warehouse significantly shortened the delivery time of fresh food. Missfresh made a commitment to deliver to its customers within two hours and, by the end of 2019, the average delivery time had been cut to 36 minutes.[16] Their front warehouse strategy made Missfresh stand out among other vertical, fresh food e-commerce operations. In May 2019, the firm announced it was adding three new categories of product to the front warehouse: meals, coffee and live seafood, and also began to offer "next day delivery" for daily necessities from its larger warehouses. By November 2019, Missfresh had 1,500 front warehouses in 20 cities across the country.[17] The online grocery shopping launched by Meituan in 2019 was an imitation of the front warehouse strategy of Missfresh.

In July 2020, Missfresh announced a new round of financing of US$495 million, which was a joint investment by CICC Capital, Tencent, and other investment institutions.[18] The Covid-19 pandemic accelerated the online penetration rate of fresh food, and this round of financing was a record high in the fresh food-to-home model. Tencent had started investing in Missfresh as early as 2015, in the A-round financing, and continued to invest in subsequent rounds.

Some e-commerce platforms that had their own delivery capabilities, such as JD, Meituan and Ele.me, created partnerships with offline supermarkets and convenience stores to launch an O2O (online to offline) model. JD launched JD To Home (京东到家) in 2015. It made agreements with offline retailers to deliver goods to consumers, offering a general delivery time of one to two hours. The delivery times of traditional supermarkets are longer than that of Hema and Missfresh. One of the reasons is that traditional supermarkets were not designed to take online shopping into account, or optimise the picking and sorting process. Moreover, goods displayed online were often inconsistent with the offline inventory and stockout and error rates were high. In August 2018, JD To Home announced the completion of a new round of US$500 million financing. This time the retail giant, Walmart, joined the investment league. At that time, JD To Home already had 1.2 million merchants and more than 50 million individual customers,[19] covering virtually all first and second-tier cities. JD also struck up partnerships with Carrefour, Family Mart, 7–11, Lawson and other international convenience store giants, as well as with domestic players such as Yonghui (永辉), CP Fresh (正大优鲜) and Our Hours (全时). However, Meituan, with its delivery capabilities in location-based service, still provided a much shorter delivery time than JD To Home. Generally, a delivery from a nearby convenient store through Meituan was around 30 minutes.

The integration of comprehensive e-commerce platforms and offline supermarkets gained traction. In August 2015, JD invested US$700 million in Yonghui, a leading fresh food supermarket. Alibaba also invested

Illustrated by Aspen Wang.

in many supermarket chains and shopping malls, such as Sanjiang (三江购物), Lianhua Supermarket (联华超市), Yintai (银泰) and Suning (苏宁). The expansion of e-commerce platforms to offline is becoming fiercer. In 2015, Wumart Supermarket (物美超市) launched DMALL (多点), providing home-delivery services for nearby residents and other collaborating supermarkets.

There have been so many developments, innovations, new models, new entrants and new approaches in fresh-food new retail, and it is almost impossible to capture them all. We have tried to summarise the "key approaches" of the different models in Figure 7.1, which will help in grasping the core attributes.

From Figure 7.1, we found something interesting with respect to the competition: Hema is competing with everyone in this field. It is operating

|  | Yiguo Fresh | Tmall Fresh / JD Fresh | Missfresh | O2O / Meituan / JD to Home | Traditional supermarkets / DMALL | OAO / Hema / 7-Fresh |
|---|---|---|---|---|---|---|
| **Type** | New venture | E-commerce platforms | New venture | Existing platform | Partner with e-commerce platforms | New venture |
| **On/offline** | Online | Online | Online | O2O | Offline (Duodian has online) | OAO |
| **YoE** | 2005 | 2013 | 2014 | 2015 | 2015 | 2016 |
| **Focus** | Fruit | Fruit, vegetables, seafood | Fruit, meals, coffee, live seafood | Diverse | Diverse | Fresh food and others |
| **Warehouse** | Large | Large | Front warehouse | No | In store | In store |
| **Delivery** | 1-2 days | 1-2 days | 36 minutes | 1-2 hours or 30 minutes | 1-2 hours | 30 minutes |
| **Logistics** | Self-established | Acquiring or self-established | Self-established | Self-established | Partnership or self-established | Self-established |
| **Price** | Expensive | High | Lower | N.A. | Low | Lower |

Figure 7.1 Varieties of models.

across the boundaries of offline supermarket, online e-commerce, delivery and even restaurant businesses. In offline it is competing with traditional physical supermarkets and restaurants; in online it is competing with JD fresh and Missfresh; in delivery it is competing with Meituan and JD To Home. It is a bit too soon to tell if their model has an advantage over the others but Hema has certainly attracted many "copycats" to its OAO (on-line and offline) concept. In 2017, JD launched 7-Fresh, Suning launched SuFresh and the traditional super supermarket, Yonghui, launched Super Species (超级物种).

The integration of online and offline businesses is, of course, not unique to Chinese e-commerce. In November 2015, Amazon opened its first offline bookstore in Seattle. In June 2017, it acquired Whole Foods, which is known for its high-quality fresh food and included more than 460 wholefood stores worldwide.[20] January 2018 saw the launch of "Amazon GO": cashier-free stores, which offered mostly snack food, where customers enjoy "Just Walk Out" shopping, powered by hundreds of cameras and sensors that record their movements and purchases. Albert Heijn, a major supermarket chain in the Netherlands, has implemented a technology which allows customers to tap their phones or credit cards on a shelf tag to make their purchases. However, what is clear is that these remain initiatives and single instances of online merging with an offline business. To date, only companies such as Hema and Missfresh have brought this new approach to scale.

The merging of online and offline in the fresh-food sector is an example of the new retail trend. Hema is a classic example of new retail in action.

## Fresh food: new retailing in action

During the 2016 Computing Conference, Jack Ma, founder of Alibaba, proposed the concept of "new retailing". He believed that the concept of e-commerce would soon be outdated and that the next one or two decades would be about "new retailing", that is, the combination of online, offline and logistics.[21] The emergence of Hema is a concrete example of Jack Ma's interpretation of new retail. In 2018, Liu Qiangdong, founder of JD, also put forward his vision on the future of retailing as "borderless retailing"; an unbounded shopping network that enables seamless communication between buyers and sellers.[22]

Fresh food is among the essentials of most Chinese people's daily life and it is the best reflection of the relationships between "people, products and places" in the retail business. Although fresh food e-commerce started late in China, it broke down the boundaries between online and offline, by constantly innovating and reconstructing the connecting points of "people, products and places". It also made people rethink traditional e-commerce.

1. **Deep integration of online and offline.** In traditional retail, online and offline are kept apart. In traditional supermarkets, consumers go to physical stores, pick their products from the shelves and pay the bill. In online shopping, customers place an order, pay and receive delivery. Online and offline retail are like two parallel lines that do not cross. The O2O model of JD To Home connected online and offline. Customers order online to buy goods from offline supermarkets. And with the Hema model, consumers can buy both online and offline; online and offline are truly integrated. People can go to Hema stores or choose to order online, depending on their mood and daily schedule. When the Hema model was being conceived, one of the biggest decisions was whether to open up stores or just to build warehouses like Missfresh. In the end, it was decided that to open up stores, as consumers were unlikely to go to a warehouse to buy something and warehouses would not be able to transform offline traffic to online. Relying solely on online traffic was considered to be too expensive, since the acquisition cost for capturing online traffic had increased exponentially. After deciding to open physical stores, another key decision that had to be taken was whether to include catering and in-store dining. Hema decided to incorporate catering and in-store dining by outsourcing to third-party merchants. To transfer offline traffic to online, Hema insists that customers use Hema app to pay for all purchases. Although this strict enforcement may turn some consumers away it is probably the most critical step. Consumers do not necessarily think about online versus offline business models; they simply go to the supermarket when they have time on hands and prefer placing an order online, enjoying the convenience of home delivery, when they are busy. For consumers, the most important thing is convenience and meeting their needs. If companies stick to the

traditional boundaries between online and offline, they will build their own artificial walls.

2. **Deep integration of logistics with online and offline.** The importance of logistics is fully reflected in fresh food e-commerce. For non-fresh food products, consumers are not so demanding on expediency and are generally satisfied with same-day or next-day delivery. Non-fresh food products are also not so prone to damage and decay during storage and transportation. Although the takeaway sector requires prompt deliveries, it relies on only one part of logistics chain – delivery to home. The handling of fresh food, on the other hand, has three unique characteristics: (1) high requirements for distribution time; (2) the logistics chain is complex and long; and (3) the goods are easily spoiled. All the fresh food market players have worked hard on logistics. To start with, they established cold chain logistics systems, with deliveries from large warehouses, which solved the transportation issue and spoilage problem. However, there was no significant improvement in distribution times. Missfresh moved the warehouse to within three kilometres of consumers, which reduced delivery times from one to two days to one to two hours. By combining warehouse and store, Hema further shortened the delivery time to less than 30 minutes. Half an hour is almost the same time it takes the consumers to shop in a physical store on their own.[23] According to a research report from iResearch, consumers purchase more frequently from Hema and Missfresh, who deliver within two hours, than from Tmall Fresh and JD Fresh, whose delivery time is one to two days.[24] After their logistics systems had been set up and the distribution speed improved, both Hema and Missfresh started expanding their product ranges beyond fresh food, adding many daily essential items. According to iResearch's report, more than 70% of users buy daily necessities at the same time they buy fresh food online.[25] Again, this is a typical case of high-frequency consumption beating low-frequency consumption. In the future, fresh food e-commerce platforms, such as Missfresh, are likely to steal market share from other, more all-encompassing, e-commerce companies.

3. **Customised models to feed different customer needs.** From the traditional fresh food e-commerce to the O2O model of JD To Home, the front warehouse of Missfresh and the OAO concept of Hema, the

business model of fresh food e-commerce has constantly evolved. In fact, another model appeared in 2018, community group buying (社区团购), and we will discuss more in Chapter 8. A "community group" refers to residents in the same community, with each having an organiser, the "head". The head is often a stay-at-home parent with children to look after and no permanent job. The head establishes a WeChat group on which they promote eight to ten products for pre-sale every day. All the orders are integrated into one large order, which is shipped directly from the supplier to the community and then distributed by the head to the buyers. Community group buying exists mainly in third and fourth-tier cities and one head can cover 300–500 families. By January 2019, Shixh (食享会), a leading community group-buying start-up firm, had set up nearly 20,000 communities in 45 cities across the country, with some 20,000 heads. The advantages of community group buying are obvious. You can use the acquaintance network of the organiser to access customers, and there is no cost for building warehouses and stores. The model is very light. At present, China's fresh food e-commerce market sees a coexistence of multiple models, each with advantages and disadvantages, covering different consumption scenarios. No model has an overwhelming advantage. Not only are the different players trying different models, Hema is also constantly improving its own model. Hema's first store was called Hema Xiansheng. Since then, it has successively hatched Hema Vegetable (盒马菜市), Hema Mini, Hema F2, Hema Station (盒马小站) and Pick'n Go, and each mode corresponds to a different scenario. For example, in contrast with the big Hema Xiansheng store, Hema Mini has only 500–1000 square metres of floor space, with fewer product categories, and its distribution range is just one-and-a-half kilometres, covering a more middle-low market. Pick'n Go mainly solves the problem of breakfast for white-collar workers. Consumers typically place an order on the subway and scan the bar code to pick up their goods when they pass the Pick'n Go at the subway exit. In November 2019, Hema even opened a shopping mall in Shenzhen, Hema Li (盒马里·岁宝). Along with shops selling clothing and daily necessities, there are also food outlets and parent-children areas, covering the needs of family activities at the weekend.

## Is there money in online fresh food?

Finally, let's come back to Hema. The Hema model looks innovative and the customers like it. But they still have not answered the biggest question — is it profitable? One of the earliest online fresh food retailers, Ocado, founded in the UK in 2000, took 14 years to make a profit. One reason that it was able to survive was that investors considered it a unicorn firm.[26] Making a profit has long been a problem for fresh food e-commerce. Amazon tried Amazon Fresh as early as 2007, in Seattle, but only began to expand to other cities in 2013, which is quite conservative considering Amazon's propensity for fast expansion. If Amazon Fresh had showed any promise, would they have still acquired Whole Foods in 2017?

The Chinese internet players are experimenting and expanding while at the same time they have not figured out how to make money. The fresh food business, given its size, is clearly of such strategic importance that it overrides short-term profit goals. Xiaomi, for example, hardly made any profit on TV sets, but still sold them as a necessary means of reaching consumers in the IOT space. Could the same logic be applied here? If Alibaba doesn't sell fresh food, a new or existing competitor will. Is this logic sufficient justification for business ventures?

Looking back at the earliest foreign players in China's retailing sector, Carrefour entered China in 1995 and Walmart in 1996. They were the pioneers and first movers in the supermarket industry in China and were very successful and profitable. Now these traditional retailers are facing intense competition from Alibaba and JD, who emerged from the technology sector. In 2019, Suning acquired an 80% share of Carrefour.[27] In 2012, Walmart acquired 1haodian.com, which merged with JD, and thus survived indirectly (Figure 7.2).

Online and offline merging is not just limited to the fresh food sector. We focus on fresh food in this chapter because it is the most difficult to do due to the short shelf life of fresh food that puts strains on the supply chain and high standards of freshness demanded by consumers. The merger of online and offline is already happening before COVID-19. The pandemic has accelerated the speed of this transformation. For most companies to survive in 2020, they had to move their businesses online. We saw the companies who had prepared for this online-offline merger before 2020 fared much better than those who were caught offhanded in 2020. The

| Challenge | Description |
|---|---|
| High-frequency transaction | Cost of delivery |
| Cold chain logistics | Increasing complexity of delivery as weight loss/size/proportions change during delivery |
| Need to see | Fresh comes in many grades |
| Large number of producers | Highly segmented |
| No clear standards | Much fresh food does not have a brand |
| Profit model | Nobody makes money on fresh food yet |
| Requirements for the delivery time | Cannot wait 2 days... or even 2 hrs |

Figure 7.2 Key challenges for fresh food moving online.

preparation is not only about building IT infrastructure and database, but also about the business model and the way the business is run. We would argue that the organisational changes are more critical to its success of this transformation. The trend has become a necessity for all sectors.

There is an old saying in China, "Mega trends can be evident in smaller details (见微知著)". Fresh food is only one of the hundreds of categories in China's retail market. But from the perspective of e-commerce, the qualitative leap of Chinese enterprises from replication to innovation is noticeable. As we saw in the previous chapter, in the "war among the thousands of group-buying companies", so many competed homogeneously, fighting their battles on advertising and financing capabilities. And yet for the competition in the fresh food arena, the fight is about business models, innovation and an understanding of customers. Innovative fresh food players such as Hema are not copycats. Instead, they innovate and experiment along consumer consumption scenarios. "Either innovate or be cast aside" is an apt description of the fierce competition in fresh food new retailing in China. If the fresh food business is going to follow trends of other industries in China, we predict that a few big players will survive and there will be many niche players specialising in certain product categories, select regions and specific customer segments.

The trend is relevant not just to retailers and logistics companies. Syngenta Group, the world leading agricultural technology company, has been trying to crack the Chinese market in a big way for 30 years by extending their business model from the West into China. In 2017, Syngenta launched a new model called MAP (Modern Agriculture Platform) in China, a platform to guide and supply farmers through the process of modernising their farms and connecting them to premium buyers. MAP provides farmers with highly innovative seeds and crop protection products, digital services, training programmes and advice to grow crops in an even safer and more environmentally friendly way. A key element of the MAP model was the "Map beSide" initiative, in which the MAP marketed crops grown by farmers in its network to commercial buyers, such as Hema Xiansheng, at a premium price. Because the MAP's digital service enabled full product traceability, consumers at Hema could scan a QR code to see product information as well as information on the farm location, environment, harvest process, etc. Leveraging China's new retail trends, its China market centric model supported by Syngenta's Global product and service capabilities enables the company to grow China business much faster than its competitors.[28]

## Concluding remarks: questions for executives to ask

1. If we have a fresh food or perishable food category, what are our major drivers to move online?
2. What are the challenges for fresh food online in my region and industry?
3. What are the benefits for the customer, brands and you to bring fresh food online?
4. How to deliver the fresh food retail proposition?
5. What's your weak link in your food value chain? Where would you invest? Is vertical integration better for you? Which product category should you invest in and which should you not? Where do you want the control of the food source to be?

## Notes

1 Converted at concurrent exchange rate, unless otherwise specified.
2 https://www.freshhema.com.
3 https://www.retailnews.asia/hema-fresh-eyes-2000-stores-by-2022/.

4   2020年6月4日盒马APP和京东商城价格.

5   http://www.ebrun.com/20200525/386993.shtml.

6   http://www.ebrun.com/20200525/386993.shtml.

7   http://news.winshang.com/html/067/6744.html.

8   http://finance.eastmoney.com/a/202006171524962330.html.

9   https://finance.sina.com.cn/stock/usstock/c/2018-09-17/doc-ifxeuwwr5264124.shtml.

10  Converted at concurrent exchange rate, unless otherwise specified.

11  https://baijiahao.baidu.com/s?id=1640536811507012613&wfr=spider&for=pc.

12  https://wenku.baidu.com/view/44022a44571252d380eb6294d-d88d0d232d43c4b.html.

13  https://www.askci.com/news/chanye/20190119/1804431140552.shtml.

14  http://report.iresearch.cn/report_pdf.aspx?id=3123.

15  http://finance.sina.com.cn/stock/relnews/us/2019-12-24/doc-iihnzhfz8079253.shtml.

16  https://www.huxiu.com/article/328165.html.

17  https://www.huxiu.com/article/328165.html.

18  https://tech.sina.com.cn/roll/2020-07-27/doc-iivhvpwx7676551.shtml.

19  https://www.sohu.com/a/253147571_343156.

20  https://www.huxiu.com/article/200260.html.

21  https://www.sohu.com/a/116110863_468951.

22  http://www.linkshop.com.cn/web/archives/2018/403267.shtml?sf=wd_search.

23  Huxiu Selection. 5 Cases help to Understand New Retail. Zhejiang Publishing Group Digital Media Co., Ltd.

24  http://report.iresearch.cn/report_pdf.aspx?id=3123.

25  http://report.iresearch.cn/report_pdf.aspx?id=3123.

26  https://www.thisismoney.co.uk/money/markets/article-7990289/Britains-Ocado-counts-cost-fire-flagship-warehouse.html.

27  http://finance.sina.com.cn/zt_d/snygsgjlf/.

28  Interview with Erik Fyrwald, CEO Syngenta Group on March 8, 2021.

# 8

## SOCIAL E-COMMERCE
### Reaching the bottom of the pyramid

China is the world's second largest economy and has been the world's largest, in purchasing-power-parity terms, since 2014. It is a rich country. It is also relatively poor, however, when comes to per capita GDP and a population of 1.4 billion. As Premier Li Keqiang said in 2020, at a press conference after the closing of the Third Session of the 13th National People's Congress, "Our country is a developing country with a large population. The per capita annual disposable income in China is RMB30,000 (US$4,208[1]). But there are still some 600 million people earning a monthly income of RMB1,000 (US$140)". This statistic shocked a lot of Chinese, especially white-collar workers living in first and second-tier cities. They could not imagine how someone could live or survive on US$140 per month. China has two faces.

Hao Jingfang (郝景芳), the author of *Folding Beijing* (北京折叠), became the second Chinese writer to take home a Hugo Award when she won the Best Novelette award at the 74th World Science Fiction Convention in 2016. In her novel, a futuristic Beijing is divided into three foldable spaces.

DOI: 10.4324/9781003205074-10

The protagonist of the story, Lao Dao, lives in the Third Space, where it is crowded, messy and quarrelsome. Two-thirds of the city's population live in the Third Space. To make more money to send her daughter to a good kindergarten, Lao Dao deliver letters to the First and Second spaces – a risky undertaking. In the process, he gets the chance to see the two other worlds. The Second Space is full of skyscrapers and is prosperous and orderly. This is where urban white-collar workers and promising students live. The First Space is pleasant and green, without any high-rise buildings, but has the best resources. Less than 7% of the population live in the First Space. The three spaces are separated from each other, and it is difficult to pass between them. Although Folding Beijing is a fantasy novel, there is some realism to it. Different spaces represent different social classes, and it is hard to break through class barriers.

Xiao Li, a white-collar worker living in Beijing earning a monthly income of tens of thousands of yuan (thousands of dollars), was shocked to hear that China has 600 million people with a monthly income of around just RMB1,000. This was a completely different world from the one in which he lived, where apartments were priced at US$10,000 per square metre. He enjoyed shopping in Hema Xiansheng; he liked to eat out often; he went to the movies once a week; and he liked to take holidays overseas. He has been to Thailand, Japan, Malaysia, the Maldives and Dubai and, if it were not for Covid-19, he would have visited Paris in 2020.

In the mountainous countryside around Bijie city (毕节), Guizhou Province, Xiao Hang lived in a mud house with his grandparents. It took him almost a full day to travel from home to the city. Xiao Hang's father died ten years ago, and his mother remarried. He and his sisters lived with his grandparents. They survived on government subsidies – slightly more than RMB10,000 (US$1400) a year. Xiao Hang was very good academically; he ranked among the top in his county, and he was admitted to Bijie No. 1 High School. However, he could not afford the tuition fees and living expenses of over RMB10,000 (US$1400) a year. Fortunately, a nonprofit organisation was able to sponsor his studies. But there are many families like Xiao Hang's in rural China, who can barely afford to shop in Taobao, and for whom JD and Meituan are well beyond their reach. As for Hema, they have never even heard of it.

With over 600 million people in economic situations like Xiao Hang's, how could they have access to e-commerce? This chapter focuses on how

Chinese internet entrepreneurs succeeded in coming up with innovative business models to develop this vast, underserved segment, enabling the likes of Xiao Hang to be a part of the new retail revolution.

Before we address how to serve people like Xiao Hang, let's meet a few interesting Chinese internet "wise men". They are not as well known outside of China as Jack Ma (who hasn't heard of Jack Ma?) but, in our opinion, they are extraordinary in their business ventures. What makes them interesting is their uncanny ability to be successful while eluding the spotlight; they are, we say, Zen-ishly wise.

## The "wise men" of the Chinese internet

Let us start with William Ding, the founder of NetEase, who rang the bell three times at the Stock Exchange.

William Ding was born into an intellectual family in Fenghua City (奉化), Zhejiang Province, in 1971. His father was an electronic engineer who had profound impact on his son. In his childhood, Ding liked to play with the radio. In 1989, he was admitted to the University of Electronic Science and Technology, majoring in electronic science and technology. After graduating, with the help of his parents, he found a job at the Ningbo Telecom Bureau of Zhejiang Province, as a technical engineer. The job at the telecom bureau was well paid but he felt somewhat unfulfilled and unchallenged. During his two years there, he became very proficient with the computer operating systems. In 1995, Ding resigned from his job, despite objections from his family, and travelled to Guangzhou. After switching three jobs in two years, he founded his own company, NetEase (网易), in 1997. This was before the advent of the BAT three (Baidu, Alibaba and Tencent). NetEase aimed to make internet access easier for the Chinese.

Ding rang his first IPO bell at the Nasdaq, in 2000, when he was just 29 years and NetEase still a portal website. In October 2019, NetEase's education sector, NetEase Youdao (网易有道), landed on the NYSE, giving him his second bell. On June 11, 2020, in the middle of Covid-19, NetEase landed on the Hong Kong Stock Exchange, with an opening price of HK$133 (US$17.2); an 8% increase from the issue price, and with a closing market value of HK$455.8 billion (US$57.5 billion).[2]

In the 20 years since NetEase went public on the Nasdaq, its market value skyrocketed more than 2,700 times, from less than US$20 million to more than US$55 billion, and its share price grew over 90-fold. The overall annual return, including dividend distribution, reached as high as 26.2%. Ding said proudly, "In the past two decades, there are only two companies in China whose annual return on capital exceeded 20%, one is Maotai (茅台; Maotai is one of China's famous liquor brands) and the other is NetEase".[3]

NetEase's performance seems quite miraculous, considering the internet bubble burst soon after it went first public. Its stock price plummeted, and the business fell into crisis. It was ordered to suspend trading shares. NetEase's stock price was fixed at US$0.64, and its market value fell to less than US$20 million. Ding considered selling the company, however, unfortunately or fortunately in hindsight, no one wanted to buy it. At this critical time, Ding met his fairy godfather, Duan Yongping (段永平), who drummed up over US$2 million to buy NetEase shares. Ding was able to navigate through the storm. NetEase transformed into an online games business and the stock price began to soar. Just one year later, in 2003, Ding became China's richest man on the Forbes ranking.[4]

## Duan Yongping: China's "Warren Buffet" behind multiple leading brands

Duan Yongping – the Chinese meaning of Yongping is "forever safe" – is also known as "China's Warren Buffett". He keeps a low profile, and no one knows his true wealth. Duan was born into an ordinary family in 1961. Both of his parents were teachers, and he grew up during the Cultural Revolution (1966–1976), which meant that he didn't receive much of an education.

In 1977, China's universities began to open up their doors to the public. However, the entrance exams were extremely competitive. Between 1977 and 1990, the acceptance rate hovered around 5%–10%. Duan was no luckier than Jack Ma in trying to get into college. In fact, it's hard to say who fared worse. The total score Duan achieved was 80 out of 500 (out of five subjects with a maximum of 100 points each). So, he tried again the following year. This time he still got 80. But it was an average of 80 among five subjects and the total was 400 that year. He was admitted to Zhejiang University, majoring in wireless radio technology. He did his master's in econometrics at the China Renmin University (People's University).

After graduating, Duan was keenly aware of the opportunities brought about by China's new "opening up" policy and its economic reforms. He went south to Zhongshan City, Guangdong Province and applied to Foshan Rihua Electronics Factory, which produced large-scale electronic game machines. In less than a year, he was promoted to director. With the business facing losses of more than RNB2 million (US$420,000), he redesigned the product and launched the "SUBOR (小霸王, Xiaobawang in Chinese)" game console in 1991.

Jackie Chan, one of the most popular martial art film stars, was tapped to endorse the new product. Chan came with a premium price tag that this unknown company could ill afford but the gamble paid off. SUBOR quickly became a well-known brand in China. In 1995, Duan's company share reform plan was rejected and he left SUBOR. He promised he would not open a similar business, in direct competition with SUBOR, for 12 months.

Duan went ahead and established a new game console company, BBK, but kept his promise by waiting a year before launching his new product. He used the same approach as he had at SUBOR: a good product design (game console brand "EEBBK 步步高"), with celebrity endorsement. This time the celebrity was Arnold Schwarzenegger, who starred in the EEBBK adverts on CCTV. For two consecutive years, Duan was CCTV's top bidder for advertising slots[5] and Schwarzenegger became the "Chinese terminator". Duan's winning formula worked again.

One of the key employees who left SUBOR along with Duan was Tony Chen, who later founded OPPO, currently one of the leading smartphone brands in China. The other leading brand is Vivo, which is owned by BBK. In the first half of 2019, OPPO and Vivo ranked numbers one and two, respectively, in the Chinese market in terms of sales quantity, surpassing Huawei, Xiaomi and Apple.[6] Both of the two brands target young people in third- and fourth-tier cities and rural regions. The two founders of OPPO and Vivo are disciples of Duan and are deeply influenced by his management and marketing philosophy. Duan also has another disciple, Colin Huang, the founder of Pinduoduo (PDD), a revolutionary social commerce platform.

## Colin Huang and his mentor

How did Colin Huang and Duan come to know each other? The two seemed to have nothing in common. When he was a student at Zhejiang University, Huang liked posting articles on the internet, which made him popular. After a class one afternoon in 2002, Huang returned to his dorm and an MSN friend request popped up from someone he didn't know. It was William Ding, the founder of NetEase. Ding asked Huang for some advice on a technical problem, which Huang was able to provide. Ding then introduced Huang to Duan Yongping, who had just bought US$2 million stocks of NetEase.

Huang grew up in an ordinary family without much money. They were not poor in the sense of needing to borrow money, but Huang often wore clothes passed down by relatives and friends. Growing up in this environment helped him understand the needs of those at the bottom of the social pyramid. Huang was very talented at his studies, and he was admitted to Chu Kochen Honors College (竺可桢学院) at Zhejiang University, one of the top five comprehensive universities in China. Chu Kochen Honors College was specifically set up for students with special talents. Huang majored in computer science and continued his postgraduate studies in the University of Wisconsin. In 2004, he graduated and debated whether he should join Microsoft or Google. Duan advised Huang to join Google, which was not yet listed.[7] Three years later, Google went public and Huang earned his first pot of gold.[8] In 2006, Duan made a bid of US$620,000 for the opportunity to have lunch with Warren Buffett. He took Colin Huang with him.

## Huang the entrepreneur

In 2007, Huang left Google to set out on his own entrepreneurial journey. That he went on to found PDD was no accident; his prior experience was very much related to e-commerce. Duan was a strong supporter of Huang's entrepreneurial skills and asked him to manage EEBBK's e-commerce business, Ouku (欧酷). After three years, Huang felt that he could not better Liu Qiangdong's JD in this field and Ouku was sold. In 2010, he founded the e-commerce operation company, "Leqee (乐其)", which provided e-commerce agency operation services for major brands such as Nestlé, COFCO

(中粮) and Unilever. In 2013, Leqee hatched Huang's third start-up, a game company called Xunmeng Information Technology (寻梦 "seeking dreams" in Chinese), which generated a good cash flow. Although he made money through games and e-commerce operations, Huang felt that he wasn't making any meaningful impact on society so, in 2015, he started his fourth venture, "Pinhaohuo (拼好货)", in fresh food e-commerce. In September, he established Pinduoduo. Pinduoduo's angel investors included Duan Yongping, William Ding, Wang Wei (SF express) and Sun Tongyu (孙彤宇), one of the founders of Taobao. Duan invested not just financially, but also was generous with advice. Huang once said quite frankly, "Among my angel investors, Duan Yongping has the most influence on me".[9] Duan Yongping also praised Huang: "Huang is a sensible person, he pays attention to the essence of things".[10]

## PDD: China's fastest growing e-commerce start-up

The establishment of Pinhaohuo and PDD, in Huang's words, was to "do something that can impact society more".[11] "Our team may be 20 years later than Alibaba's team. I think we still have a chance… to make a different Alibaba".[12] Despite the dominance of the likes of Alibaba and JD in China's e-commerce space, Huang believed that it was still possible to compete with them head-on, if he could address the needs of the segment of Chinese consumers who were essentially being ignored by the titans of the industry.

In September 2015, Huang merged Pinhaohuo and PDD into one company, PDD. PDD's target was the millions of underserved, price-sensitive consumers.

How did PDD serve customers like Xiao Hang? Here's one example: a dress priced at RMB39 on Taobao was only RMB19 on PDD and, if the customer could invite five friends to buy as a group, the price fell to only RMB9.9, including delivery. RMB9.9 is about US$1.50. How could anyone make money by selling US$1.50 dresses? (Figure 8.1a–c)

With rock-bottom pricing, PDD's active user base not surprisingly went from zero to 100 million in its first year and then to 200 million in its second. By the end of March 2020, PDD boasted 628 million active users on its platform, making it probably the world's fastest-growing company in

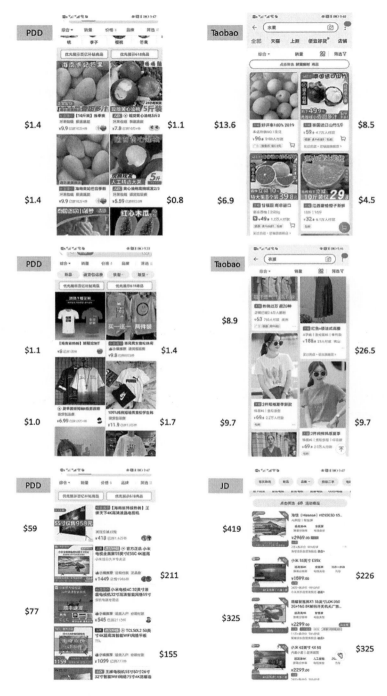

Figure 8.1  Searching fruit, clothing and TVs on PDD, Taobao and JD.

terms of client acquisition.[13] (According to the latest annual report, Alibaba had 711 million active users in China in 2019[14] and JD had 362 million active customer accounts.[15]) As PDD's user base expanded, its trading volume also grew exponentially. In the 12-month period ending December 2019, PDD reported a gross merchandise value (GMV) of RMB1,006 billion, or US$144.6 billion, which represented a whopping 213% increase from the previous year.[16] In the same period, Alibaba reported a GMV of RMB5,727 billion (US$823.2 billion)[17] and JD reported a GMV of RMB2,085 billion (US$299.5 billion).[18] Now in its fifth year of operation, PDD is a solid third in the fiercely competitive e-commerce market in China, after Alibaba and JD (Figures 8.2 and 8.3).

With such a rapid growth, PDD attracted a lot of attention as well as money from the capital market (Figure 8.4).[19]

On July 26, 2018, PDD launched its initial public offering on the Nasdaq market.

Known for rock-bottom-priced products that it sold on its online platform, PDD had been the target of much criticism and even ridicule relating to the quality of its products. Despite the controversies and seemingly bad reputation, PDD's stock prices shot up by more than 30% on the first day of trading and its market value reached nearly US$30 billion, or more than half that of JD, the second largest Chinese e-commerce player behind Alibaba.[20]

Huang didn't travel to the United States for the day of listing. Instead, he invited some of his customers to ring the bell at the Nasdaq. He stayed in Shanghai and participated remotely, as if it were just another ordinary day. It took Alibaba five years to go public, eight years for Vip.com, ten years for JD and only three years for PDD.

| Time | 201609 | 2017 | 2018 | 2019 | 202003 |
|---|---|---|---|---|---|
| Active users (millions) | 100 | 200 (Sep) | 300 (Jun) | 585 | 628 |
| GMV (billion US$) | | 21.6 | 68.7 | 144.6 | |
| Revenue (million US$) | | 267 | 1,912 | 4,329 | |
| Profit (million US$) | | -76 | -1,500 | -1,000 | |

Figure 8.2  Key statistics of PDD.

|                              | Alibaba | JD    | PDD   |
|------------------------------|---------|-------|-------|
| Active users (millions) 2019 | 711     | 362   | 585   |
| GMV (billion US$)            | 823.2   | 299.5 | 144.6 |

Figure 8.3  PDD vs Taobao and JD.

| Time   | Round    | Investors                                                                                      | amount           |
|--------|----------|------------------------------------------------------------------------------------------------|------------------|
| 201603 | A        | Gaorong Capital                                                                                | million dollars  |
| 201607 | B        | Gaorong Capital, New Horizon Fund, Tencent Investment, Shunwei Capital, Xiaomi Technology, IDG, etc | US$110 million   |
| 201701 | C        | Sequoia Capital                                                                                | US$215 million   |
| 201804 | D        | Tencent, Sequoia Capital                                                                       | US$1.369billion  |
| 201807 | IPO      |                                                                                                |                  |
| 201909 | Strategy | Convertible bond                                                                               | US$1 billion     |

Figure 8.4  Financing history of PDD.

In June 2020, Huang, at age of 40, became the second richest man in China, valued at US$45.4 billion (ranking 22nd richest in the world), while Pony Ma of Tencent was valued at US$51.5 billion (ranking 19th in the world), Jack Ma at US$43.9 billion (23rd in the world) and Liu Qiangdong of JD at US$12.7 billion (Figure 8.5).

Interestingly, in April 2020, Jack Ma was valued US$38.8 billion, Pony Ma at US$38.1 billion and Colin Huang at US$16.5 billion. Within two months, Huang had increased his value by US$28.9 billion.

An IPO does not necessarily represent success, however. PDD was unable to make any profit, even after five years. Amazon also didn't make its first profits until 2015, 20 years after its establishment, which meant its investors were extremely patient and confident for a period of two decades. They believed that the company would eventually make some money. The question for PDD, though, is just how long can it withstand losing money?

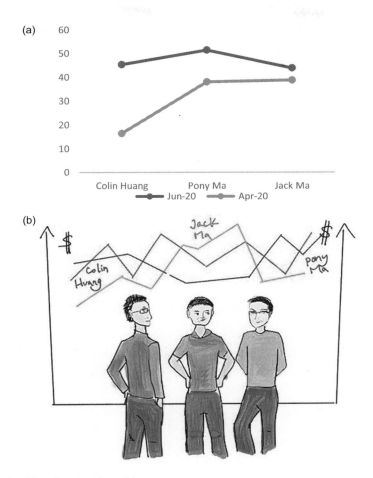

Figure 8.5  The change of wealth.
Illustrated by Aspen Wang.

## People in low-tier cities got online: timing matters

The Chinese believe "timing, conditions and capability (天时、地利、人和)" are all indispensable to achieve success. PDD's timing was ripe.

- Since 2015, low-cost smartphones sold by Xiaomi had quickly enabled users in third- to fifth-tier cities to connect to the mobile internet, increasing the internet penetration rate of the rural population.
- In 2013, the monthly active user (MAU) rate for WeChat was 355 million; in 2015 it was 697 million; in 2017, 989 million; and in

2019, 1.165 billion. The increase largely came from low-tier cities and rural regions. This made it possible for PDD to use online social communication.

- The launch of WeChat Pay made it very convenient to pay by mobile.
- The coverage of the logistics system grew more extensive, from first- and second-tier cities to the lower-tier cities.
- Taobao did not use WeChat's social traffic, because Alibaba and Tencent were fierce competitors, and JD's prices were too high for the low-income population.

When PDD was born, the entire social e-commerce infrastructure had already penetrated into low-tier cities, yet Taobao and JD had not yet begun to deploy. Timing is everything!

## A market unbeknownst to the middle class: positioning matters

The most common products sold on PDD include multi-packs of paper for RMB14.9 (US$2.1); pieces of luggage for tens of yuan (several dollars); and five pounds of fruit for RMB9.9 (US$1.4): commodity prices on the plat-form are extremely low. In categories like mobile phones, the best-selling products are mobile phones for the elderly, with an average price of only RMB30 (US$4.3).

PDD, known for its low prices, has always received criticism for product quality. When the news came out that it had submitted a listing application, the internet immediately exploded with calls of "fake goods", "counterfeits", "consumption downgrades", "low-end customers", "low-tier cities".... In 2016, the number of complaints about PDD accounted for 13.12% of the in-dustry, ranking it an ignominious first.[21] Just a week before PDD went public, nappy manufacturer "Daddy's Choice" filed a trademark infringement lawsuit in a federal court in New York. The indictment alleged that PDD allowed counterfeit products with the company's trademark to be sold on its platform.

In response to the questioning and criticism, Huang said, "People living within the fifth ring road of Beijing would say that this (PDD's customer) is a sinking (bottom of the pyramid) population. We are targeting the most common people in China". "People living within the fifth ring road cannot understand our core (philosophy)".[22] (In Beijing, there are several highways circling the inner city, called ring roads. The fifth ring road is 10 kilometres from the city centre. People living within the fifth ring road are well-to-do middle class.) "Consumption upgrades", Huang continued, "are not for Shanghainese people who live the lives of Parisians, but let the people in Anqing City (fourth-tier city), Anhui Province, have kitchen paper towels and good fruit to eat".[23] The low prices on PDD made it possible for many users to be able to afford products that they would not have been able to before – fruit juice cups for RMB28 (US$4.0), electronic blood-pressure monitors with voice-reporting function for RMB39 (US$5.6), large-screen smartphones for RMB398 (US$57.1), etc.

According to the National Bureau of Statistics of China (NBSC), China's per capita disposable income in 2019 was RMB30,733 (U$4,405),[24] which translates to US$367 per month. While in China's affluent coastal regions income levels are much higher than the national average, its vast inland provinces and particularly its rural population are nowhere near this figure. The reality is the average monthly income of 600 million people is only US$140, and there are approximately one billion Chinese living in small cities and townships who are much more price sensitive than the shoppers you meet at a Gucci store in a first- or second-tier city. Indeed, at least two-thirds of PDD's customers come from outside the target audience of a typical e-commerce outlet.[25]

In China, there are clearly two groups of people: those living inside and those living outside the fifth ring road. On the internet, however, the separation between the two is invisible. Xiao Li, who lives inside the fifth ring road, bought Boston lobster for RMB89 (IUS$12.8) in Hema Xiansheng. Xiao Hang, who lives outside the fifth ring road, was happy with the five pounds of mangos he bought on PDD for RMB9.9 (US$1.4); he had never eaten mangos before. This is the reality of China – indeed the reality of many developing countries – a pyramid market with a mass of people at the bottom.

## Low-end supply chain

Since the 1980s, China has developed a huge manufacturing capacity. In 2015, many Original Equipment Manufacturer companies (OEMs) that supplied the foreign trade contracted within China, began to fall short of orders. A large surplus of production capacity was created, and it needed to shift to the domestic market. However, this process was not easy. JD's focus had always been on licensed products, and it didn't do any business with the OEM factories; and Taobao was deeply involved in "fighting fake products". The OEM factories had extra capacity and needed cash. This is where PDD came in.

PDD significantly reduced the factories' marketing costs by providing them with free traffic. The "group-buying" products – low in price but high in volume – could not only utilise the factories' production capacity but could also help manufacturers quickly win the trust of consumers through and establish a brand image. Some factories were willing to reduce profits or even lose money, in order to build up sales and their brand. In December 2018, PDD launched a "new brand" plan to support those factories who wanted to shed their OEM status.

Matsutek was a manufacturing company with more than 70 international patents, located in Shenzhen. The robot cleaners it produced were for big brands such as Honeywell, Whirlpool and Philips and were sent all over the world.[26] In 2015, after manufacturing for other brands for 20 years, Matsutek launched its own brand, "Jiaweishi 家卫士". However, having the technology and production capacity didn't mean that they knew the market needs or consumer preferences. Consumers would rather spend four times as much to buy a big-name brand based on OEM products, than buy a Jiaweishi. In 2018, Jiaweishi joined PDD's new brand plan and, within six months, sales volume had exceeded 100,000. Jiaweishi is a typical example of many small and medium-sized manufacturing enterprises in China.

Another popular category sold on PDD is agricultural products. This is where is the RMB9.9 (US$1.4) five-pound free-delivery fruit comes in. In 2018, white garlic from Zhongmu County (中牟县) had no effective distribution channels and the Zhongmu government sought cooperation with PDD. The merchants who collaborated with PDD bought seven million pounds of garlic and sold it to PDD customers at a preferential price – five pounds for RMB9.6 (US$1.4) and ten pounds for RMB18.9 (US$2.8). This model was copied by other producers who had either over-produced or had no direct market access. All kinds of agricultural products from Yunnan, Guangxi, Henan, Hainan and other areas were directed towards PDD consumers. Farmers could also open stores themselves on PDD, eliminating the need for intermediates and greatly reducing the spoilage rate, due to a shortened timeframe. PDD worked with the agricultural regions to help them train e-commerce operators. They trained over 100,000 migrant workers who had left their hometowns to find work in the city. Following the training, they returned to their rural towns and villages and worked with PDD to sell their local produce. When a particular product was in season, big data was used to identify the customers who were most likely to buy it, and large quantities were shipped at low cost. By November 2020, PDD had 12 million farmers connected to its platform, and it expected to sell RMB250 billion (US$37 billion) agricultural products by the end of 2020.[27]

This new supply chain for perishable agricultural products met the needs of the underserved population in low-tier cities. In this way, PDD made a dent in the e-commerce market that so far had been monopolised by Alibaba and JD.

## How did PDD play with social e-commerce?

### Social + e-commerce

PDD's business model is reflected in its name. Pin means "group purchase" and duoduo means "many". The process of inviting friends to join is made very easy on Tencent's WeChat messaging platform and many people are drawn to PDD from a WeChat group, where family members or friends ask them to "help cut the price", or to buy the same product together for a deep discount. The user who initiates the "price cutting" process can even get the product for free − including delivery − if he or she manages to invite enough people to click on the link within 24 hours. This model inspires users to share links on WeChat, invite friends to join in with group buying and helps to bargain and share reciprocity. While they are helping to lower prices or join a group purchase, the unsuspecting newcomers who click on the link are completing the PDD registration process, without hardly noticing it (Figure 8.6).

The shopping process of PDD is also designed for easy social communication. Almost all products on PDD are delivered free. This makes the user's decision-making time shorter and the process easier. Both JD and Taobao have a shopping cart function, which PDD doesn't. A PDD user doesn't have to think about buying multiple products together to save on delivery costs

Figure 8.6  Group buying.
Illustrated by Aspen Wang.

because, basically, every product comes with free delivery. In this way, they can click directly onto the link sent by others and join in the group buying. Features, such as ultra-low-priced products, no price comparison, no shopping cart, free delivery, etc., offered by PDD greatly reduced the threshold for users to shop on their mobile phones.

### Game + e-commerce

PDD thought of many ways to attract customers more frequently. The "daily check-in" is one. This feature encourages users to open the app every day by rewarding them with redeemable points each time. Users can redeem their vouchers for cash deductions when making a purchase.

In May 2018, PDD also launched an in-app game to motivate users to engage with the app for fun, even if it didn't immediately translate into a purchase. The game was named Duo Duo Orchard/Pasture and allows users to "raise" chickens (or "plant" fruit trees – the choices vary depending on seasonality), "feed" them and "play" with them. After a period of time, a certain amount of eggs can be harvested and exchanged for real products. Online gaming coupled with monetary rewards doubled the happiness.

To earn feed for the chickens, players need to fulfil a variety of missions such as viewing commodities, sharing products and inviting friends to join PDD. Players can also see how their friends' chickens are doing. They can either help them feed them or "steal" their food (Figure 8.7).

*Figure 8.7* Duo Duo Pasture.

Over 60 million users log on to Duo Duo Pasture and play every day.[28] It is not only a tool to incentivise consumers to log on, browse and purchase more often, but also allows users to interact and enjoy shopping with friends.

That PDD introduced gaming into e-commerce is not surprising. The firm's predecessor, Xunmeng Information Technology, was a gaming company, and PDD had a profound understanding of the appeal of games and how they could be successfully incorporated. PDD's game provides customer satisfaction in completing tasks. The game is also sociable – finding enough people to take advantage of the lowest price possible. It provides the satisfaction of knowing "I am getting the best deal" and by seeing the "hen" you have raised lay "eggs" that you can exchange for real products gives people a sense of accomplishment. The psychological satisfaction in turn creates app stickiness.

### *Recommendation + e-commerce*

Compared to Taobao and JD, PDD is designed quite differently. When a consumer has something in mind that they would like to buy, say hiking boots or something more specific like hiking boots of a particular brand, they go on Taobao to search for it. When they type in women's hiking boots, thousands of hiking boots by hundreds or thousands of third-party vendors appear on the screen. It takes time for the buyer to review the list and compare prices before making a decision. When a consumer goes to PDD, they do not have a specific item in mind. Based on their viewing histories, shopping behaviours and what people with similar tastes like to buy, PDD recommends relevant deals to you. If Taobao is search based, then we can call PDD recommendation based. People go to Taobao because they have something specific in mind, and people go to PDD because they are looking for the best deal.

## The successful factors of PDD

Colin Huang once said that PDD is "a combination of Cosco and Disney"[29] – providing consumers with low prices and fun.

By November 2020, the number of users on PDD had exceeded 731 million.[30] With the completion of user accumulation through social communication, PDD no longer needed to rely on viral communication to acquire users. The mode of inviting relatives and friends to form a group to cut prices also changed. Users no longer had to rely on friends, they could now also form a group with strangers. Duoduo Orchard/Pasture continues to bring people the fun of socialising and gaming.

Why PDD emerged and how it became successful is described in Figure 8.8. With people in low-tier cities coming online and within reach of e-commerce platforms, and supply chains providing low costs, low prices and acceptable quality (relative to price) products, PDD identified and captured the white spot of 600 million people with an average income of US$140 per month, which all other e-commerce players ignored, by integrating social e-commerce, gaming entertainment and recommendations together in one core value proposition: value for money.

PDD is different from traditional e-commerce not only by customer segment but also in how they engage their customers. Direct selling has the appeal of instant gratification. PDD provides the thrill of the best deal and a sense of accomplishment, whether it is in the form of raising a virtual hen or inviting friends to join in with group buying. You could argue that PDD provides the kind of user experience that increases stickiness.

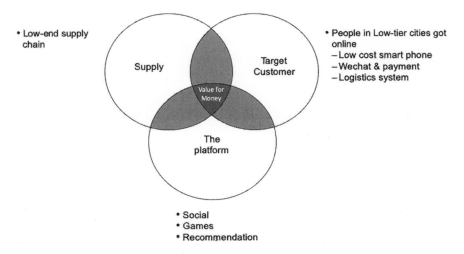

Figure 8.8  Factors of PDD's success.

## All kinds of models of social e-commerce

PDD, with group buying as its main feature, developed so rapidly that it managed to ascend into the top three e-commerce companies in China within a very short time. Group buying is just one form of Chinese social e-commerce, however.

For example, in Chapter 7 on fresh food, we mentioned community group buying, which is also a typical social e-commerce. The community group buying platform is responsible for product selection, warehousing, logistics and after-sales support. Community group buying mainly uses the acquaintance relationships of the head of the group, who organises the residents of their community. The head promotes the product information through a WeChat group, and residents place orders through the WeChat Mini program. The individual orders are then integrated into one large order, which is shipped directly from the supplier to the community and distributed by the head to the buyers. The products are mainly daily necessities such as fresh food and other goods with high repurchase rates. The community group buying became a turf war by the end of 2020. Almost all internet giants poured resources into this sector. Alibaba invested in Nice Tuan; PDD had Duoduo Grocery; Meituan launched Meituan Preference; Didi established Chengxin Preference; JD came up with Xi Pinpin, all these new community group buying are in the form of mini program.

There is also a "membership social e-commerce". In this concept, the platform is responsible for the entire supply chain process including product selection, distribution and after-sales. Consumers can become members by paying membership fees or fulfilling the required purchase order quota. They can also become distributors. The members only need to share links and recommend products to earn income. Many members are previous WeChat business people (微商) individuals who sell goods through their WeChat Moments). An example of membership social e-commerce is Yunji (云集). By 2018, there were already 6.1 million members and 23 million active users on the platform.[31]

There is also "content social e-commerce". Unlike the previous models, content social e-commerce does not rely on acquaintance relationships, but stimulates users' enthusiasm for purchase through common interest. The key opinion leaders (KOLs) on the platform attract users through content such as graphics and text, short videos and other forms, and users can directly click to the corresponding e-commerce platform to make a purchase while viewing the content. Some users share their comments after the purchase, which further enriches the content. A typical example is Xiaohongshu (小红书), which focuses on tourism and food.

Although a type of e-commerce, social e-commerce is very different from traditional e-commerce. If PDD followed the traditional e-commerce path, it would have found it difficult to break into a space dominated by two giants, Taobao and JD. The reason why social e-commerce can offer different opportunities is because it has unique advantages.

1.  **The customer acquisition of traditional e-commerce is a funnel structure, and social e-commerce is a fission structure.** In traditional e-commerce, consumers are just buyers. In social e-commerce, consumers are both buyers and promoters. Through the viral marketing among consumers' acquaintance relationships network, the cost of acquiring new customers is low and fast. In traditional e-commerce, consumers search and browse, click to view and make purchase decision. This is a funnel structure, where some customers get lost as they pass through each layer. Social e-commerce is a net structure, and every consumer node can split into multiple consumer nodes. PDD's users grew from zero to 100 million in one year, and to 700 million in five years. This would be inconceivable if it had relied on the traditional ways of customer acquisition. Furthermore, acquaintance relationships imply a certain level of trust. If an acquaintance is considered to be a shrewd buyer, then what they are buying should be a good deal. This kind of reasoning is more persuasive than the official ads created by companies. With the incentives of discounts and commissions, the willingness to actively spread and share is also high, which can push the fission further.

2.  **Recommending instead of searching; promoting single products instead of brands; "wanting" instead of "needing".** In traditional e-commerce, most consumers shop with a purpose. They have something in mind and go online to search for it. They evaluate the options among many search results and choose the ones that most match their needs and expectations. Social e-commerce is based on individual's social networks, and the products are pushed towards

them. These are unplanned purchases motivated by the best deal recommended by friends. Compared with traditional e-commerce, people buy things in PDD that they "want" rather "need". Sometimes it is hard to say which is more exciting: buying something you need or buying something you want. Getting a good deal generally creates positive feelings. Acquaintance recommendations can also weaken dependence on brand. The larger the sales volume, the lower the cost, the more competitive the price. The lower the price, the higher the sales volume. This is a virtuous circle. To a certain extent, PDD generates new demand – goods that people would not have bought if it wasn't for PDD.

Recommendation algorithm plays an important part in PDD's business model. One may argue that other e-commerce players such as Taobao and JD also use various forms of algorithm, but rather as a supporting tool, the extent that PDD business model is largely built upon the recommendation algorithm is a key differentiator. It uses data to predict what users would like to see and to buy. Because the recommendation is so accurate, the users could make an immediate purchasing decision based on the individualised recommendation, without ever needing to use the search function. The more you use it, the more accurate the recommendation is presented to you; the more you feel you get the best deal every time you log in, the more you will use it. A positive cycle is formed and people are hooked to it. It becomes a habitual behaviour – not necessary the loyalty described in the traditional marketing textbook. We also question whether there is such a thing called loyalty in the e-commerce space?

3.  **PDD not only attracts consumers in low-tier cities but also appeals to people in first-tier and second-tier cities who are cost conscious.** PDD's value proposition is to serve people who care about value for money. There are hybrid consumers in China who will buy a Hermes bag and stay in a five-star hotel but will also buy RMB9.9 (US$1.4) five pounds of mango. This is more about consumption philosophy than consumption capability. Huang said that his mother was "already rich, but she still cares about the difference of one or two yuan (a few cents) when she goes out to buy food or paper towels, but then she also buys a high-end iPhone".[32]

## The incumbents' responses: at home and abroad

In response to the rapid rise of PDD, both Alibaba and JD struck out. In March 2018, Alibaba launched the "Taobao Special Edition" app, targeting the third- and fourth-tier cities and the elderly. The same month, JD launched JD Group Purchase (later renamed as Jingxi 京喜, the Chinese pronunciation is like "nice surprise"), where the product price was lower than on JD. It also stimulated users to share through group purchase prices and social media. With the entry of Alibaba and JD, the penetration rate of e-commerce in third- and fourth-tier cities became close to saturation. PDD transformed its strategy from customer acquisition to customer retention.

Does the United States have something similar to PDD? Brandless, established in 2014, was the closest to PDD. As the name implies, the products sold at Brandless had no brand, and all products were sold for just US$3. Brandless also made full use of social network promotion. Users recommended Brandless to friends and when the friends completed an order, the users who made the recommendation received US$6. Brandless implemented a membership system, with an annual fee of US$36, which gave members free delivery; non-members had to make a minimum purchase of US$72 to be eligible for free delivery (this later dropped to US$39). Brandless was also very popular among investors. In July 2018, it received a US$240 million Series C financing from the Vision Fund. In February 2020, however, Brandless announced its failure.[33]

If you compare Brandless with PDD, based on the three factors of "timing, conditions and capability", we could hypothesise why Brandless was not as successful as PDD. The population infrastructure, e-commerce infrastructure, and supply chain infrastructures of the United States are very different from those of China. First, logistics infrastructure has covered the whole China. Second, while the low-income population cannot afford iPhones, they have Chinese-made smart phones. Third, the ease of using mobile payments is at their fingertips. Fourth, social platforms like WeChat are part of Chinese people's daily lives and link friends together easily. Fifth, China's manufacturing sector as a world's factory has the capability and capacity to produce on a large scale. These conditions barely exist in the United States.

For example, the high logistics costs in America made it impossible for Brandless to offer free delivery for everything and everyone. To get free delivery on Brandless, consumers had to buy 13 items in one go, which made the purchasing decision complicated. To find low cost and acceptable quality products at US$3 per item is a struggle. The number of users of Brandless began to decline in 2019, the main reason cited being "quality decline".[34]

## Challenges for MNCs

It is understandable for multinational companies (MNCs) to ignore or dismiss PDD because it is deal-driven and its prices are so low that it doesn't warrant consideration. In our view, PDD is the most likely to bring disruption to the industry. We introduced you to Matsutek, a domestic player that launched its own robot cleaners, Jiaweishi, with the help of PDD, after being an original equipment manufacturer (OEM) for multinational brands for 20 years. Matsutek's is not a unique case. It is the strategy of PDD to help local manufacturers to establish their brands and develop the local market. Jinhui (金辉) is another OEM for world-class kitchenware brands such as Zwilling and WMF. It tried to build up their own brand 10 years ago but failed, due to weak brand awareness. This time, with consumer statistics provided by PDD, Jinhui redesigned its products and repositioned itself. It promoted its kitchen knives under the brand of "Wang Mazi (王麻子)" on PDD. The kitchen knives used the same materials as Zwilling and WMF and had more functions. They are priced at one-quarter of the international brands. "Wang Mazi" was a great success on PDD, achieving RMB50 million (US$7.5 million) sales revenue in less than six months.[35]

When most companies practice the push-based supply chain – producing the products first, then pushing the products through the channels to the market – PDD experiments with pull-based logic. It uses an algorithm to predict users' demand and the price they are willing to pay. Then it works with local brands to design and develop the products. More and more, Chinese companies are collaborating with PDD, and these domestic players are likely to challenge MNCs.

PDD has 731 million users. With its low prices and subsidies to consumers, will they be able to make a profit? Unlike JD and Tmall, which take a percentage cut from each transaction on their platforms, PDD makes its money mainly from advertising income. Its business model and value proposition make it difficult to take a percentage cut of an already "dirt-cheap" sales price. While PDD has the strong backing of powerful players in China including Tencent and SF Express, they still need to make money to be sustainable. The investors seem to hope that over time, PDD will be able to find new revenue sources from its huge client base without fundamentally changing its business logic. The good news finally came in the third quarter of 2020, when PDD made a profit of RMB4.66 billion (US$698 million). After five years, they were able to break even. However, this was only for one-quarter and not the whole year; the more important question is whether they can continue this positive trajectory.

PDD has collected tremendous data on its platform. Huang believes PDD can use the data to help increase the efficiency of supply chain. He said: "Supply chain upgrade will be our strategic focus for a long time. The final model of PDD is to enable the upstream to do mass customised production".[36] From this point of view, improving products and reducing costs to make room for profits should be the next most important step for PDD.

On July 1, 2020, Huang announced that he would formally step down as CEO of PDD, while continuing to serve as chairman, and the new CEO would be Chen Lei, the company's co-founder who was previously CTO. Chen Lei holds a bachelor's degree in computer science from Tsinghua University and received his PhD in computer science from the University of Wisconsin-Madison. He led the development of PDD's distributed artificial intelligence technology, an innovative technology system that has now become the underlying backbone for its recommendation algorithm. The recommendation algorithm will continue to play an outsized role in PDD's future.

## Concluding remarks: questions for executives to ask

1. How large is your potential bottom of the pyramid market? How much new addressable market can you imagine for your business? What is the percentage of cost-conscience consumers of your products? Social e-commerce not only attracts consumers in low-tier branches but also appeals to people in first-tier and second-tier branches who are cost conscious.

2. How can social recommendation mechanisms support your business growth? Recommending instead of searching, promoting single products instead of brands, "wanting" instead of "needing".

3.  What is the role that gamification plays in your customer engagement?
4.  How can you reconsider your customer acquisition strategy? The customer acquisition of traditional e-commerce is funnel structure, and the social e-commerce is fission structure.
5.  Can your logistics process and overall operations support social commerce end-to-end? What are the weak inks and how can you strengthen them?

## Notes

1   Converted at concurrent exchange rate, unless otherwise specified.
2   http://www.forbeschina.com/business/49295.
3   https://mp.weixin.qq.com/s/4nA7RYU7YHq19cYxYZ8bug.
4   https://baijiahao.baidu.com/s?id=1669204608834318338&wfr=spider&-for=pc.
5   https://baijiahao.baidu.com/s?id=1634487486618755294&wfr=spider&-for=pc.
6   https://www.sohu.com/a/329498620_126540.
7   http://finance.sina.com.cn/chanjing/gsnews/2018-10-25/doc-ihmxrkzw3550516.shtml.
8   https://baijiahao.baidu.com/s?id=1665639260996080706&wfr=spider&-for=pc.
9   https://tech.qq.com/a/20190605/001019.htm.
10  https://www.sohu.com/a/257712592_618348.
11  Colin Huang's article published on his own Wechat Account "Why Start New Business Again".
12  Colin Huang's article published on his own Wechat Account "Why Start New Business Again".
13  https://www.pinduoduo.com/home/about/.
14  https://tech.sina.cn/i/gn/2020-02-13/detail-iimxxstf1186815.d.html.
15  JD 2019 annual report:
16  PDD 2019 annual report.
17  Alibaba annual report.
18  JD 2019 annual report.
19  http://finance.sina.com.cn/stock/s/2018-07-26/doc-ihfvkitx3344110.shtml.
20  http://finance.sina.com.cn/stock/usstock/c/2018-07-27/doc-ihfvkitx4267904.shtml.

21  http://finance.sina.com.cn/chanjing/gsnews/2018-07-31/doc-ihhacrcc9002088.shtml.

22  http://tech.chinadaily.com.cn/a/201804/13/WS5b88e-27ca310030f813e7493.html.

23  https://www.huxiu.com/article/272900.html.

24  http://www.stats.gov.cn/tjsj/zxfb/202002/t20200228_1728913.html.

25  https://baijiahao.baidu.com/s?id=1649514985942945700&wfr=spider&-for=pc.

26  https://baijiahao.baidu.com/s?id=1619652550412323977&wfr=spider&-for=pc.

27  https://finance.sina.com.cn/stock/relnews/us/2020-10-17/doc-iiznctkc6107685.shtml.

28  https://pinduoduo.gcs-web.com/static-files/afa5ca3e-247c-44a9-b05d-8e9e191f3119.

29  https://www.sohu.com/a/236956321_116903.

30  https://new.qq.com/omn/20201115/20201115A0AAHV00.html.

31  http://report.iresearch.cn/report_pdf.aspx?id=3402.

32  https://mp.weixin.qq.com/s/GTV9OwzoKjvWjgGwRACbhA.

33  http://finance.sina.com.cn/stock/relnews/us/2020-02-22/doc-iimxyqvz5051822.shtml.

34  http://finance.sina.com.cn/stock/relnews/us/2020-02-22/doc-iimxyqvz5051822.shtml.

35  https://k.sina.com.cn/article_1652484947_627eeb530200121jn.html?subch=onews.

36  https://baijiahao.baidu.com/s?id=1621172647339605726&wfr=spider&-for=pc.

# 9

## LIVESTREAM CELEBRITY SELLING

### Taking retail by storm

In the first half of 2014, Taobao's operations team began to notice a new phenomenon. A few of the online stores on its platform seemed a bit different to the others. They didn't seem to rely on Taobao's traffic or participate in any of its promotional activities but, nevertheless, their sales were good. Excellent in fact. Data showed the sales figures concentrated around just one or two days a month, with little activity at other times. The peculiar sales pattern and rapid growth rate of these stores quickly caught Taobao's attention. Upon investigation, they found out that the owners were "key opinion leaders" (KOLs) with a lot of followers who they interacted with on Weibo and other social media platforms, attracting many of them to their Taobao stores.

Ming Zeng, chairman of the Alibaba Academic Committee, once said that "new things might be late but they will inevitably come".[1] He instructed Taobao's operations team to keep an eye on the platform and to watch for emerging new trends. Internet celebrity selling via livestream platforms was one of the "new things" that inevitably arrived.

DOI: 10.4324/9781003205074-11

## China's divergent livestream celebrities

As with most things in China, there is no such thing as the internet celebrity. Chinese internet celebrities come in many forms. One type is "the CEO" – a recent brand of internet celebrity that felt it could no longer ignore the power of livestreaming. Another type is the professional sellers – "the Pros" – who didn't want to miss this opportunity and transitioned from the physical selling to online selling. In doing so, they found themselves reaching a much wider audience. Then, a new breed of celebrities emerged, a group of "Underdogs" that were not even interested in selling or livestreaming; they just loved to talk about and share their products. There is also a type called "the Official" – government officials using livestreaming to promote their local produce and bolster their region's economy (Figure 9.1).

*Figure 9.1*  China's divergent livestream celebrities.
Illustrated by Aspen Wang.

## "The CEOs": rejuvenating business through livestreaming

On June 11, 2020, William Ding, the founder of NetEase, must have been one of the busiest people on the planet. In the morning, his company completed a second listing on the Hong Kong Stock Exchange, where he performed the customary bellringing with the help of a "cloud" from his headquarters in Hangzhou. An IPO is one of the most important milestones for any founder of a business. So how did Ding celebrate his big day? He made his first livestream sales pitch in the evening on both the NetEase Yanxuan (网易严选, NetEase's e-commerce business) and Kuaishou (快手) apps. What better way to capitalise on this special occasion than being a celebrity in the e-commerce space? Ding was very picky when it came to the products he wanted to sell in his new role. During the three hours he was live, from 8pm to 11pm, he recommended only six items, although the original plan had been 22.

Ding was not the first Chinese entrepreneur to try his hand at livestream selling. On April 1, 2020, when the nation was recovering from the Covid-19 pandemic, Luo Yonghao (罗永浩), another CEO, began his first live broadcasting on Douyin.

Luo Yonghao, known as Old Luo (not that he is old; Chinese people like to put the word "old" in front of the last name to show respect, or to acknowledge someone who is experienced), is an interesting case among Chinese entrepreneurs. Old Luo was born in Yanji (延吉), Jilin Province, in 1972. We don't know if he was good academically, but he dropped out of school when he was around 15 or 16 years. After leaving school, Luo did many things for living, such as selling books, grilling shish kebab, manual labour and selling tonic water. Luck was not yet on his side and he didn't make a lot of money. Later, by chance, Luo heard from a friend that English teachers at the New Oriental School (新东方) could earn up to RMB1 million (US$140,000) per year, and he was much impressed. He was already 28 years old.

Luo enrolled in English classes at the school and studied hard. Within a few months, he thought he was ready to become a teacher. He wrote a ten-thousand-word letter to Yu Minhong (俞敏洪), the founder of the school, requesting an opportunity to teach. But his first two trial lectures were a disaster. Not willing to admit defeat, he went to Yu's office and asked for a third chance. This time, he passed the assessment. In 2001, Luo, who had not graduated from high school or studied abroad, became an English teacher at the New Oriental with an annual salary of RMB600,000 (US$84,000), which placed him in a high-income bracket. Thanks to his witty humour, Luo was a very popular, engaging teacher.

After teaching at the New Oriental for six years, he left the school and established a blog site called Bullog (牛博网), which was not commercially successful. After that, he founded an English training school, penned his own autobiography and gave speeches all over the country. In 2012, he found something worth devoting his efforts to wholeheartedly – Smartisan Technology (锤子科技). He hoped that his Smartisan phone would become the "best mobile phone in the eastern hemisphere". At one point, Smartisan Technology was valued over US$100 million. However, the Smartisan phone didn't become the "best mobile phone". The company was poorly run and fell heavily into debt. In 2019, Smartisan Technology was sold to ByteDance, the parent company of Toutiao and Douyin.

While it is easy to see why William Ding took to livestream selling to promote his NetEase Yanxua, what was Old Luo's sales pitch about, with Smartisan Technology already sold? In November 2019, Luo was issued a "consumption restriction order" by the court, due to arrears owed to Smartisan Technology's suppliers. On the same day, he published a letter, "The Confession of a CEO debtor".[2] The letter stated that Smartisan Technology owed RMB600 million (US$87 million) to suppliers and banks, dating back to the second half of 2018. Luo was not willing to "go through a bankruptcy process which would dissolve his financial responsibility but would disappoint creditors who had helped him". He had already paid off RMB300 million (US$44 million) of debt. He said, "please rest assured" that he would "continue to work hard to pay off the remaining debt".

So, this is why Luo, at the age of almost 50, made his first attempt at livestream selling. He had plenty of fans that admired his life story and his uncanny honesty. During his first live stream, he made pitches for a total of 22 brands, with a cumulative viewership of over 48 million people and sales volume of over RMB180 million (US$25 million).[3] The first product he recommended was RMB9.9 (US$1.4) for ten Xiaomi pens, which sold out within seconds. And at the end of the live broadcast, Luo even shaved his beard to promote a razor. Brands competed fiercely for slots in Old Luo's first live broadcast. Only 1 in 100 brands were selected, and they had to pay RMB600,000 (US$85,000) each.[4] In other words, before the live broadcast had even started, Luo already received more than RMB13 million (US$1.8 million) upfront. Optimistic, he estimated that he could pay off his debt in a year and a half, and then he could consider buying back the Smartisan brand.[5]

While Old Luo does not fit the usual "seriousness" image of a Chinese CEO, Ms Dong Mingzhu, chairman and president of Gree, a global fortune 500 company, is a well-respected businesswoman, who has the image of an iron lady. Dong was born in 1954 into a modest family in Nanjing, a coastal city that served as the capital of various Chinese dynasties, kingdoms and republican governments dating from the 3rd century up to 1949. She went to an ordinary college and, after graduating in 1975, took on an administrative role at a chemical research institute. In 1984, when her son was two years old, her husband passed away and she raised her son single handedly. Up to this point, she led a life no different to any ordinary person growing up in one of China's coastal cities. But Ms Dong is anything but ordinary.

In 1990, at the age of 36, Dong decided to leave her relatively stable life behind and moved to ZhuHai, a city neighbouring Macao, to work for Gree Group. Starting in an entry-level role, Dong pretty soon caught the attention of the then general manager when she managed, through sheer persistence, to collect a debt of RMB420,000 (US$87,807), a huge amount for the company at that time. In 1992, she achieved individual sales of RMB16,000,000 (US$2,901,389), which was an eighth of the company's total sales. In 1994, when Gree Electronic Appliances Inc. was experiencing financial difficulties, she was unanimously voted in as head of sales. In the same year, Gree was listed on the Shenzhen Stock Exchange. Under her leadership, Gree became the number one air-conditioner manufacturer in China, a position that was sustained for many years. With such an outstanding record, it was not surprising that she became CEO of Gree in 2007 and chairman in 2012. At the age of 61, in 2015, Dong led Gree into the ranks of the world's top 500 companies and Gree became the world's number one in home appliances. Gree makes all types of air-conditioners and small household appliances. In 2019, it had 88,846 employees and revenues of RMB198 billion (US$28 billion).[6]

As young as she is in appearance and at heart, Dong had reached the golden age of 67 when she ventured into online streaming. On June 1, 2020, she sold RMB6.54 billion (US$915 million) worth of products, which was equivalent to one month total company revenue during covid-19.[7] This was already her fourth livestream appearance, with the first in April, in collaboration with Douyin. Lack of experience and a poor network connection made the first try not so successful, however; her sales reached just RMB230,000 (US$32,000).[8] Dong was not the only CEO trying out livestream selling. On May 17, William Li, founder of NIO (an electric car company), landed 320 car orders and 5288 test drive appointments during his 40-minute livestream broadcast on Taobao.[9] The year 2020 was a very popular year for entrepreneurs and livestream selling.

In fact, the impact of the Covid-19 pandemic forced many Chinese entrepreneurs to rely on livestream selling in order to survive. With all his stores shut, Sun Laichun (孙来春), CEO of Lin Qingxuan (林清轩, a cosmetics company), realised that the cash in the company's account could barely sustain the business for two more months. He decided to give livestream selling a try on Taobao. Unexpectedly, for a first-time appearance, he attracted an audience of more than 60,000 and he sold nearly RMB400,000 (US$57,000) worth of camellia oil. Sun wrote a letter to Taobao, "At this very dark moment, (Taobao Live) gave me a glimmer of hope".

## "The Pros": solid sales on steroids

While Old Luo was selling food items and daily necessities on Douyin, another celebrity sales phenomenon, Viya, who we introduced in Chapter 1, was selling rocket-launch services – for example, sending something to the space, or having the naming right of the rocket, or the viewing privilege of the rocket-launch – on Taobao. Launches for real rockets, not toy rockets. The original price of the rocket-launch service was RMB45 million (US$6.4 million), and the price quoted on the live broadcast was RMB40 million (US$5.7 million). Buyers had to pay a RMB500,000 (US$71,000) deposit to book the service. Soon after the broadcast began, more than 800 people had paid a deposit. Minutes later, slots for the rocket ride were sold out.[10] One wonders if there is anything that cannot be sold on a livestream broadcast.

In addition to Viya, the other most popular livestreaming online celebrity in 2019 was Li Jiaqi. China's top seller of lipsticks, Li Jiaqi earned RMB200 million (US$29 million) in commissions for himself in 2019. In comparison, more than 60% of China's listed companies earned less that year.[11] Prior to selling lipsticks on Taobao Live, Li Jiaqi was a beauty adviser (BA) at a L'Oréal cosmetics counter. In 2016, L'Oréal and a multi-channel network (MCN) organisation launched the "transformation of BA to online celebrities" campaign. Li Jiaqi stood out among all the participants. On 2018 Singles' Day, Li outdid Jack Ma in terms of livestreaming sales volume. He earned himself the nickname "lipstick brother" – or Mr Lipstick – for a good reason.

Why are Viya and Li Jiaqi so successful? What are their secrets? One is that they know the product category or the products they sell very well. Before starting livestream selling, Viya had 15 years experiences in clothing retail and Li Jiaqi used to be a beauty adviser for L'Oréal. Second, they know their customers, and they know how to sell to a targeted audience. Before launching their careers online, they were already very successful in their offline businesses. They are simply good salespeople, and they have a natural knack for sales. Although they have very different styles, they both have the trust of their followers. Viya's are mainly female, who buy all kinds of products for themselves and their families. Viya is like a caring sister who helps them find good things at an unbeatable price. Li's followers are young girls who want to look good. In his dramatic, online performances, Li pronounces that "Chanel N°116 instantly changes you from ordinary girl to sophisticated western style girl" and tells them to "Buy it". "Buy it!" "Buy it!" Who can resist the clarion call? The battle is over even before it starts. Even CEOs that do live broadcasts often pair with professional celebrities to help boost sales.

Both Viya and Li Jiaqi are nationwide celebrities with followers all over China watching their livestreams and buying the products they recommend. However, China is a big country, with 672 cities and 21,297 towns, as of 2019,[12] which leaves some clear gaps for local players to fill. Chao Song is an internet celebrity that focuses on Xuzhou, a third-tier city in Jiang Su Province, where he was born and still lives. He operates 15 stores selling deep-discount products, such as 80% discounts off backlogs of Paul Frank clothing. Since 2011, whenever customers came into his stores, he asked his employees to add their WeChat accounts. During the Covid-19 crisis in early 2020, almost all stores in China were shut down, and Chao's 15 were no exception. He had no choice but move his business from offline to online. He started selling via online streaming.

Chao set up 8,000 WeChat groups to manage and serve his 500,000+ followers, with each group no more than 80 customers. His 24 employees managed the 8000 WeChat groups using over 100 mobile phones. Chao announced in advance what products he would be selling in his livestreaming broadcast, and the prices. Before the start of the broadcast, he sent a livestream link to each WeChat group. Customers clicked the link to watch the stream and could ask the employees any questions privately via WeChat. Chao required his employees to reply to each customer question within one minute and to speak in the Xuzhou dialect, to make the customers feel connected. Chao began to put out three to four broadcasts each month and ensured all his customers had received their goods correctly from the previous broadcast – and that there were no after-sales problems – before starting the next broadcast. In one of his live streams, he sold RMB4 million (US$586,000) worth of Sulwhasoo products within two hours, which is equivalent to 150 days of sales from one of his offline stores.[13]

"As a native of Xuzhou, I know very well what the local Xuzhou people like, what brands they like, which brands sell well and what type of goods they prefer. I know very well what Xuzhou people need", commented Chao.[14] Chao is just one of the localised internet celebrities in China that focus purely on their own cities or towns.

The rise of internet celebrities has been rapid, and many film stars have also joined them selling products online. Taobao Live signed Liu Tao (a popular film and television actress) as their "Chief Selection Officer" and, on her debut, she sold RMB148 million (US$21 million) worth of products within three hours.[15]

## "The Underdogs": the rise of the exponential amateur

Mr Bags, whose real name is Tao Liang, is noted for his sense of fashion and his unique insights into handbags. He is an opinion-maker and a blogger with more than seven million social media followers.[16] In contrast with Viya and Li Jiaqi, who were successful salespeople before they became online streaming celebrities, Mr Bags studied international relations at Columbia University in New York. He loves bags and has spent lot of time studying the products. When Chinese people want to buy luxury bags such as Hermès, their English is not always proficient enough for them to do any in-depth research – or they may simply not have the time for research – which makes it difficult to decide which brand to buy. Mr Bags educates

Illustrated by Aspen Wang.

buyers and provides them with useful advice; he began to write articles about handbags, their various brands, design and the latest trends.

He opened Weibo and WeChat accounts and later a Xiaohongshu account to spread his knowledge of fashion. In due course, the luxury handbag market made him a go-to source among China's burgeoning affluent consumer groups for in-depth trend analysis and advice. He quickly garnered a strong following of Chinese readers both nationally and from overseas. Luxury brands such as Louis Vuitton, Hermès, Chanel, Christian Dior, Valentino and Gucci all noticed his expertise as well as his influence among his followers and started to collaborate with him. In 2018, Tod and Mr Bags launched the co-branded handbag, Wave backpack. In his WeChat Mini-program "BAOSHOP", 300 limited edition bags, each worth RMB10,800 (US$1,574), sold out in six minutes. Strawberry and Givenchy also launched limited-edition bags jointly with Mr Bags, with remarkable success.

Does Mr Bags differ fundamentally from Mr Lipstick? Of course, there are differences. Mr Bags not only works directly with luxury brands, but he also has his own quasi-brands by co-designing with them. His bags are worth US$1,500, while the lipsticks that Mr Lipstick sells are less than US$50.

Mr Bags is not alone in the game. He is ranked the third most influential fashion blogger. Another internet fashion blogger, Ye Si, also known as Gogoboi, has seven million followers, and commands Louis Vuitton.[17] Between them, they are rumoured to charge up to US$100,000 per campaign to "support" brands. Similar to Mr Bags, the fourth most influential fashion blogger, Li Beika, has no formal training, just an interest and oversized hobby. She tells her middle-to-upper-income-class readers where they should spend their money. Gucci, Chanel, Jo Malone and many others are eager to work with her. Although the fashion brands might complain loudly about their cost, Mr Bags, Li Beika and Gogoboi do more than just talk about the latest fashion brand products; they persuade the customers that they *deserve* them.

While America has influencers like Chiara Ferragni and Kylie Jenner, their followers are mostly on Instagram, unlike China's new-wave media magnates, who have built multifaceted empires across China's digital landscape, pushing compelling storytelling through Weibo, WeChat and Douyin.

## "The Officials": government officials understanding the digital game

In 2020, the sudden outbreak of Covid-19 provided a unique opportunity for another type of internet celebrity to emerge. On February 19, 2020, PDD launched its "agricultural products sales" livestreaming activity, in which many government officials took part. Tang Feifan (汤飞帆), the mayor of Quzhou City (衢州市), Zhejiang Province, explained the history and local cuisines of Quzhou Ponkan to 530,000 consumers. Wu Kangxiu (吴康秀), head of Xuwen County (徐闻县), Guangdong province, China's largest pineapple grower, sold around 250,000 catties of pineapples.[18] On March 15 alone, more than 100 county or township leaders went on Taobao Live to promote and sell local specialities.[19]

Anhua County (安化县), Hunan province, with its many mountains and very few fields, is China's famous "home of black tea". Out of a population of 1.1 million, some 360,000 earn a living from black tea-related business. Chen Canping (陈灿平), 47 years old, is the deputy head of Anhua County. He has been posting short videos on Douyin since 2018 to promote tea on behalf of local farmers. He has more than 100,000 followers. During the Covid pandemic, with no distributors coming to Anhua to purchase tea, the tea farmers became exasperated. Chen thought of an online sales pitch. On March 1, 2020, he started livestream selling and more than 2,500 people watched his debut. Since then, he has broadcast almost every day, on all kinds of platforms including Douyin, JD, Tmall and PDD. He also sent private messages to internet celebrities and asked them for help to promote black tea. On April 3rd, in a livestream selling event on Douyin, RMB2.55 million (US$360,000) of black tea was sold. Now, Chen Canping is an internet celebrity and the "hope" of Anhua's tea farmers.[20]

Today, if you open the Taobao, JD and PDD apps, many stores are livestream selling and many farmers introduce their own agricultural products and launch promotional activities through live broadcasts. More and more people are joining the livestreaming activities.

## The livestream landscape: e-commerce vs short video

The large e-commerce platforms are a natural starting point for livestream selling. Taobao was the first to combine livestreaming with selling. In March 2016, it tried out the new model by inviting a group of "anchors". This was when Viya joined Taobao Live. In 2018, Taobao launched the "Super IP" programme to encourage anchors to attract new internet traffic. In 2019, the Taobao Live app was officially launched and was no longer just a functional module within the Taobao app. On Singles' Day in 2019, Taobao Live reached a sales volume of RMB20 billion (US$2.9 billion), which accounted for 7% of Taobao's total transactions that day.[21] Over 50% of Tmall merchants were selling goods on Taobao Live.[22] Livestream selling became so popular that PDD and JD also joined in. JD announced that it would invest at least RMB1 billion (US$140 million) nurturing internet celebrities.

But this is only part of the livestream landscape. On Douyin, Mr Lipstick, Li Jiaqi, attracted 14 million followers within two months. [23] In addition to e-commerce platforms, short video platforms represented by Douyin and Kuaishou also entered the field of livestream selling.

## Kuaishou – recording the world and you

Su Hua (宿华), the founder of Kuaishou, was born in 1982 in a rural village in Hunan. Su Hua was good at academic studies. In 2000, he was admitted to the College of Software Engineering at Tsinghua University – China's equivalent of MIT. After finishing his undergraduate studies, he began postgraduate and doctoral programmes, majoring in software engineering. However, he didn't finish his PhD as planned, dropping out after his master's degree. Rumour had it that Su was depressed by the rapid rise of housing prices in Beijing and felt that there was no use in studying if an academic couldn't afford to buy a house. He left university and joined Google, where he stayed for two-and-a-half years before starting his own business.

Su's first start-up project was video advertising on websites. Video advertising is commonplace nowadays but back then it was still a new phenomenon. His first attempt failed in 2008. In the following year, he continued to start new businesses and fail, several times. He finally gave up and took a job at Baidu, as the system architect of Baidu Phoenix Nest (凤巢, Baidu's AdWord-like bidding system). Two years later, he left Baidu and started up on his own again. This time, his new business was related to search engines and was later acquired by Alibaba. Su had found his financial freedom. Buying a house was no longer just a dream. However, where would his next inspiration come from?

In 2013, Su met Cheng Yixiao (程一笑), the founder of GIF Kuaishou, and set up a new company, Kuaishou, with Su as the CEO and Cheng responsible for customer acquisition. The positioning of Kuaishou was as a platform for ordinary people to record and share their life stories. The users were "young people in small towns" that could make short videos and share them. Generally, people liked to "be seen and admired" and therefore were happy to record themselves and post it on Kuaishou. From the beginning, Kuaishou used smart algorithms to recommend short videos that users might want to watch. In two years, the business saw an explosive period of growth. In 2015, users rose from 100 million to 300 million within eight months. In 2020, Kuaishou's daily active user (DAU) figure reached 300 million.

Kuaishou started livestream broadcasting in 2017, with revenue coming from both livestream selling and gifts showered on the anchors by fans during the broadcast. In accordance with Kuaishou's positioning, the celebrities were mostly grassroots. The top celebrities, such as Brother Sanda (散打哥), Xinba (辛巴), Erlv (二驴) and Uncle Benliang (本亮大叔) were blue-collar workers or farmers in third and lower-tier cities. They bonded well with their followers and they showed strong selling capability. The first few celebrities on Kuaishou each earned commissions of over RMB100 million (US$14 million) in 2019. Most of the transactions were through third-party e-commerce platforms such as Taobao and PDD, with Kuaishou charging commission on each one. Only a few of the transactions were completed on Kuaishou's self-operated e-commerce platform.

## Douyin – recording precious moments of life

Before we start talking about Douyin, we need to introduce Zhang Yiming (张一鸣) and his Toutiao. Zhang Yiming was born in 1983 in Longyan City (龙岩), in the province of Fujian. He and Wang Xing (founder of Meituan) were fellow townsmen. In 2001, Zhang was admitted to Nankai University (南开大学), one of China's top ten comprehensive universities, majoring in microelectronics. He later transferred to software engineering. After graduating in 2005, Zhang began his entrepreneurial journey. His first start-up was to develop a collaborative office system, which ended in failure. In 2006, he joined the travel search website Kuxun and was responsible for the development of Kuxun's search functions. While working at Kuxun, there was one event that had a great influence on Zhang. He wanted to book a train ticket to go home. At that time, there was no ticket-grabbing software, and it was difficult to buy tickets online. Zhang spent one hour writing a program to automatically search for tickets according to his requirements. In this way, Zhang got his train ticket in half-an-hour. He thought that, if his algorithm could find the required information in time and he could push it to the customers, it would be a great business.

In 2008, Zhang left Kuxun and joined Microsoft. He soon left, however, to join his fellow townsman Wang Xing's company, Fanfou, and was put in charge of Fanfou's search function. In 2009, when Fanfou was shut down, Zhang set up a vertical real estate search engine "99Fang" (九九房). Zhang had already shown interest in information products when he was in 99Fang. There were some content products in 99-Fang such as "house visiting diary" and "real estate information".

By 2012, the mobile internet was poised to take off. Zhang found a new CEO to replace him, and left 99Fang. He set up ByteDance. In August, the Toutiao app, a smart content distribution platform, was launched. Toutiao's unique feature was that it provided the reader with the most personalised news experience. Its machine-learning algorithm monitored users' reading habits and offered customised feeds including articles, videos and ads. First-time users were shown general content, which they marked "like" or "dislike". They could also make comments or re-post items after reading them. The machine-learning algorithm remembered the user's choices and reading time, as well as other reading habits and interests. The more frequently the user viewed Toutiao, the more accurate the machine's judgement and the more relevant the recommendations the user received. Toutiao proved popular. Within 90 days of its launch, it obtained 10 million registered users. By June 2019, its monthly active user (MAU) figure had reached 260 million.[24]

Toutiao's data showed that users were viewing short videos for longer periods of time. In 2016, ByteDance began to enter into short videos. ByteDance's style is what they call "bulk incubation" and it launched three products simultaneously: Huoshan short video (火山小视频), Xigua video (西瓜视频) and Douyin. These three products all followed Toutiao's underlying logic: customised recommendations. Unlike Kuaishou, Douyin targeted users in first- and second-tier cities. In November 2019, among the mobile short video apps, Douyin and Kuaishou ranked first and second with 530 million and 425 million MAU, respectively, and Xigua video and Huoshan short video ranked third and fourth.[25] In the top four short video platforms, three belonged to ByteDance (Kuaishou was the exception).

Until 2019, almost 70% of ByteDance's revenue came from advertising. Finding a strong business model to monetise its huge traffic was critical. Douyin entered livestream selling in 2018. However, lacking the internet celebrities like Viya and Li Jiaqi on Taobao, or Xinba on Kuaishou, progress was pretty slow. It wasn't until Douyin signed with Old Luo in 2020 that it made a splash in livestream selling. Like Kuaishou, most transactions involved users switching to third-party platforms, such as Taobao and JD, to complete their purchase. However, there were small changes in Luo's livestream selling, in which users unknowingly completed the transaction process for the first time on Douyin's own e-commerce platform, the Douyin store. During the Singles' Day Shopping Festival 2020, Douyin achieved GMV of RMB18.7 billion (US$2.8 billion),[26] which was 200% of the GMV for the whole of 2019.

Kuaishou was established three years before Douyin but trailed the latter in terms of traffic. Fundamentally, Douyin and Kuaishou are very similar: people watch short videos in the short snippets of time they can grab during their busy day. But there are some differences. Kuaishou, which targets people in lower-tier cities, has content that might be considered somewhat coarse, or unrefined. There are videos about people eating live snakes and even sex-related content. Kuaishou might be perceived to be uncultured. Douyin, on the other hand, targeted young people from the first and second-tier cities from the very beginning. Its short videos appear to be exquisitely produced and the characters are filtered to be good-looking. Users on Kuaishou are more involved and like in the community, they are audience as well as participants, while users on Douyin are audience following the latest fashion trends. From this perspective, Kuaishou has more stickiness than Douyin, which makes it a good base for livestream selling (Figure 9.2).

In 2020, Taobao led the way in China's livestreaming e-commerce, while Kuaishou and Douyin made efforts to catch up. In 2019, the general merchandise value (GMV) of Taobao Live was around RMB250 billion (US$36 billion), Kuaishou RMB40–50 billion (US$6–7 billion) and Douyin RMB10 billion (US$1.4 billion). JD and PDD were just about to start. Short

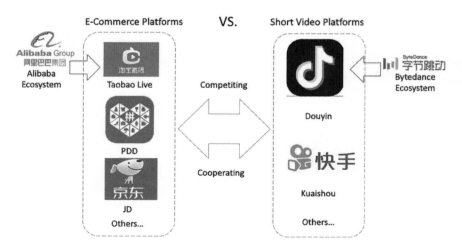

Figure 9.2 The livestream battle.

|  | Taobao Live | Kuaishou | Douyin | PDD | JD |
|---|---|---|---|---|---|
| **GMV ($ billion)** | 36 | 6-7 | 1.4 | ~ | ~ |
| **DAU (million)** | 250 | 300 | 400 | 200 | 50 |

Figure 9.3  The livestream platforms (2019).

video platforms and e-commerce platforms have their own advantages and disadvantages for livestream selling. The short-video platform is an off-the-shelf livestreaming platform with super-high frequency. In terms of daily active users (DAU), Douyin had 400 million, Kuaishou 300 million, Taobao 250 million, PDD 200 million and JD 50 million.[27] It is well known that Li Jiaqi attracted a large number of followers from Douyin, which was critical to his success. However, short-video platforms typically have no back-end supporting systems such as supply chains and after-sales services, which were the advantage of traditional e-commerce platforms. That's why the short-video platforms continue to collaborate with e-commerce in livestream selling, while they build their own supply chain system. In 2020, WeChat also launched its short video function, users can apply for a video account to publish short videos and share them in WeChat. Tencent is officially in the game and expected to be a strong contender (Figure 9.3).

## No longer just a Chinese game

There are also livestreaming platforms in the United States. For example, YouTube, Instagram, Twitter and Facebook all have live broadcast functions. However, they attract very few viewers (except for game broadcasting). In 2019, Amazon also launched Amazon Live but again, there are few broadcasts and viewers. Amazon's consumers are typically of a more traditional e-commerce mindset; they know what they want and use direct searches to find a specific product and place an order, and its done. They don't have time to hang out on the platform or watch live broadcasts.

There are also internet celebrities in the United States. For example, there are many American bloggers in the fields of travel, food and beauty, but their content is still mainly based on text and graphics and videos. The income of the celebrities is from advertising fees and commissions from platforms. There are celebrities as well as live broadcasting platforms in the United States, but there are few celebrities livestream selling.

"Internet celebrity" is a broad term. There are bloggers and online streaming celebrities. In China, graphic and short-video bloggers are different to the livestream-selling celebrities. Bloggers share their lifestyles, which ordinary netizens can only dream of. Their opinions influence their followers and indirectly they drive brand sales. The online streaming celebrities, on the other hand, are super-salespeople. They transformed themselves from being super-sellers in the physical world to super-sales celebrities online. Both Viya and Li Jiaqi honed their sales skills offline for many years. Online streaming allows them to reach a wider audience and build up a much bigger fan base. Of course, Taobao and MCNs contributed to their successes by providing the platform and professionalising the concept of online selling. The question is whether the same model could be replicated outside China.

Recently, the international expansion of TikTok (the overseas version of Douyin) has given people new ideas about the development of celebrity livestream selling in other countries. TikTok appears in the top 20 free apps in many countries and regions around the world.[28] In May 2020, Kevin Mayer, the Disney executive who oversaw the launch of the streaming service Disney+, became chief operating officer of ByteDance, the parent company of TikTok, and was charged with driving its global development. However, things can change very quickly and the increasing friction between China and America led to President Trump announcing his intention, in July 2020, to ban TikTok. Kevin Mayer left ByteDance in August. TikTok was already banned in India. The silver lining came through in December 2020: Walmart hosted its first live shopping event on TikTok.

## Celebrities sell, but who is buying?

By March 2020, the number of online shoppers in China had reached 710 million and the number of online livestreaming users was 560 million.[29] Among them, livestreaming e-commerce users accounted for 265 million – or 37.2% of online shoppers and 47.3% of livestreaming users.[30]

- In terms of age demographics, 80% of livestreaming e-commerce users were born after 1985 and 50% were born after 1990.

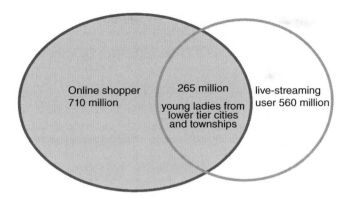

*Figure 9.4* Livestreaming e-commerce users.

- In terms of location, users from second-tier cities ranked first, accounting for more than a quarter, followed by third-tier cities, accounting for about 20%, and users from the super first-tier cities such as Beijing, Shanghai, Guangzhou and Shenzhen were the fewest.[31]
- Gender-wise, consumer of livestream selling is dominated by women. 91% of Li Jiaqi's followers, and more than 61% of Viya's followers, are female.[32] People call them "Li Jiaqi's girls" and "Viya's ladies" (Figure 9.4).

This diagram shows that celebrity marketing seems to be driven by young females from lower-tier cities and townships. They are often price-conscientious, have time on their hands to watch livestreaming programmes and, above all, enjoy this new shopping experience. Their income may not be high, but they do not have the same pressure of high housing prices that face those living in first-tier and super-first-tier cities and have some disposal income to consume.

## Celebrities sell what, exactly?

Although Viya famously sold rocket-launch services in her livestreaming broadcasts, that was more of a publicity drive than anything else. Most products sold via livestreaming are fast-moving consumer goods such as cosmetics, food items, 3C digital products, clothing and jewellery. And online selling seems to be highly concentrated. For example, analysis by WalktheChat revealed that for June and July 2020, cosmetics, food and home appliances accounted for 90% of total GMV from the top 100 Douyin KOL campaigns.

The conversion rate using live stream tends to be higher for the product category that requires visual demonstration accompanied by vivid explanation. Based on one research, the conversion rate increased by 66% after consumers viewed the livestreaming broadcast.[33] For small brands or unknown brands, livestreaming broadcast could help by building consumer awareness.

According to Viya and Li Jiaqi's selling record in March 2020, the average unit price of Viya's sales was RMB78 yuan (US$11) and for Li Jiaqi it was RMB74 yuan (US$10).[34] In Old Luo's first livestream selling on Douyin, although his products included some RMB4999 (US$706) Xiaomi mobile phones, his average unit price was only RMB197 (US$28).[35] Li Jiaqi sells third-party products, including international brands such as L'Oréal, Unilever and P&G, as well as domestic brands such as Pechoin, and lesser known products such as Huaxizi. Moreover, we should not forget even though the livestreaming happens predominantly on new platforms like Douyin and Kuaishou; conversions take place pretty much on the traditional platforms, Tmall and JD (Figure 9.5).

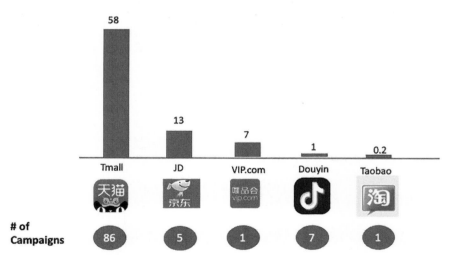

Figure 9.5 GMV generated from top 100 Douyin KOL campaigns on different marketplaces ($ million).

Brands have complicated feelings for livestreaming celebrities: they both love and hate them. After all, celebrity selling provides brand exposure in a short period of time. Fifty-two million people watched Mr Lipstick's live broadcast on March 5, 2020 and a large number of them were targeted customers. The sales figures can be very alluring potentially reaching millions of dollars in one night. But this is just the one side of the coin. On the other there are high fees – the slot fee for a top celebrity can be tens of thousands of dollars; high commissions – ranging from 20% to 40%; low selling prices – top celebrities have greater bargaining power and usually ask for the lowest price for some products, which could mean 50% discount. In addition, there is one more cost that cannot be ignored: the cost of product returns. In categories like clothing, in particular, the return rate can be as high as 30%. Put all these costs together, for most of the goods sold via celebrity livestream broadcasting, the brands may not make much profit or any profit at all.

So, making a profit through livestream selling is not always the case for the brands that are being sold. Then why do it, if you cannot make a healthy margin? One of the purposes for brands is to increase brand exposure and influence, to attract traffic to their online stores. For some new brands, matching targeted customers with corresponding internet celebrities to promote one or two items could generate explosive effects and help establish good brand reputation. For example, Huaxizi, a domestic cosmetics brand, became a top 10 cosmetics brand in Tmall Beauty through its connection to Li Jiaqi. In Singles' Day 2019, Li sold more than 700,000 boxes of Huaxizi powder in his live stream and the sales revenue exceeded RMB100 million (US$14 million) within an hour.[36] Another example is Perfect Diary, whose positioning is low pricing, and which became popular among young people following KOL-sharing on Xiaohongshu. By working with internet celebrities, many new domestic brands have risen rapidly in the fields of beauty, food and beverage and small appliances. Another reason to work with celebrities is "destocking" – to quickly dispose of some overstocked inventory goods at a lower price through a livestream event.

## Why livestream selling disrupts logistics

Unlike Mr Lipstick, Viya has her own factory, which generates more than 30% of her sales. If a factory makes 30,000 skirts a day, and a celebrity like

Viya can sell all of them overnight, there needs to be a new style available the next day. The rise of Taobao Live posed a great challenge to the traditional clothing supply chain. Traditional garment manufacturers designed several styles a year. Though international brand Zara is much more efficient than traditional fashion houses, taking only two to three weeks from design to production, it is still hard for them to compete with livestreaming models that introduce a new style every day. The factory has to make samples within half a day, the anchor counts the number of orders while selling and then, as soon as the live broadcast has ended, the orders are sent to the factory to produce and deliver quickly. "One live streamer often needs 40 styles during one broadcast, and 20 broadcasts a month translates into 800 styles. For ten live streamers there needs to be 8,000 styles". The number of new styles per month on Taobao Live exceeds 160,000.[37] Zhao Yuanyuan, head of Taobao Live, said that the characteristics of "multiple styles and small inventory" place high requirements on the speed of the supply chain.

Clothing design, production, selection, live broadcasting, delivery, inventory digestion … there are many sections to livestream selling. However, the life cycle of a new style is as short as one month. To ensure the stability of supply chain, many internet celebrities moved to places closest to the supply chain, where they could complete the whole process of selecting, broadcasting and selling in one location. Changshu City (常熟市), Jiangsu Province, less than 200 km away from Hangzhou, is a well-known distribution centre for textile and clothing. Taking advantage of livestreaming e-commerce, the city has become the first choice of clothing supply chains for Taobao, Kuaishou and others. In Changshu, many factories initially were suppliers to other live streamers. Then later, the factories' bosses took to livestream selling by themselves, with pretty good results. Over time, an ecosystem emerged in Changshu, where different brands from all over the country appeared, along with many internet celebrities. In addition to Changshu, Hangzhou, Guangzhou and other cities all established large-scale clothing supply chain bases. With factories and live streamers all coming together, the entire process of livestream selling could be completed from one base.

At the end of 2019, Viya established her own supply chain base, or "homestead", in the Alibaba park in Hangzhou. The two-level office building has a total area of about 10,000 square metres and was transformed into a large selection venue, with multiple counters and shelves. It is very similar to a shopping mall except for the fact that there are no price tags. The homestead invites merchants to come and display their products for the live streamers to choose. It not only serves Viya, but also all the live streamers that are in demand. The homestead is expected to accommodate thousands of brands and tens of thousands of SKUs, including beauty, food, apparel, accessories, shoes, bags and other categories that are common in livestream selling. It can also help the live streamers to find the goods that suit them more quickly and help the merchants to save the time of matching live streamers. The live streamers can then complete the whole process in one location, including live broadcasts.

## And the show goes on: celebrity nurturing

The company that Viya established is Qianxun. The chairman of Qianxun is Viya's husband. In addition to Viya, the company has more than 30 internet celebrities. It is a typical multi-channel network (MCN). An MCN is an intermediary agency that connects internet celebrities, merchants and platforms, providing training and other resources. Only the very top internet celebrities have the capability to directly connect to the merchants, and most other internet celebrities need to rely on MCNs.

Since 2019, MCNs have exploded and nearly 7,000 have emerged in China.[38] Ruhan, established in 2015, was the earliest and first listed MCN in China. It listed on the Nasdaq in April 2019. Zhang Dayi was Ruhan's most famous celebrity. However, the stock sank on the day of listing. People seemed not to trust Ruhan's business model. The business mainly covered the three major areas of internet celebrity brokerage, e-commerce business and advertising services. Although Ruhan signed more than 150 Internet celebrities, Zhang Dayi alone still contributed more than half of the company revenue. The nurturing of new internet celebrities is not easy.

Internet celebrities, livestream selling platforms, brands, supply chains and MCNs have all jointly created the ecosystem of China's celebrity selling.

Not any celebrity sells. Li Xiang, a well-known presenter in China, once tried to sell mink coats in her live broadcast. The merchant paid RMB800,000 (US$113,00) in slot fees but not even one coat was sold. It's not just the identity of internet celebrities or the tool of live broadcasting that wins consumers, but:

1. Low price, low price, low price: important things are worth repeating three times. The real core competitiveness of livestream selling is value for money. Among the top-selling products on Douyin, the most popular are priced at RMB1–50 (US$0.14–7.1), followed by RMB50–100 (US$7.1–14) and RMB100–200 (US$14–28). The prices of 85% of products are below RMB200 (US$28). RMB200 (US$28) is the breaking point for people's impulsive consumption. The more capable the celebrities are, the better prices they can get from the merchants. The product prices are so transparent online that consumers can choose to buy on Tmall or JD so the reason they buy from celebrities is the competitive price. This logic is the same as social e-commerce. In a survey about the reasons for buying on livestream selling, the top five reasons are (from high to low):

   1. Value for money of the products.
   2. Liking the displayed products.
   3. High discounts.
   4. Discounts only within a limited time.
   5. The live streamers explained the value of goods well.

   Three of the top five reasons are related to price and two are related to the product itself. Li Jiaqi once was so furious that he asked his followers to return a product, simply because his competitor Viya got the same merchandise for RMB5 (US$0.70) cheaper. Celebrity selling's secret recipe is value for money.

2. Trust, Trust, Trust: the reason why so many people buy the products recommended by Viya and Li Jiaqi is because they believe that the products recommended by them cannot go wrong; "I can place order with closed eyes". This trust includes the trust in the internet celebrities themselves, as well as in their ability to select products and bargain down prices. From product selection to broadcast planning and from payment settlement to logistics and to after-sales processing … if any one link is not handled well, problems occur. Consumers' criticism on the internet can instantly pull the celebrities down from their altar. Behind every internet celebrity who has succeeded, there is an excellent and efficient operations team. Viya has a team of about 500 people

working for her. They are responsible for product selection, merchant invitation, pre-screening and after-sales. They have strict procedures and processes. Every day, Viya's team receives more than 1,000 products for registration. Two or three hundred products will be presented to Viya after a blind selection by the team, and then Viya tries the products herself before she decides to recommend them in her live broadcasts. Viya's working schedule is very intense. Throughout the 365 days of 2019, she completed more than 350 broadcasts, each three to four hours long. Her day starts in the afternoon. She gets up at 4pm and prepares for the broadcast after a meal; makeup starts at 7:30pm and the live broadcast starts at 8pm, usually ending at midnight. She then meets with the merchant's team to try new products; signs off work at six or seven in the morning; eats breakfast; and then goes to bed. Only in this crazy hard-working way, can Viya ensure that the quality and price of the products are the most favourable to her followers so she can win their trust to place orders. The trust followers have for the celebrity is so fragile that, for a live streamer it is like skating on thin ice; they dare not make any mistakes. In one of his live broadcasts, Old Luo recommended a particular variety of roses, with the intent that the consumers can have a sweet 520 (May 20 is pronounced in Chinese sounding like I love you). Unexpectedly, when they received the goods, consumers found that the roses had seriously wilted, and they were hugely disappointed. Luo immediately issued an apology letter and asked the merchant to re-fund the consumers. In addition, he himself also paid more than RMB1 million (UIS$140,000) compensation. This is trust.

3. Brands self-broadcasting: internet celebrity selling presents a big challenge for brands. The internet celebrities own the customers; brands do not own customers. In the long run, internet celebrities are becoming more and more expensive and their bargaining power is getting stronger. They take more of the value of the products – the part that originally belonged to the brand premium. The brands will become the "factory" of internet celebrities. Some brands have already begun to do their own livestream selling. Three Squirrels (三只松鼠), established in 2012, is a typical "Tao brand", which means it is a brand developed on e-commerce platforms such as Taobao. Three Squirrels sells all kinds of nuts as snacks. Since it was born as an internet brand, Three Squirrels is particularly sensitive to the trend of e-commerce and new retailing. In 2018, it began to collaborate with Li Jiaqi and Viya,

and later began to do livestream selling on their own stores. By June 2020, Three Squirrels Tmall flagship stores had more than 40 million followers and ranked first among all of the Tmall stores (Viya's store had 27 million followers, Xiaomi 31 million, Nike and Adidas 28 million).[39] Three Squirrels has its own live streamers, who make live broadcasts almost every day, on Tmall, JD and some other platforms. At least thousands of people watch its live broadcasts, sometimes as many as tens of thousands. Compared with working with professional celebrities, the advantages of brands self-broadcasting are obvious: there are no slot fees, no commissions, the price is self-determined, and the overall cost is so much lower; the brand can broadcast whenever it needs to, in conjunction with its own marketing rhythm and other marketing channels. Since it takes a long time to nurture and groom internet celebrities, brand self-broadcasting also requires a longer period of time to grow followers. But taking care of their own broadcasting also has another huge advantage: the distance between production and consumption is unprecedentedly close. The broadcast can take place in the factory. Self-broadcasting not only cuts unnecessary intermediate links but can also save time and related costs. There is great value to be had in companies improving their offerings by interacting with customers in the live broadcast and obtaining real-time feedback.

Clearly, for brands, this phenomenon of livestream celebrity selling is changing not just the way brands interact with customers but is disrupting their business model. No longer do brands own the customer touchpoint, it is livestream celebrities that increasingly win the valuable screen time and attention of the customer. While the digital revolution and omnipresent platforms and ecosystems are often thought to "take out the middlemen", we see exactly the opposite happening now in Chinese retail. It is not surprising, as with an overload of information and instant and on-demand access to almost every piece of information in the world, customers are looking for trustworthy "filters". The livestream celebrity becomes the middleman – one that is much more powerful, with more leverage, than the traditional value-chain middleman that brands are used to. A new agent has been introduced into the retail business model.

This is not the end of the story of new retail. In this chapter, we documented and analysed important new actors in retail business models, such as Viya and Li Jiaqi. In the next chapter we see how Chinese retail has reached a completely different level. In our final chapter, we discover how an implicit and highly sophisticated new actor was introduced, thereby transforming retail from commerce to craft.

## Concluding remarks: questions for executives to ask

1.  How is livestreaming playing a role (or not) in your region and industry? What are the main competitors doing and what are the leading relevant platforms in your region?
2.  If you were to experiment with livestreaming in your region, which product category would you choose, what price would you offer, who are the potential star streamers that you would consider using and which platform would you choose?
3.  What benefits can livestreaming bring to you and your customers?
4.  Do you have the, or have access to a, relevant e-commerce ecosystem to support your livestreaming efforts?
5.  Do you have the, or have access to a, relevant livestream platform with connected e-commerce channels for your livestreaming efforts?

## Notes

1   Zeng Ming, Intelligence Business.
2   https://baijiahao.baidu.com/s?id=1649189979274197844&wfr=spider&-for=pc.
3   https://xw.qq.com/cmsid/20200417AoJKL000.
4   https://xw.qq.com/partner/gdtadf/20200327A06XKS/20200327A06XKS0o?ADTAG=gdtadf&pgv_ref=gdtadf.
5   https://t.cj.sina.com.cn/articles/view/2023016805/7894c965055o0nalv?-from=tech.
6   Gree 2019 annua report.
7   https://www.thepaper.cn/newsDetail_forward_7787468.
8   https://www.sohu.com/a/399308024_120576742.
9   https://mp.weixin.qq.com/s/842c1Le73powvqPlv2O1Rw.
10  https://baijiahao.baidu.com/s?id=1662889577041163658&wfr=spider&-for=pc.

11    https://www.sohu.com/a/365436522_114941.
12    https://www.sohu.com/a/334079098_115423.
13    https://mp.weixin.qq.com/s/kUgIGh-13SW1UHXBmlKzA.
14    https://mp.weixin.qq.com/s/kUgIGh-13SW1UHXBmlKzA.
15    http://column.iresearch.cn/b/202006/890561.shtml.
16    https://www.businessoffashion.com/community/people/tao-liang.
17    https://www.ft.com/content/dfa1c90e-f82f-11e6-bd4e-68d53499ed71.
18    https://baijiahao.baidu.com/s?id=16596815185384520 47&wfr=spider&-
      for=pc.
19    https://new.qq.com/omn/20200316/20200316A0HOT500.html.
20    http://k.sina.com.cn/article_2072969551_7b8f014f00100029m.html.
21    https://www.thepaper.cn/newsDetail_forward_9956631.
22    https://baijiahao.baidu.com/s?id=1683123305982411111&wfr=spider&-
      for=pc.
23    https://view.inews.qq.com/a/20200514A0S6D500?tbkt=I&openid=-
      004IBAM_zryqtMfudBN6XoyJ8E2U&uid=&refer=wx_hot.
24    https://www.csdn.net/article/a/2018-04-04/15944820.
25    http://column.iresearch.cn/b/202006/891611.shtml.
26    https://baijiahao.baidu.com/s?id=16831556064281329 60&wfr=spider&-
      for=pc.
27    https://finance.sina.com.cn/stock/relnews/hk/2020-03-26/doc-
      iimxxsth1943581.shtml.
28    http://column.iresearch.cn/b/202006/891611.shtml.
29    https://mp.weixin.qq.com/s/842c1Le73p0wvqPlv2O1Rw.
30    https://36kr.com/p/708721070938120.
31    In the new definition, Beijing, Shanghai, Guangzhou and Shenzhen are
      super first-tier cities, Hangzhou, Chengdu and others are first-tier cities,
      and most provincial capitals are second-tier cities.
32    https://www.sohu.com/a/365924119_100252997.
33    https://mp.weixin.qq.com/s/Aub2az2uieVhcxl5XA92-g.
34    http://finance.ifeng.com/c/7vdToQzSokT.
35    http://www.xker.com/a/32435.html.
36    https://www.douban.com/note/767055845/.
37    http://finance.sina.com.cn/stock/relnews/us/2019-03-26/doc-
      ihtxyzsmo581068.shtml.
38    http://news.iresearch.cn/yx/2020/04/321159.shtml.
39    Tmall real time data.

# 10

## ULTIMATE EXPERIENCE RETAIL

### When craft meets e-commerce

All the new retailing formats we have covered so far in this book, including Meituan, Hema, PDD and celebrity selling, have been product focused. Li Jiaqi might be very knowledgeable about the cosmetics industry, but his method is still very much product oriented. Likewise, the illustrious Mr Bags. In the end, they are selling products that fulfil material needs. In this chapter, we introduce a different way of selling, where craft meets e-commerce. The protagonists here are exceptional people who have a passion combined with unusual talents. They started out by sharing their passion for something online and later were able capitalise on their unique talents, captivating their followers via various social media. On the surface, they don't appear to be pushing a product. But fans are still eager to buy a piece of the lifestyle that they portray.

### Yearning for Shangri-la

As China develops, people inevitably fret more and more about pollution in the big population centres. In addition to environmental concerns, city

DOI: 10.4324/9781003205074-12

dwellers, especially professionals in tier one and tier two cities, are under intense pressure from competition, work and economic conditions, such as rising housing prices. Is there such a thing as a work/life balance in China? Jack Ma once provoked a viral online debate with his controversial views on the "996 work culture", which refers to working from 9am to 9pm, six days a week. Do white-collar workers have a choice to work less? Not really, not in such a competitive environment.

Once people reach the middle classes or above, the increase in their material satisfaction comes with a void, a yearning for pure and simple things, like clean air and organic food – an idyllic lifestyle, a little like Shangri-la, the earthly paradise described in the popular 1933 novel, Lost Horizon, by English writer James Hilton.

Chinese ancient literature contains many poems that echo the same yearning. Tao Yuanming (365?–427), also known as Tao Qian, was one of China's greatest pastoral poets. Renowned as the "ancient and modern recluse poet", he glorified a return to country living. Some 1500 years later, in the New World, the author, naturalist, transcendentalist and philosopher, Henry David Thoreau (1817–1862), also expressed a profound fondness for pastoral life. To be close to nature, he lived alone in the woods for two years. His famous book, Walden, records the two years spent living primitively by Walden Pond, deep in the woods outside his hometown of Concord, Massachusetts. He built his own house with natural resources and farmed his own crops. He observed the beauty of nature contained in the changing seasons and reflected in the pond's immensely clear water. In essence, Walden is a book of worship for nature and a simple life. The yearning for a pastoral lifestyle is appealing and universal. It is a need; and where there is a need, there will be someone, somewhere, who fulfils it for us.

Today there is someone living the life described by Thoreau, in a way that is more visually and artistically alluring. This is Li Ziqi, the "Queen of making everything from scratch". And in 2020, under the cloud of Covid-19, she became our "Quarantine Queen".

## Li Ziqi – living an idyllic dream

At first glance, Li Ziqi seems quite plain, but she exudes an inner peacefulness that makes you want to look a little more. One of this book's authors is a big fan and could watch her channel all day. For another, her pastoral fantasies have become a reliable source of escape and comfort.

*Illustrated by Aspen Wang.*

As a Chinese food blogger, Li Ziqi's videos are integrated with nature. Raw materials are either dug out of the ground or picked from trees; she washes them in a mountain spring and cooks on a log fire pit (no gas stove, no modern kitchen appliances). The camera shots are of rain falling on the roof, flowers blossoming, roosters crowing, a dog sitting quietly at her feet and rustic utensils on a wooden table.

When peaches were in blossom, she picked them to make peach liqueur.

When bamboo shoots ripened, she made a bowl of hot and sour Liuzhou snail noodles.

When tomatoes came to fruit, she made a bright red and delicious tomato sauce, along with a veritable banquet of tomato-based dishes.

When it was the Dragon Boat Festival, she made glutinous pork dumplings.

On Chinese New Year's Eve, she smoked bacon and salami.

She removed wood from an old house and built a small bridge and a swing set.

She raised silkworms and sewed a silk quilt. Yes, she demonstrated how to raise silkworms and how to make a silk quilt – each step of the process.

After harvesting grapes, she used the grape skin to dye cloth for a purple dress.

In March 2019, Li Ziqi published a 12-minute video of her making a pen, ink, paper and inkstone. Filming started in the autumn of 2017 and took almost two years to complete. When making ink, the soot coagulation that is produced after burning the tung-oil needs to be stored for more than a year, and it needs to be dried for at least six months after the ink has been made. Making brush pens starts with cutting bamboo and shearing wool. When making paper, she started by cutting the tree and peeling the bark. The inkstone she carved herself.

Li Ziqi is more than a disciple of Hestia, goddess of the kitchen, or of Demeter, goddess of the harvest, or Hephaistos, the god of artisans. There seems to be no end to what she can create from scratch and turn into entertainment.

Li Ziqi was born in Mianyang (绵阳), Sichuan Province, in 1990. Her parents divorced when she was young, and she lived with her father. When she was six, her father died, and her stepmother was unkind to her, so she was taken in by her grandparents. Li Ziqi's grandfather was a cook and jack-of-all-trades. He made all sorts of things out of bamboo and was also good at farming. While she lived with her grandparents, Li helped her grandfather with his carpentry and helped her grandmother with cooking and farm work. She accumulated a wealth of experience that she would later tap into for her videos. When she was 14, her grandfather passed away. Her grandmother had to raise her alone and times were hard. Li had to drop out of school and earn a living. She slept in the park and worked as a waiter, earning RMB300 (US$40) a month. She taught herself music and worked as a DJ in a bar. However, in 2012, her grandmother fell ill, and Li decided to return to her hometown to be with her.

Back in Mianyang, Li opened up an online store on Taobao, but the business wasn't that good. To increase sales, she made some short videos. In 2015, she started to make films of what she was good at, such as cooking. She self-directed and self-filmed short videos about food, which she released mainly on the Meipai app, an imaging and video-editing social media platform. In 2016, she spent three months learning how to cook Lanzhou beef noodles and produced a video that became hugely popular – it was played more than 50 million times. Slowly, Li Ziqi became more and more well-known and she began to build a fan base.

A multi-channel network (MCN) agency discovered Li's talent. In 2016, she joined Hangzhou Weinian Technology company. While she concentrated on creating her videos, Weinian Technology was responsible for their promotion and online operations. In 2017, the Sichuan Ziqi Culture Communication Co. Ltd. was established, with Li Ziqi and Weinian Technology holding 49% and 51% of the shares, respectively.

With the support of Weinian Technology, Li's career took off. Her videos were shared on various platforms, including YouTube. By the end of 2020, she has 26 million followers on Weibo and 38 million followers on Douyin.[1] Her videos aren't translated into English but nevertheless, her number of followers on YouTube is over ten million (which is equivalent to CNN). She was the first Chinese "creator" with more than ten million fans outside of China. It is interesting to see the comments on her YouTube channel that are written in English, Russian, French, Spanish and Korean.

Although she has such a huge following, Li does not represent any big brands aside from her own, neither does she sell goods like Viya and other celebrities. The word "buy" never appears in her videos. Her income comes mainly from YouTube commission and sales from her Tmall flagship store. According to statistics from InflueNex, she earns around US$730,000 on YouTube every month.[2] Her Tmall store opened in August 2018 and sells the food products that appear in her videos. By 2020 there were more than 40 different products. Monthly sales of Liziqi Liuzhou Snail Noodles – three bags for RMB39.7 (US$5.6), have exceeded 1.5 million, and monthly sales of Liziqi Osmanthus Nut Lotus Root Starch, priced at RMB59.7 (US$8.4), have exceeded 200,000.[3] The rough estimate of her monthly income is over RMB100 million (US$14 million). This is just the sales in her Tmall store and doesn't include sales through other channels, such as community group purchases. Some netizens estimated that, in 2019, Li Ziqi's personal income was over RMB160 million (US$23 million).[4]

It is not just the Chinese buying Liziqi products. According to official Tmall overseas data, nearly 500,000 bags of Liziqi Liuzhou Snail Noodles were sold in a year to more than 100 countries and regions around the world.[5] (Figure 10.1)

Li Ziqi's products are not cheap – her prices rank at the top of each product category. For example, 360 grams of Liziqi Sesame Walnut Powder on her Tmall flagship store is RMB59.9 (US$8.4) – or US$.023 per gram, whereas 500 grams of COFCO Sesame Walnut Powder is RMB69 (US$9.7) – or US$.019 per gram. That's a 20% price premium.

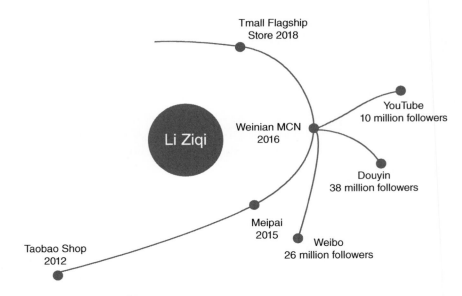

Figure 10.1 Li Ziqi milestones.

Li Ziqi once said in an interview, "Most people are living under huge pressure. I hope when people are tired and stressed, they can watch my videos and feel relaxed. I hope my videos will take away their anxiety".[6]

## Are there other Li Ziqi's?

Li Ziqi's popularity was not necessarily accidental. In neighbouring Yunnan Province, a young woman named Dong Meihua – better known as Dianxi Xiaoge (滇西小哥) – followed a similar path to success. The Chinese meaning of Xiaoge is "little brother". Also, a food blogger, Xiaoge has plenty of fans outside of China too but is quite different to Li; Xiaoge is the girl next door, warm, chatty and casual. Her simplicity draws people in; it's as if your friend is cooking with you, in the type of ordinary Chinese rural house that you can still see when you visit your relatives. In stark contrast to Li's dreamlike videos, which seem to be shot almost too perfectly, Xiaoge's videos look unrehearsed and feature real people in the background going about their daily business, who appear oblivious to being filmed. She cooks simple and interesting dishes with fresh local produce from her village. She uses a steel bucket – a staple of every rural family – whereas Li uses an "antique" wooden bucket, which you might find in an interior-designed house. Besides the differences in style, Xiaoge's business model is the same as Li Ziqi's. She has five million followers on Weibo and YouTube, where she posts videos, and a Taobao shop selling the food products featured in her videos.[7] Both portray a serene pastoral life with wonderful food and enticing dishes. They are successful entrepreneurs that leverage our dreams of living simply but also fulfil our desires for quality produce and sensory experiences. In particular, they have tapped into the Chinese people's fondness for great food. Their talents have been financially rewarded.

There is also a "Li Ziqi" in northern Europe: Jonna Jinton. In 2010, she dropped out of school and left the city to begin a life of seclusion in the Swedish forest, which she portrayed poetically in her videos, almost like a fairy tale. There were mountains and snowfields, woodland and lakes, aurora in the sky, ancient herding calls to welcome the spring and the traditional Swedish "ice bath". Many people took solace from Jinton's videos; some viewers said, "your videos make me want to live, not just exist".[8] Now, Jinton has 1.68 million followers on YouTube and 640,000 followers on Instagram. Like Li Ziqi, she also has her own e-commerce brand. She opened two online stores. One is an art gallery where she sells her paintings. The other is a silverware store run by her husband. In her videos, she often wears the silver ornaments that he has made.

Li Ziqi, Xiaoge and Jinton fulfilled people's yearnings for their Shangri-la. They are successful because they genuinely love living in their natural surrounds, and they know where their talents lie. Li Ziqi is good at cooking and making things, and she uses her eye for aesthetics to present what she is doing. If there is something she is not familiar with, she will take time to learn all about it before filming the videos. She spent several months learning how to make Lanzhou beef noodles, how to dye clothes, and how to make paper and ink. Jinton has a beautiful voice and is good at art. The knowledge, expertise and talents of these three are indispensable to their success and their passion and authenticity draw people in.

Such dreams exist everywhere. A few weeks into lockdown during the pandemic in 2020, a curious thing happened on Instagram, Tumblr, Pinterest and Facebook. Many people started to post images of pretty cottages adorned with flower-laden trellises, bright sunbeams streaming through dense foliage, dappled wooded pathways and earthy mushrooms growing in abandon... The phenomenon is called cottagecore. The idea lays heavily on a mix of rural self-sufficiency and idyllic decoration, with a dose of nostalgia. The popularity of cottagecore is also indicative of a desire for inner Shangri-la. The yarning for Shangri-la has the universal relevance.

Li Ziqi fulfils people's dreams for an idyllic lifestyle. But a simple, rural life is not for everyone, particularly younger age groups such as teenagers, who have their own dreams and fantasies.

## Luo Tianyi – my dream girl friend

Every year brings the tragic news of students in colleges, high schools and even middle schools committing suicide. In China, teenagers are under pressure: the pressure of studying hard to enter a prestigious university; the pressure to meet the lofty expectations of parents; the pressure of peer-to-peer comparisons …. On top of that, they have to cope with all the drastic physiological changes that come with being a teenager. Is there a way for them to escape this reality, to create their own fantasy?

If there is a need, someone will provide a solution. Let us introduce Luo Tianyi.

*Illustrated by Aspen Wang.*

Born in 2012 under the sign of Cancer, Luo Tianyi is 15 years old, forever. She has grey tinted hair (currently fashionable in China) tied up with jade ornaments. She has unproportionally large eyes with green pupils. She wears a beautiful Chinese knot to her waist. She looks sweet, innocent and pretty.

Luo Tianyi is a virtual singer, created by Shanghai Henian Information Technology Co., Ltd. She was concocted in the lab and is a Vocaloid. She is also like a clean slate, upon which fans can project all their desires. They write songs that she sings. They write novels that become her life stories. They draw cartoons that she acts out. For example, the set behind her character "Her Royal Highness of Eating" was created by fans, who hand-painted her eating in various ways. Ninety-nine percent of Luo Tianyi's songs are produced by fans who have some talent for musical production and in order for Luo to sing the songs they write; they have to purchase sound library software. In other words, anyone can ask Luo to sing a song for them. Luo has more than 10,000 user-generated content (UGC) songs on Bilibili,[9] and a song titled "Ordinary DISCO" has been played over 10 million times.[10]

Although Luo Tianyi is just a virtual singer, she is nonetheless hugely popular, with 4.62 million followers on Weibo and 1.9 million followers on Bilibili.[11] In June 2017, Luo and other virtual singers held a concert at the Mercedes-Benz Centre in Shanghai. The first batch of 500 SVIP seats, at RMB1280 (US$187) per seat, and limited-edition tickets for the concert all sold out within three minutes. The concert was broadcast exclusively on Bilibili. The number of viewers was 4.5 million, a figure comparable to that of top stars.

You might wonder who would be a fan of a virtual idol. Luo's followers are typical Generation Z (born between 1995 and 2009). Compared to people born in the 1970s and 1980s, Generation Z were born in an era that was materially rich. Many of them are well educated and knowledgeable about music and art. They have their own talents and like to show them off. They produce songs that they relay to Luo, which she sings for them. Gen Z grew up as "digital natives", familiar with animation and comics, and they are comfortable with virtual reality. They are vocal and willing to express themselves in art forms. One-way communication and uni-directory consumption are not enough for them; they need to participate and co-create content. They like real film stars and real singers too, but they cannot actively participate in creating them – they are just at the receiving end. Luo Tianyi, however, is different. She was created by her fans. The fans themselves defined her image. They projected their own aesthetic values onto her. Luo Tianyi is the perfect idol reflecting their inner selves. Human idols might fall into disrepute and disappoint their fans; virtual idols do not have this problem.

It's hard for adults, who are not digital natives, to understand this new trend. Many fans refer to Luo Tianyi, as "my wife". You can see comments like "Wife is always good" on her channel. For an ordinary boy, it is almost impossible to have a girlfriend like Luo Tianyi in real life. For an ordinary girl, they like to imagine themselves as Luo Tianyi. Imagination does not blur their boundaries and virtual conversations with Luo become part of their daily lives. Many fans express their emotions in the online community: "Only people who are really lonely can understand that feeling. Whatever emotion you are having, frustration, being misunderstood, anger, or indignation, angelic Luo Tianyi will always be there comforting you with her electrifying voice". Real stars are good to worship but it is a one-way relationship, with no emotional reciprocity. Luo Tianyi is like a bright moon shining above the mountains, which is still within your imaginative reach. As one fan expressed succinctly, Luo Tianyi brought her a long-lost hope: "She is pure and simple".[12]

Gen Z, who love Luo Tianyi, are growing into a major consumer group. Gen Z are more likely to pay for content that they like than any other generations. Luo Tianyi's popularity quickly transformed into commercial value. She has endorsed many well-known brands such as Nestlé, Pechoin (百雀羚), Pizza Hut, and Mirinda (美年达).

In 2020, Luo Tianyi even went onto Taobao Live. On May 1, she appeared in her first-time livestream selling with Le Zhengling, also a virtual idol. During the one-hour live broadcast, they recommended a total of nine products, including Bausch & Lomb contact lenses, L'Occitane shower gel and Midea self-heating bento boxes – all products selected to suit the preferences of young people.

Luo Tianyi was the first virtual idol to try livestream selling. On the day of her broadcast, the number of online viewers was as high as 2.7 million, and nearly two million rewarded her by buying her gifts during the broadcast. It is said that the slot fee for Luo Tianyi's Taobao livestream selling is as high as RMB900,000 (US$126,000).[13] Before Luo Tianyi, the highest slot fee record was Old Luo, at RMB600,000 (US$84,000). Taobao hasn't announced the sales result for Luo Tianyi's first broadcast but, from the perspective of slot fees, it appears the virtual celebrity commands a higher fee than a real celebrity.

Luo Tianyi is not the only virtual idol making money. Lil Miquela, widely popular in the United States, is another. She has 2.8 million followers on social media and has had promotion deals with Calvin Klein, Prada and other fashion labels and for these she charged a fee of US$8,500 per sponsored post.[14] It is estimated that Lil Miquela will make around US$11.7 million for her creators in 2020.[15]

## The world's tech-driven first VOCALOID idol, that sells!

Luo Tianyi can perform alone or with a real pop star on the same stage. Technology makes the unreal appear to be real. The most important factor in the birth of a virtual singer like Luo Tianyi is the digital copy technology, which reproduces the human voice. The Yamaha Group of Japan's VOCALOID is one such singing voice-synthesis technology and software, which can record a human voice for entry in a sound library. The users of the software input musical notes and lyrics to make a complete song, and the software's virtual sound library sings it out. The principle is similar to a voice navigation map. In the whole process of song creation using VOCALIC software there is no real person singing; it is just the arrangement of "data" of the tones in the sound library.

Luo Tianyi is the world's first virtual idol with a VOCALOID Chinese sound library. The sound comes from voice actor, Shan Xin (山新). Hatsune Miku, the world's first virtual singer, was born in 2007 and also used VOCALOID technology. The sound source is from Fujita Saki, a Japanese voice actor. Users of VOCALOID software compose songs for virtual singers. They also draw comics, make videos and create novels etc. for them. This is how virtual idols were born.

Of course, virtual singers can hold concerts, participate in large-scale TV shows and even make live broadcasts, all of which require more than just sound technology. To make virtual idol video transmission and performance possible, it is also necessary to have augmented reality, virtual reality, artificial intelligence, holographic projection, motion capture,

3D production, voice synthesis and other technologies. Industry sources indicate that the cost of putting on a virtual singer concert can be quite staggering; a 12-song concert, for example, could be up to RMB20 million (US$2.8 million),[16] whereas the production costs for a Jacky Cheung concert are around RMB6–8 million (US$0.8–1.1 million).[17] Virtual idols are built on the latest technology and new business models and are expensive to operate, at least for now. Will the costs go down in the future? With the maturing of technology, we believe so.

## The deeply soothing ultimate retail

We included Li Ziqi and Luo Tianyi in the same chapter because they leverage the same thing – meeting the high level of human needs that go beyond material things.

1. **Functional needs vs emotional needs.** Viya became a channel, while Li Ziqi became a brand. Viya spends time explaining the features of products during her livestreaming. She not only appeals to the functional needs of human beings but also leverages the psychological needs of getting a good deal or more importantly, not missing a good deal. She promises her fans that what they are getting is the best deal, using plain language and the lowest price for a product. Li Ziqi aims to meet the emotional needs of educated and well-to-do city dwellers and their yearning for an idyllic life. Viya is direct and instantaneous – what you see now is what you should buy immediately because the great deal will soon disappear. Li Ziqi does not mention anything about buying. She makes content-rich and visually appealing documentary short films. If you want to experience part of the rural life she presents, you can buy her products in her online stores. Hers is indirect selling – selling without actively "selling". When the human beings' basic needs are satisfied, fulfilling the emotional needs plays an oversized role in the purchasing decision. In the future, we are more gravitated towards Li Ziqi type of selling – selling without selling.

2. **Co-creating the star vs following the star.** The creation of Luo Tianyi followed a UGC model; her image, her persona, the clothes she wears

and the songs she sings, are all created by fans. Fans can participate in the development and shaping of idols as they wish. Although Luo Tianyi comes across as innocent, sweet and cute, it is easy for young people to project their desires and wants onto her. Luo Tianyi can be anything you want her to be. The emotion that fans invest in drawing the virtual idol and producing music for her, deepens their feelings for her. Buying the products she endorses is kind of affirming your own creation. It is another kind of indirect selling, via emotional connection. User participation is also indispensable in the development and success of Xiaomi. In fact, user participation was one of Xiaomi's important strategies. The firm built up a 100,000-person development team through the MIUI (Xiaomi mobile's operation system) online forum. Many of the MIUI functional designs are decided by the users on the online forum. Based on the mechanism of user participation, MIUI gained a surprisingly good reputation and growth rate. Wikipedia is also a product of the user participation model. In the mobile internet environment, the products that attract users the most are those can provide them with a sense of participation and a pleasant experience. It is no longer what the product can do for me but what I do with this product. The centre is on the "I", not the product.

3. **Competing for Gen Z.** The rise of virtual idols such as Luo Tianyi signifies another formidable force in the plethora of e-retailer formats. QuestMobile data shows that in October 2018, the number of China's Gen Z users exceeded 369 million, and Gen Z accounted for more than 30% of all internet users, contributing nearly half of the growth rate of the mobile internet. What kind of people are Gen Z? Gen Z pursue "house culture". Games, anime, comics and other user-generated content have shaped idol culture. As a result of this, we have the idol economy. In 2018, the consumption scale of Gen Z driven by idols exceeded RMB40 billion (US$5.9 billion), and nearly half of the consumption was on products that idols had endorsed or recommended.[18] Gen Z likes to watch anime on mobile phones. It is the dependence of Gen Z on the phone screen and their love of "two dimensions" that built the base for the popularity of virtual idols. Gen Z are more willing to spend money via mobile phones. Taobao Live invited Luo Tianyi to their platform with the express intention to attract Gen Z. If you Lose Gen Z, you lose the future.

## Concluding remarks: questions for executives to ask

1. What benefits can ultimate selling bring your customers today? What kind of emotional needs does your product fulfil? Or what kind of emotional needs do your customers derive from buying and using your product?
2. Do you have the capability in-house to create digital content or do you work with digital agencies so that you can leverage what an ultimate seller in your industry and geography – similar to Li Ziqi – can create in terms of buzz and attention for your product category?
3. To what extent do you already co-create content and digital influence with and through your customers?
4. To what extent do you see influencers like Li Ziqi play a role in your industry at large?
5. What are the future consumers of your product or service? What kinds of behaviours challenge the way you engage with your customer today that might need to change in the future?
6. If you were to experiment with ultimate selling in your region, which product categories would you choose, what price would you offer, what story would you tell, who are the potential celebrities you would consider using, and which platform would you choose?
7. If you were to create a virtual idol for Gen Z, please sketch it and imbue with a personality. How would this virtual idol help connect your product with Gen Z?

## Notes

1 The end of June 2020.
2 https://www.sohu.com/a/363607796_120142809.
3 June 2020 Taobao Realtime data.
4 https://xueqiu.com/3780544971/137603751.
5 http://www.cnr.cn/rdzx/cxxhl/zxxx/20200605/t20200605_525118027.shtml.
6 http://www.nbd.com.cn/articles/2020-01-18/1401421.html.
7 Sep 2020 Weibo realtime data.
8 https://mp.weixin.qq.com/s/bQoikNYDwR8tvgtiwWIPpg.
9 Speaking of Bilibili, it is the iconic brand of online entertainment for young generations in China. Bilibili started in 2009 as a website-based content

community inspired by anime, comics and games (ACG), and evolved into an entertainment platform covering videos, live broadcasting and mobile games. Bilibili is famous for PUGC (Professional user generated content). In 2019, PUG video views accounted for 90% of total video views (2019 annual report). Compared to Douyin and Kuaishou, whose videos are short and mostly about 15 seconds or 60 seconds, Bilibili does not impose the length of videos posted, which offers the creators more space to create high quality content. The high-quality content attracts loyal users. According to QuestMobile, Bilibili is the "most liked" APP in China for young people under 24 years old. For the second quarter of 2020, Bilibili had an average of 172 million monthly active users (Bilibili website).

10   https://a.sendbp.com/redui/article/198432/23ee42c55620.

11   June 2020 Weibo, Bilibili Realtime data.

12   https://weibo.com/p/23134743719272328 69263/wenda_home?sudaref=www. baidu.com&display=0&retcode=6102#_loginLayer_1593523473910.

13   https://baijiahao.baidu.com/s?id=1665730051889191418&wfr=spider&-for=pc.

14   https://www.onbuy.com/gb/blog/the-highest-earning-robot-influencers-on-instagram~a243/.

15   https://www.onbuy.com/gb/blog/the-highest-earning-robot-influencers-on-instagram~a243/.

16   https://baijiahao.baidu.com/s?id=1599780213086051084&wfr=spider&-for=pc.

17   https://zhidao.baidu.com/question/138168401728766938o.html.

18   https://baijiahao.baidu.com/s?id=1620346459153081360&wfr=spider&-for=pc.

# Part III

MAKING SENSE OF NEW RETAIL

# 11

## THREE KINGDOMS

### The invisible hand of ecosystems

The rise of new retail in China has been driven by innovative companies that recognised emerging and unmet needs of consumers. Firms such as Meituan, Hema and Pinduoduo have been instrumental in pushing the boundaries of new retail beyond the e-commerce of Alibaba and JD. Moreover, individual internet celebrities such as Mr Lipstick, Mr Bags and Li Ziqi brought retail to a new level of experience. So far, they have all been doing well. For instance, Meituan's valuation is over US$235 billion in January 2021, almost 60% higher than half a year ago.[1] and Pinduoduo, just five years old, reached a valuation of over US$230 billion in January 2021, while half a year ago the valuation is US$100 billion.[2] Mr Lipstick generated US$145 million in sales on 2019 Single's Day alone.[3] Not bad for a guy who specialises in cosmetics — and much to the envy of many public companies. Looking at the new retail landscape in China, we can see that it is both diverse and highly dynamic. There are many new ventures and opportunities are everywhere. And at the core of it all is entrepreneurship.

DOI: 10.4324/9781003205074-14

Behind the scenes of Meituan, Hema and Pinduoduo, and behind the individuals of Mr Lipstick and Li Ziqi, there is an invisible hand operating a handful of business ecosystems. Well, three business ecosystems to be precise, which is somewhat reminiscent of China's epic novel, the *Three Kingdoms*. We can draw some parallel between the classical tale of the three kingdoms and the three retail kingdoms. Let us look at one of the most interesting historical periods in the history of China.

## Romance of the three kingdoms

The book titled *Three Kingdoms* is a 14th-century historical novel attributed to Luo Guanzhong. It is set in the turbulent years towards the end of the Han dynasty and the Three Kingdoms period in Chinese history, which started in 169 AD and ended with the reunification of the land in 280 AD.

The story – part historical, part legend and part mythical – romanticises and dramatises the lives of feudal lords and their retainers, each of whom are trying to replace or restore the dying Han dynasty. While the novel follows hundreds of characters, the focus is mainly on the three power blocs that emerged from the remnants of the Han dynasty, which would eventually form the three states of Cao Wei, Shu Han and Eastern Wu. The story follows the plots, personal and military battles, intrigues and struggles of these states to achieve dominance, over a period of almost 100 years.

The novel has countless fascinating and exciting plots, but the ones readers remember the most are those associated with the number "three". "Three" is a magic number in China. Taoism, a school of philosophy as popular as Confucius in ancient China, has a famous saying,

> The Tao is unmatched. Its primal activity produced the two opposing principles in nature - negative and positive. These two principles interacted with each other and produced a balanceable state of "three". All things of the universe came into being in this state.

In Chinese, it is "道生一，一生二，二生三，三生万物".

If anything, the story of the Three Kingdoms illustrates the ongoing battle and search for equilibrium between power blocs and it seems that the magic number three is needed in order to reach a relatively stable status.

In a similar fashion, the new retail kingdoms have gone through turbulent times to reach the magic three.

## The old three kingdoms: Alibaba, Tencent, Baidu

At the end of the 1990s, three young men saw the rise of the internet and started crafting business ideas. While one was based in Beijing and was part of a bustling technology scene, the two others were in the newly emerging cities of Hangzhou on the east coast and Shenzhen on the south coast. Independently, they built three internet platforms at a time most Chinese had not heard of the internet and or own computers, or even credit cards for that matter. Within less than two decades these three platforms grew into China's largest business ecosystems, encompassing online and offline businesses. By the end of 2020, they had a combined estimated market capitalisation of over US$1.5 trillion. These three young men were Jack Ma, Robin Li and Pony Ma and, respectively, they established Alibaba, Baidu and Tencent.

Jack Ma's business has its roots in trading and e-commerce, mostly focusing on facilitating small and medium-sized enterprises (SMEs) in global marketplaces. Robin Li's core business is search technology and it is often dubbed the Google of China. Pony Ma's business has its roots in instant messaging and online communication. Regardless of their origins, all three platforms have been diversifying in recent years into new areas such as internet finance, digital healthcare, culture and entertainment, enterprise services and location-based services. Moreover, they have incubated a combined total of over 1,000 new ventures. Transforming their businesses from three independent platforms into three competing business ecosystems, these three pioneers are commonly known as BAT (Baidu, Alibaba, Tencent).

## Business ecosystems

Business ecosystems are boundaryless organisations of interdependent businesses with customer-centric offerings across different industries. The idea is that each entity in the ecosystem affects and is affected by the others, creating a constantly evolving relationship in which each entity must be flexible and adaptable to survive, as in a biological ecosystem. Rather than following strict and deliberate top-down strategic directives, business ecosystems are managed by heuristic principles and data-driven insights[4] Fundamentally, business ecosystems consist of an orchestrator, a set of complementing businesses, or complementors, and a system – usually a digital coordination mechanism – that holds everything together, making the sum of the parts greater than the whole. Or, in business terms, the offerings of business ecosystems meet the needs and wants of the customer better than individual offerings. Let's have a look at BAT's business ecosystems and how they orchestrate the new retail revolution.

## Alibaba

The Alibaba Group is the world's largest and one of the most valuable retailers with operations in over 200 countries. With over 50,000 employees and a market cap of over US$636 billion (January 2021),[5] it is one of the top ten most valuable and biggest companies in the world. The success of Alibaba can be largely attributed to its new organisational form – a business ecosystem – which has fostered the rapid growth and transformation of its businesses since the company began life in 1999.

Alibaba's core business centres around building online trading platforms. Launched in 1999, Alibaba.com is the flagship of the Alibaba Group, a leading English-language wholesale marketplace for global trade. Buyers are located in over 200 countries and include agents, wholesalers, SMEs, retailers and manufacturers. By 2017, the platform included two distinct businesses: Alibaba.com International and 1688.com (formerly Alibaba.com China).

In May 2003, Alibaba launched Taobao. Taobao offers a comprehensive range of products, from collectables and hard-to-find items to consumer electronics, clothing and accessories, sporting goods and household products. In less than ten years, Taobao became one of the world's most popular consumer to consumer (C2C) e-commerce marketplaces. In April 2008, it launched Tmall (B2C). Tmall's aim was to be the online platform for quality, brand-named goods, serving the needs of increasingly sophisticated Chinese consumers.

In 2004, Alibaba's ecosystem began its first large-scale transformation. In the decade that followed we saw the maturing of the business ecosystem and an extension of all the services to support the core, in order to create a fully functioning e-commerce ecosystem. In particular, we can distinguish three phases: (1) extending SME client services: Alipay, Alimama, Alicloud; (2) extending consumer services: Aliexpress, Juhuasuan, eTao; and (3) consolidating and upgrading. In the latter phase we notice, in particular, the upgrading of the logistics division, from dependence on external providers to initiating a smart logistics network (Cainiao), and the extension of Alipay's online payment system to a fully fledged, online financial services sub-ecosystem.

In 2013, Alibaba's ecosystem saw its second large-scale transformation, with large investments in less mature companies and more diverse fields. As a result, the company diversified from e-commerce into internet-related businesses, financial services, social networking services, digital healthcare, and culture and entertainment. Not satisfied with just running online shopping marketplaces, Alibaba built an e-commerce ecosystem to enable and support an expanding range of commercial activities. The goal was to make the internet part of the Chinese consumer's everyday shopping experience: mobile apps like Alipay and Taobao let users pay electronically in physical shops, order movie tickets and takeaway noodles, book transportation and buy merchandise online – picking up their orders from bricks-and-mortar outlets. While online and offline retailers were often traditional enemies, in China the rapid growth of e-commerce and mobile shopping has encouraged collaboration. For instance, Alibaba invested US$4.3 billion in Suning, a household electrical appliances vendor, and US$736 million in Intime retail, one of the largest shopping mall operators in China.

## Alibaba driving new retail

It is in this last phase of Alibaba's transformation into a full-blown ecosystem that it started to play a significant role in driving the phenomenon of new retail.

In 2016, Jack Ma proposed the concept of "new retailing", that is, the combination of online, offline and logistics.[6] In the same year, Hema's first physical store was opened in Shanghai and residents living within three kilometres of the store could place their orders online and receive delivery within 30 minutes. Hema captured a lot of attention and is interpreted as Alibaba's way of reinventing the new retail.

As you might remember (see Chapter 6), Alibaba is also a main player in lifestyle/location-based services. It invested in Meituan in 2011, which it later lost to Tencent in 2015. To compensate, it paid over the top to acquire Ele.me in 2018 (US$9.5 billion was considered an outrageous overvaluation) and soon merged Ele.me with Koubei, a restaurant-reviewing company in which Alibaba had invested back in 2006.

So, the opposing teams of Alibaba and Tencent are:

*Ele.me + Koubei vs Meituan + Dianping.*

However, Alibaba's footprints in new retail go far beyond the above:

- launched Tmall Fresh in 2013, and invested in Yiguo Fresh (Chapter 7);
- launched the "Taobao Special Edition" app in 2018 to compete with PDD (Chapter 8);
- launched Taobao Live in 2016 and cultivated celebrities such as Viya and Li Jiaqi (Chapter 9) — even Luo Tianyi did her first livestream selling on Taobao Live and Li Ziqi has her flagship store on Tmall (Chapter 10);
- invested in many supermarket chains and shopping malls, such as Sanjiang (三江购物), Lianhua Supermarket (联华超市), Yintai (银泰) and Suning (苏宁). (Chapter 7).

It is no exaggeration to say that Alibaba occupies half of the new retail space in China.

## Tencent

Tencent is currently Asia's most valuable company and one of the world's largest internet companies. It focuses on social communications. Tencent's most popular instant messaging service, WeChat, has over 1,164 million active monthly users (MAU) in China and abroad in December 2019.[7] In

2019, the company's total revenues reached US$54 billion (a year-on-year growth of 20%), with a net profit of US$14 billion. Its market capitalisation is an estimated US$710 billion (January 2021).[8] Over the last decade, Tencent has diversified into culture and entertainment (gaming), cloud, digital healthcare, and internet finance and it is highly active in overseas investments and acquisitions. In 2007 and 2014, Time magazine called founder Pony Ma one of the world's most influential people.

Inspired by ICQ, the world's first internet instant messaging service that was founded in Israel in 1996, many Chinese companies developed similar products, such as the Sina Pager and PICQ. However, Tencent's OICQ was much simpler and more user friendly than its competitors' offerings. Moreover, the product was small in size in the sense that it was easy to download, which was crucial considering the limited internet speed and costly bandwidth at that time. In the face of an America Online (AOL) lawsuit in 2000, Tencent changed the name from OICQ to QQ.

In 2009, it started to move its products to mobile platforms. In 2011, Xiaomi, a smartphone producer founded in 2010, launched a mobile instant messenger called Miliao (see Chapter 5). Tencent was in danger of losing its market advantage to a newcomer. Of course, it would have been possible to move QQ to mobile platforms. However, instead it decided to launch a new product, one which could perfectly meet the social and communication needs of users in the mobile era, not just a modified version of a last-generation PC product. It was a team led by Allen Zhang (founder of Foxmail and one of the most talented programmers in China), which had been formed originally to focus on developing the QQ mailbox, that was behind the innovation of a whole new product: WeChat.

Tencent had begun to expand its business portfolio beyond communication and chat early on. In 2003, it released its own portal, QQ.com. Extending its revenue model, the company began to sell membership services, such as virtual goods, via QQ. By 2016, it had become the largest online gaming company by revenue.[9] Its online gaming platform started selling virtual goods, such as virtual weapons, as well as emoticons and ringtones, which later became the company's largest revenue stream. The gaming platform and portal were all connected to QQ and formed the core of Tencent's emerging ecosystem.

Tencent's growth strategy changed course in 2011. It employed two mechanisms to diversify into new but related sectors. First of all, it initiated several innovative products and services. These were developed mostly by the company itself and focused on new product development. As we saw with the development of WeChat (Chapter 5), Tencent encourages internal competitions with multiple teams engaging in the same product development. The second mechanism was significant investment in new companies and technologies. This strategy of investment led to Tencent being the most proactive firm in diversification: over 200 companies across a wide variety of sectors and phases joined its business ecosystem. Five business areas stand out amongst these: e-commerce, digital healthcare, culture/entertainment, internet finance and location-based services (LBS).

## Tencent driving new retail

It is in this last phase of its transformation into a full-blown ecosystem that Tencent started to play a significant role in driving new retail.

Although deemed to be an instant messaging and gaming company, Tencent has not sat silent in the wave of e-commerce and new retail. As early as 2005 it launched the C2C platform, Paipai, although it was not ultimately successful, and the company eventually dropped its plans to develop its own e-commerce business. Instead, in 2014, it acquired a 15% stake in JD and, in 2015, invested in Missfresh. But that's not all.

Tencent's ambition in the high-frequency lifestyle services is evident in the way it grabbed Meituan from the hands of Alibaba (Chapter 6). In 2014, it invested in Dianping and, in 2015, succeeded in merging Dianping with Meituan. It invested US$1 billion into the newly merged company and another US$400 million in 2018, just before Meituan's IPO. According to Meituan's 2019 annual report, Tencent holds more than a 20% share of Meituan.[10] Alibaba fought back by acquiring Ele.me, as we saw earlier, at an over-inflated price.

"The enemy of my enemy is my friend". The saying works well in business. Tencent invested in PDD in 2016 (Chapter 8), just one year after PDD had been established, and invested again in 2018, before PDD's IPO. According to PDD's 2019 annual report, Tencent holds a 16.5% share of PDD.[11] Tencent is indispensable to PDD, who relied on the social media effect of WeChat to accumulate its huge customer base. With JD targeting higher-end customers and PDD targeting lower-end customers, it looks like Alibaba's Taobao is squeezed rather uncomfortably in the middle.

# Baidu

Baidu is China's largest online search engine, with a focus on Chinese-language search. By Q1 2020, the Baidu app had 22 million active daily users (DAU) (about 60% of Baidu's search requests are on its app),[12] which is about 65% of China's online searching market.[13] In 2019, Baidu's total revenues were US$15 billion, which was increase of 5% on 2018. And 2019 was the first year since its IPO in 2005 that the company showed a loss in its financial report, of US$328 million.[14] In January 2021, Baidu's market capitalisation was an estimated US$70 billion[15] – not on the same level as Alibaba and Tencent, who are both over US$600 billion. However, Baidu is no longer just an online search engine. It now boasts successful businesses in internet finance, digital healthcare, online education, location-based services, driverless cars and more. In 2016, the MIT Technology Review recognised Baidu as one of the top 50 most intelligent companies worldwide.

Baidu competed strongly with Google, especially in 2001 and 2002. In 2001, Baidu also started to promote a revenue model based on paid listings, i.e., a bidding system for advertisers on how much they would be willing to pay to appear at the top of results in response to specific searches. In early 2002, Baidu announced a "flash plan". Its purpose was to be level with Google in terms of search technology within nine months. At this stage, Baidu was still a start-up and Google already a strong player, with five million users in China. Baidu eventually became the top Chinese search portal. It is important to realise that this was well before the Chinese government started to take control of the internet and block Google's services.

The core of Baidu's ecosystem is Baidu Search. However, in its first decade, the company developed a large range of services for consumers and businesses that were complementary to Baidu Search. One such was community-based services, including the successful Baidu Tieba, which was launched in 2003, and Baidu Knows, an online search-based, interactive Q&A platform. Besides consumer-focused services, Baidu also developed business services for websites and developers, including Baidu Cloud Observation, which monitors website safety, the Baidu Index, which performs key-words data analysis and the Baidu API Store, which provides an API service for developers and others.

Baidu's diversification into related but different fields of business started to take off in 2011. Although Baidu Games started back in 2007 and Baidu's e-commerce platform, You'a, was launched back in 2008, both had had little impact and failed. Baidu's growth is driven by, on the one hand, the peer pressure of Alibaba and Tencent and, on the other, a strategic need to diversify beyond the core of search business and find new revenue streams. According to observers, Baidu has significantly diversified into the following four business areas: digital healthcare, online education, internet finance and location-based services. Not all of Baidu's diversification initiatives went well, however. For instance, some of the toolkits it developed for internet users such as a browser, a Chinese input system, a virus scanner and a media player, have not achieved much success in the market.

In recent years, Baidu has invested significant resources in the research and development of artificial intelligence (AI) technology and has made significant progress in the commercialisation of AI technologies, such as AI-powered voice assistant platform DuerOS, autonomous driving platform Apollo, Baidu Cloud, Baidu Search and Baidu Feed.

It is in this last phase of transformation into a full-blown ecosystem that Baidu could have started to play a significant role in driving new retail. However, its initiatives have been limited by mixed results. For example, its food delivery subsidiary, Baidu Waimai, which was established in 2014 and for a time formed a three-way competition with Meituan and Ele.me, eventually lagged behind and was acquired by Ele.me in 2017, who renamed it "Star. Ele.me" (Chapter 6). Looking back, one possible explanation for the failure of Baidu Waimai could be that its payment system was not as successful as WeChat Pay and Alipay. Another important trigger was Robin Li's announcement, in 2016, that the company would focus on AI. Baidu Waimai seemed too far removed from a company that was pivoting towards AI.

## End of the old three kingdoms?

We thought for a long time that the BAT constellation was a stable and de facto a set of monopolists in China. Moreover, with their increasing diversification and expansion, it appeared that they had all become too big to fail. However, history would prove us wrong. By 2020 it became clear that

Baidu had become the "little brother" of the three, in terms of valuation, impact and business reputation. So, what went wrong?

In our analysis and discussion with executives from BAT and through our detailed tracking of investments and growth, we ascertained that compared to Baidu, Alibaba and Tencent started to follow a different growth path.

First, Alibaba and Tencent began to invest in companies in the same fields as each other, such as in lifestyle services, fresh food new retail, etc. In the case of Meituan and Ele.me, Meituan Dianping (also referred to as China Internet Plus or XinMeiDa in Chinese), is a location-based service (LBS) platform that focuses on catering. Meituan, established in 2010, received two rounds of investment from Alibaba, and Dianping, China's earliest consumer review platform, was supported by Tencent with two rounds of investment. In 2015, the two companies merged into Meituan Dian-ping. By 2016, Tencent, and others had invested US$3.3 billion. Hence both Tencent and Alibaba supported the rise of another firm in their fields. Mei-tuan Dianping has become a national champion itself. In February 2018, it added a taxi-hailing service, pitching itself in direct competition with Didi Chuxing and, in April 2018, it acquired Mobike, thereby becoming a ma-jor player in the mobility sector. Its latest valuation of over US$235 billion makes Meituan a serious contender for one of the top seats in China's new retailing space.

Tencent has been an active investor in LBS companies, many of which were top unicorns. For example, in 2015 it was part of a joint investment, with JD and other partners, in Ele.me of US$350; it has pumped several rounds of investment into Didi Chuxing since 2013; and obtained 20% of Dianping, the leading restaurant review and LBS platform, in 2014. In total, Tencent has invested in 25 companies in the LBS sector, which is led by a younger generation of changemakers. Tencent plays a significant role in providing fuel for these ventures.

An impressive example is the case of Ele.me: a food delivery venture founded by several Shanghai Jiaotong University students that combined a Taobao-like marketplace with a full-blown logistics system. By the end of 2017, Ele.me boasted its own 15,000-strong delivery force and extended its presence into over 2000 Chinese cities, connecting 200,000 restaurants and delivering 16 million orders a day.[16] Alibaba couldn't sit idly by and let Tencent win the LBS space. So, it acquired Ele.me in April 2018, with a valuation of US$9.5 billion.

Baidu might seem to have been left out but that is probably partly by choice. Baidu has been aggressively betting on its future in AI, starting with the hiring of Andrew Ng in 2014 but, so far, has not been able to monetise much of their innovation. Although Baidu is continuously recognised as one of the world's most innovative companies, it has yet to prove the scalability and applicability to create business growth. Clearly the focus of Baidu is still on developing pioneering technology, competing with Google and Microsoft rather than Alibaba and Tencent. Perhaps this strategic choice pushed them out of the domestic game, leaving Alibaba and Tencent to march ahead.

Lastly, we also believe that lack of competition is a reason for the decreasing competitiveness of Baidu. The fact is that Google – uncomfortable with complying with Chinese regulation – is de facto blocked in China and there is no alternative to the Chinese searching engine other than Baidu. This may have made Baidu complacent and shows that creating competitive companies in China requires a competitive environment.

## The new three kingdoms: Alibaba, Tencent, ByteDance

When we look at what has been fuelling the internet celebrities, it is clear that the company ByteDance has played a crucial role. In particular, one of ByteDance's businesses, Douyin/TikTok, has been crucial in enabling Mr Lipstick and Li Ziqi to expand new retail concepts into livestreaming. It was said that ByteDance 2020 revenue may reach RMB239 billion (US\$ 37 billion).[17] In December 2020, ByteDance had a private valuation of over US\$180 billion.[18] Meanwhile, Baidu's valuation dropped sharply, to around US\$70 billion. Moreover, in January 2021, Baidu considered delisting from the Nasdaq to find ways to bolster valuation.[19] It appears that Baidu is no longer one of the three kingdoms and that ByteDance has become a good contender as its replacement.

So how does a newcomer quickly become a rival of the two biggest internet giants?

The key, in our view, is for competitors to use Alibaba and Tencent's size against them. As these giants have grown – and today they are massive companies – they have steadily lost two critical elements that formed the foundation of their success. First, they have become less agile, as it is harder to maintain agility with 50,000 employees than it is with, say 5,000. Second, their ability to understand and respond to niche groups of consumers has diminished with size and scale.

ByteDance is quickly on the way to becoming a new "super-app". Founder Zhang Yiming's first product, Toutiao, quickly became China's largest news aggregation service, surpassing traditional media and internet giants within five years of its launch. ByteDance's other venture is the short video-sharing service TikTok, currently the world's highest valued start-up, with 20% of its 500 million users based outside of China. ByteDance launched services such as Duoshan, gogokid and Wukong in 2018, all directly competing with Alibaba and Tencent.

However, a lean camel is bigger than a horse (in Chinese, 瘦死的骆驼比马大). Alibaba and Tencent are still three or four times larger than ByteDance, so why should ByteDance be considered alongside them. The answer is algorithms, which have been in the blood of ByteDance since its birth. While BAT put everything in front of you for you to search and choose, ByteDance does the opposite. Based on algorithms, it seems to understand what you like and want and pushes it to you, without you having to bother to search and choose. Allen Zhang once said, "Pushing is changing the world, as the users are lazier".[20] Pushing based on algorithm is more in line with human nature; in this sense, the gene of ByteDance is more advanced than Alibaba and Tencent. Algorithms will help ByteDance to be part of the tripartite confrontation.

## ByteDance or Meituan?

It is hard to say if the new equilibrium is stable. The reality is that Meituan, with a valuation of over US$235 billion and large numbers of users, is building up a significant ecosystem that is increasingly gaining attention and popularity. Also, consider the reasons why Baidu has left the three kingdoms: to be independent from Alibaba and Tencent and focus on new − yet to be commercialised − technologies. This sounds familiar: ByteDance was launched independent of Alibaba and Tencent and actively competes with them. Moreover, ByteDance has a singular technology focus

*Illustrated by Aspen Wang.*

on recommendation algorithms based on AI. With the increased global political scrutiny and pressure on ByteDance's TikTok overseas, there may be
a window of opportunity for Meituan. (Figures 11.1 and 11.2)

In China, never say never.

|  | Tencent | Alibaba | Meituan | PDD | JD | Byte Dance | Baidu |
|---|---|---|---|---|---|---|---|
| Market Value[i] (B $) | 710 | 636 | 235 | 230 | 137[ii] | 180 | 70 |
| Revenue 2019 (M $) | 54,082 | 56,152 | 13,980 | 4,329 | 82,867 | N.A | 15,429 |
| Profit 2019 (M $) | 16,724 | 13,053 | 419 | -1,000 | 1,750 | N.A | -328 |

---

[i] July 21st 2020
[ii] January 2021

Figure 11.1 Market value of Alibaba, Tencent and other players.

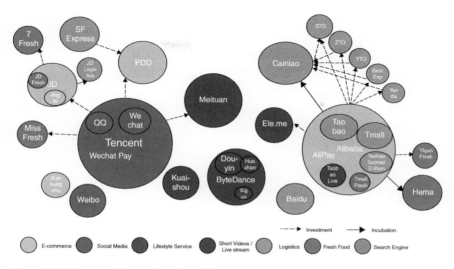

*Figure* 11.2  The new "three kingdoms".

## Notes

1   https://new.qq.com/omn/20200708/20200708A0QR1I00.html.
2   http://finance.eastmoney.com/a/202006161523836628.html.
3   https://www.scmp.com/magazines/style/news-trends/article/3074253/
    who-millionaire-li-jiaqi-chinas-lipstick-king-who.
4   Mark J. Greeven/Wei Wei, Business Ecosystems in China, 2017.
5   http://quote.eastmoney.com/us/BABA.html?from=BaiduAladdin
    20200816.
6   https://www.sohu.com/a/116110863_468951.
7   Tencent 2019 annual report.
8   https://www.laohu8.com/stock/00700?f=baidu&utm_source=-
    baidu&utm_medium=aladingpc 2020 0819.
9   http://www.chinadaily.com.cn/interface/zaker/1142841/2017-03-24/
    cd_28668367.html.
10  Meituan 2019 annual report.
11  PDD 2019 annual report.
12  https://m.chinaz.com/2020/0708/1155307.shtml.
13  https://zhuanlan.zhihu.com/p/77228887.
14  https://xw.qq.com/cmsid/20200320A0FFUR00.

15   https://www.laohu8.com/stock/BIDU?f=baidu&utm_source=-
     baidu&utm_medium=aladingpc.
16   http://news.iresearch.cn/content/2018/04/274127.shtml.
17   https://mp.weixin.qq.com/s/IwlUKw76Xg3CN17v7cv-cg.
18   https://36kr.com/p/955199108576902.
19   https://markets.businessinsider.com/news/stocks/baidu-stock-nasdaq-
     delisting-boost-valuation-amid-congress-pressure-2020-5-1029224027.
20   http://money.163.com/20/0109/11/F2ER8TOV00259DLP.html.

# 12

## THE CONCLUSION

### Retail reinvented in China for the world

#### New retailing, what is it all about?

Jack Ma once said: "The past 200 years are the age of knowledge and technology, and the next 100 years will be the age of smartness, experience and service".[1]

**Smartness** refers to the important role of big data and the IoT (Internet of Things). Smartness is at the core of the new retailer. For example, it's a "smart" recommendation that is largely responsible for our fixation on Douyin and TikTok. And when we look at what is behind Tmall's processing of mass transactions on Singles' Day, or Meituan's "super brain" coordinating its speedy 30-minute deliveries, or Hema's electronic price tag containing all sorts of commodity information … what we find behind all these visible experiences are invisible big data and IoT technology. The leading new retail companies all have first-class, cutting-edge data processing and analysing capabilities.

DOI: 10.4324/9781003205074-15

So, what are the concrete impacts of smartness on user **experience** in this world of new retail? First is the fast delivery. Second is the convenience of one-stop shopping. Third is accurate product recommendation. Fourth is the seamless integration of online and offline. Fifth is fun. Sixth is a sense of belonging to a large community of like-minded people. People can use the Meituan app to order a food delivery, book movie tickets and hail a taxi. Consumers can choose to either visit Hema's physical stores or open the Hema app, place an order and get home delivery. PDD integrates the fun of playing games into shopping. Viya's fans feel they are getting the best deal. Li Ziqi satisfies people's inner yearnings for nature and beauty and Luo Tianyi allows people to participate in the creation of herself. The new retailers thrive on providing incredible user experience.

In the past, retailing and **services** were two separate industries but, in the era of new retail, the two are deeply integrated. Needless to say, logistics, express delivery and takeaway delivery are the most typical services of new retail. But we also see how Viya and Li Jiaqi spare no effort in bargaining with brands for recommended products to ensure maximum bang-for-their-buck for their followers, and how Li Ziqi spends up to two years to make a 14-minute video. Although these efforts are invisible to consumers, they constitute the ultimate services. (Figure 12.1)

We coin new retailing as experience-focused, service-oriented retail, based on big data and artificial intelligence, fulfilling the needs of specific customer segments. The relationship between the three elements of retail (products, places and people) has evolved from the earlier

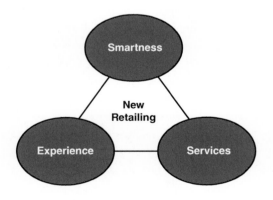

Figure 12.1 Smartness + experience + service = new retailing.

"products-places-people (product is king)" to "places-products-people (channel is king)" and to the more recent "people-products-places (user is king)". The trajectory is the inevitable result of economic development and material wealth, as well as technological advancement and the wide coverage of the internet. In the future, new retail around the world will not necessarily follow the same model and form as it is currently found in China, but the trend led by economic and technological development – where the user is king – would most likely be the same.

## New retailing: all from customer needs/pain points

Four pillars supported the foundation of new retail: e-commerce, express delivery, third-party payment and social media (Figure 12.2). While new retail may have still developed without these four pillars, it may not have been able to scale up so rapidly.

In chapter 2 to chapter 5, we reviewed the development of e-commerce platforms in China, starting with the founding of Alibaba in 1999 and the building of the other pillars: express delivery, online third-party payment and social media platforms. The period from 1999 to 2009 was the era of traditional e-commerce. During this ten-year period, e-commerce

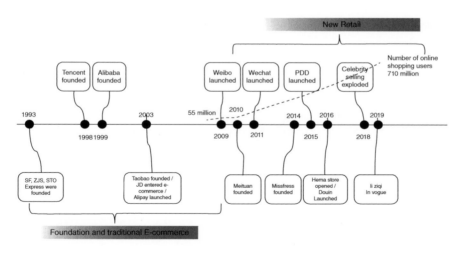

Figure 12.2  The development of e-commerce and new retail in China, towards "user is the king".

developed rapidly in China and the idea of buying things online became widely accepted and put into practice. Around 2010, smartphones became increasingly prevalent and social media platforms, especially WeChat, started to dominate people's daily lives. The soil was cultivated, and the seed was planted. New retail began to sprout in a whole variety of different forms.

From Chapters 6 to 10, we studied the five stages of new retail in China; the first being lifestyle/location-based e-commerce; the second, fresh food – both online and offline; the third, social e-commerce; the fourth, celebrity selling; and the fifth, ultimate selling. All these five stages are different in many aspects, but they have two things in common:

- They leverage the four foundations: e-commerce platforms, third-party payment, express delivery and social media platforms.
- They exist because they are trying to satisfy needs of certain segments of customers.

**Stage 1: lifestyle/location-based e-commerce.** With the ever-expanding ranks of the middle class armed with rising disposable income, there were more people eating out more often, seeking entertainment, socialising with friends and travelling. This was particularly the case with relatively well-to-do, white-collar young professionals. They cultivated a new lifestyle that was quite different from that of their parents. Traditional e-commerce just sold general commodities; it did not offer a new lifestyle. Meituan and Koubei came along to satisfy those customer lifestyle needs, by providing restaurant reviews, takeaway deliveries, travel bookings, movie tickets, bike rental and more, and developed into super-platforms that offer almost every type of lifestyle service and entertainment.

**Stage 2: fresh food, online and offline.** Taobao, JD and Meituan seemed to have already moved everything online, except for one very high-frequency basic demand category – fresh food. Fresh food such as vegetables, fruit, meat, eggs, poultry and seafood are the most indispensable things in the daily lives of ordinary Chinese people. However, due to high logistics costs, low price points and easily perishable products, the online penetration of fresh food had been very low. New, different models began to emerge for fresh food e-commerce. Hema combined offline stores/warehouse and online purchasing; Missfresh deployed the front warehouse concept and achieved within-hour delivery; JD To Home launched their O2O model and partnered with supermarkets to deliver fresh food within one to two hours. The most challenging part for fresh food is logistics and all the major players in this arena expended great efforts to improve logistics efficiency. Interestingly, no one seems to have asked the question: when they will break even and start to make money?

Stages 1 and 2 expanded the product categories of online retail to lifestyle and fresh food, which traditional e-commerce could not cover.

**Stage 3: social e-commerce**. While the middle classes in first and second-tier cities enjoyed the convenience of new retailing from companies like Meituan and Hema, there were still one billion Chinese living in small cities, townships and rural areas who were much more price sensitive. Some 600 million people reported monthly income barely above RMB1,000 (US$140), and they were underserved by e-commerce. PDD tapped into this segment by utilising the social network of WeChat. There were also community group-buying firms that used the network of community organisers. Social e-commerce focused on serving these 600 million underserved consumers with affordable products, made possible by China's 40-year mission to become the "world's factory".

**Stage 4: celebrity selling.** Celebrity selling and social e-commerce have one thing in common: competitive pricing. While PDD relied on social networks such as WeChat to attract consumers into group buying, celebrity selling relied on high-profile personalities to attract customers to buy certain products. This was not a coincidence; celebrities who have a good reputation and a close relationship with their fans are more reliable than the search bars of sites such as Taobao. In China, there is a general trust deficit and certain public figures fill this void. What is worth noting is that it is not only professional celebrities but also CEOs and government officials that participate in livestream broadcasting to sell their wares. In this era, whoever has fans and followers can be a candidate for celebrity selling.

Stages three and four expanded the coverage of e-commerce from first and second-tier cities to third to sixth-tier cities and provided a venue for low-income consumers to participate in new retail.

**Stage 5: ultimate selling.** This stage is notable in that talented people started to share their passions online. In some way, it went beyond just sharing a passion. They turned their enthusiasm for something into an art form that ordinary people could admire or desire. Their followers were

Figure 12.3  The four foundations and five stages of new retailing.
Illustrated by Aspen Wang.

lured in by their evident talent and deep knowledge and wanted a piece of it themselves.

Figure 12.3 illustrates the four foundations and five stages of new retailing.

## What does this mean for global players in China – a deep dive into L'Oréal China

From Meituan to Hema and JD, from Mr Lipstick to Li Ziqi and Luo Tianyi … all of them are Chinese. How does this new retailing impact global players in the Chinese market?

In 2018, L'Oréal China achieved an increase of 33% over the previous year – a record best.[2] In 2019, it set another 15-year record – an increase of more than 35%.[3] At present, 35% of the L'Oréal Group's sales come from China, making it L'Oréal's second largest market after the United States.[4] Considering the rapid development of China's domestic beauty brands in recent years, L'Oréal's performance is outstanding. In 2019, it ranked first in the high-end cosmetics sector in China with a market share of 15.2%, second only to Procter & Gamble, which leads the mass cosmetics sector with a share of 7.5%.[5]

What was behind L'Oréal China's strong performance? In 2018, online sales contributed more than 35% to its sales, up from 25% in 2017. On-line sales represented 11% of L'Oréal's global sales in 2018. Former L'Oréal China CEO, Stephane Rinderknech, said that e-commerce drove L'Oréal China's overall growth in 2018, especially with e-commerce reaching con-sumers in lower-tier cities. "I haven't seen consumption degradation; third and fourth-tier cities are upgrading consumption".[6] Take L'Oréal's high-end beauty brand, Yves Saint Laurent, as an example: 48% of YSL's sales in beauty products comes from cities without physical stores. In other words, a large chunk of sales is completed entirely on its online e-commerce platform.[7]

To get a sense of how L'Oréal achieved this super performance in the Chinese market, let's look at what it did on Singles' Day.

Singles' Day is no doubt the most important shopping festival in China. Dating back to 2009, the grand opening event of the online shopping festival took place against the backdrop of the severe global financial cri-sis that engulfed much of the developed world. China was not exactly immune to the economic challenges of the time. Alibaba, with its modest headquarters in the eastern city of Hangzhou staffed by a dozen people, selected November 11 as the date for the occasion. The number 11.11 sig-nifies single status among young Chinese, and Alibaba had set its sights on this segment of the population. It was a marketing gimmick, and no one could guess how big of a success it would turn out to be. However, by midday many Tmall (Alibaba's B2C e-commerce site) merchants were reporting that they were out of stock. On that first Singles' Day, aggregate sales were RMB52 million (or about US$USD7.5 million), an incredibly large amount compared to previous daily sales of a few thousand yuan, which was for better-known brands on Alibaba's Taobao platform.

When the second Singles' Day rolled around, it had obviously become the most important day of the year for Alibaba. That year's record-breaking sales figure of RMB936 million (US$141 million),[8] was 18 times that of 2009.

For Singles' Day 2019, Alibaba continued to extend its reach into day-to-day Chinese life. The final tally of Tmall's one-day trading volume was 1.29 billion packages and US$38 billion − an increase of 25% over the

US$31 billion recorded in 2018.[9] In 2020, Alibaba extended the one-day shopping festival to 11 days, starting on November 1. The total trading volume of Tmall for the 11 days was 2.25 billion packages and US$75 billion — an increase of 25% compared with the same period of 2019. And the shopping festival is no longer just online purchases on Tmall and Taobao but also on JD, PDD and other platforms.

Singles' Day is a significant event for any brand in China.

On Singles' Day 2019, L'Oréal China continued to defend its title as the number one beauty group on Tmall, with its brands L'Oréal Paris and Lancôme taking the first and second place, respectively, and with both brands achieving over RMB1 billion (US$143 million) sales in just one day.[10] By 2020, L'Oréal had been the number one beauty group on Tmall for four consecutive years. It sent out over 20 million packages. Among the top 15 brands on Tmall On Singles' Day 2020, five belonged to L'Oréal,[11] with Lancôme and L'Oréal Paris each achieving over RMB2 billion (US$299 million) in sales.[12]

Let's look at how L'Oréal China prepared for its 2020 Singles' Day campaign:

- In September, L'Oréal started the warm-up to Singles' Day with an announcement on its **Weibo** account.
- It invited film stars such as Wang Yuan, Deng Lun, Zhu Yilong as **spokespeople**. The spokespeople also shared the announcement on their own Weibo accounts, and it was forwarded over one million times.
- Starting at midnight on October 21, major e-commerce platforms represented by Tmall all launched their Singles' Day pre-sale activities. L'Oréal worked closely with Viya and Li Jiaqi; Viya herself was responsible for over 20% sales of Lancôme (US$66 million) and Viya and Li Jiaqi together were responsible for almost 50% sales of L'Oréal Paris products (US$149 million).[13]
- The offline Singles' Day pop-up store of L'Oréal Maison Gate opened on November 1, 2019, in the Hangzhou West Yintai shopping mall. For 2020 Singles' Day, L'Oréal reopened the Maison Gate so that the offline pop-up stores and L'Oréal's online flagship stores could attract traffic to and from each other.
- From October until Singles' Day, L'Oréal launched promotional activities on platforms including Douyin, Xiaohongshu, Weibo, WeChat,

Toutiao, etc. Many KOLs published content on the various platforms to influence consumers' desire to buy.
- From October 21 up to Singles' Day, L'Oréal invited many celebrities to perform live broadcasts on its Tmall flagship store. They attracted the consumers' attention through various activities such as lucky draws, coupons and other promotional events.

From the Singles' Day campaign, we can see how L'Oréal China used the tricks of new retail to achieve growth in a red-sea (highly competitive) market. It utilised traditional e-commerce platforms, an online and offline integration model, celebrity livestream selling, flagship store self-broadcast selling and social media content marketing. In fact, live broadcast was created and initiated by L'Oreal China in a quite specific way. Li Jiaqi was transformed from a beauty adviser (BA) at a L'Oréal cosmetics counter to an online celebrity, in the "transformation of BA to online celebrities" campaign initiated by L'Oreal China and MeiONE, a Multi-Channel Network (MCN) organisation. You could say that L'Oréal, despite being a foreign company, was a pioneer in the trend of new retailing in China.

In September 2018, L'Oréal China and Tmall's New Product Innovation Centre reached a strategic cooperation agreement. Both parties agreed to co-create products based on big data provided by Alibaba. "Revitalift Filler", launched in 2019, was the first C2B product created by this collaboration.

## What does this mean for global players around the world?

New retail in China is relevant to global players, even if their business is not in China. Looking at its development, China's new retail offers interesting lessons that have general applications.

### Lesson 1: go beyond the customer pains

Each stage of the new retail phenomenon in China started with identifying customer pain points. Those companies that survive tough competitions find solutions to pain points. The logic is not new. Western companies have looked for pain points for many years. What is different is that these new retail companies ask a second critical question after the "pain" question – that is, the customer's willingness and ability to pay. Everyone wants an iPhone, but the majority of Chinese can't afford it. The Western customer-centric model is built on the logic that we find the pain, we create a solution and then build a business model to extract value. The Chinese logic is that we start with the pain, we find a solution, we ask what the customer can afford, and we build a business model that works within the parameters of the size of their willingness to pay. But with this Chinese logic, how can firms hope to make a profit? Initially, they do not. They bet that once they have enough customer traffic, they can make money by expanding their products and services. Taobao and JD took this path. Meituan, Hema and PDD all followed. The "number one sister of livestreaming" – Viya – clearly understands the importance of her fans' willingness to pay.

Even if they overcome this first obstacle – the size of the customer's wallet – the successful Chinese retailers go to great lengths to remove any physical or emotional barriers and to make an online purchase (impulsive or not) painless to execute. They achieve this through optimal productisation. Here, productisation is not about physical product offerings and delivery, it is to productise the whole consumer experience from research, searching, pushing the right product based on their preferences and shopping behaviour, interaction with the app, trust building, payment, delivery and after-sales services. The optimal productisation removes any physical inconvenience that prevents potential customers from completing an order. The effortlessness translates into psychological confidence in placing an order online. All the components of optimal productisation eventually come together as super-apps (Meituan, PDD, WeChat, Alipay).

## Lesson 2: go beyond the boundary of shopping

Traditional retail is about an exchange of money and goods. In the pre-new retail era, customers went to JD or Taobao because they needed to buy something. Today, when the young people in the third or fourth-tier cities watch Viya's livestream on their phone, they don't have specific products in mind, but they certainly don't want to miss out on a good deal. When they check in to the PDD app (several times each day), it is not that they have a specific shopping agenda. They log on to play the minigames that help them accumulate credits to exchange for actual goods. When they watch short videos on Douyin or TikTok, they are not thinking about shopping.

But, when they see something interesting on Douyin, they don't hesitate to click the link to buy it. It is hard to distinguish shopping from entertainment. Shopping is part of the entertainment.

New retail is about relationships and trust. In traditional retail, we trust brands. In new retail, we rely on our trust in friends. PDD accumulated over 700 million active users in five years because it used the power of acquaintance relationships on WeChat. The staying power of internet celebrities rests on the trust of their fans, who believe they have worked really hard to negotiate the best deal and provide the best service. They are as good as the last deal they brought to the table.

New retail is about co-creation. Especially for Gen Z, who are confident with self-expression and not satisfied with the limitations of one-way communication. They don't want to be just passive receivers; they need to participate in co-creating the offerings. Luo Tianyi, for example: everything about her is created by her fans, who project their desires and wants onto an elusive, composite persona. Yes, we are happy to pay for something we help to create. It is no longer what the product can do for me, but what I do with this product.

### Lesson 3: go beyond the successful business models of Apple and Amazon

When talking about successful business models we think of Apple, who wins by its product, and Amazon, who wins by scale. It is great to learn from and emulate Apple and Amazon, but not every company can be an Apple or an Amazon. There are many more digital business models available, beyond these two. Let's look at five other winning business models.

- Meituan wins by building a super-app that includes almost all lifestyle services.
- Hema wins the fresh-food segment by combining online, offline and logistics. Within this segment, there are different retail formats serving different communities.
- PDD wins by utilising social networks to expand its customer base and link customers to manufacturers.
- Viya and Li Jiaqi win by establishing personal trust and offering the best value.
- Li Ziqi wins by fulfilling people's dreams of their inner Shangri-la.

In today's world, it is not one-size-fits-all. For any company that wants to win over the Chinese market, it is important to consider the portfolio of channels and business models.

## Lesson 4: go beyond inhouse experimentation

Let's see how L'Oréal used China as test bed for a new product. They re-cruited around 1,000 female consumers in the 18–35 age bracket who had purchased facial creams on Tmall or Taobao within the previous year. These consumers were from first to fifth-tier cities. L'Oréal collected their ideas for "ideal facial creams". The final product was a cream based on the needs of staying up late, called "Revitalift Filler"; in Chinese it is "12am cream". It took only 59 days from consumer research to product launch. If they had followed the normal corporate innovation process, it would have taken between one and two years.[14] More than 100,000 Revitalift Fillers were sold on the first day of its launch.

You might remember, in Chapter 1, we gave you the example of how Nestlé collaborated with the Tmall Innovation Centre to produce its first fruit-flavoured Nescafé. This was quite different from the traditional way most MNCs go about innovation, where they develop and perfect new of-ferings inhouse before launching.

Today, the new retail landscape in China shortens the distance between brands and customers. Whether it is L'Oréal launching Revitalift Fillers in 59 days or Nescafé launching three flavoured teas in four months, China offers the opportunity of low-cost and fast experimentation. While the formal, inhouse, rigorous research-based innovation and experimentation have its place and merits, there is an alternative of imperfect, quick, learn-as-you-go experimentation that most Chinese companies' practice.

## Lesson 5: go beyond the front end of retail

On the surface, these new retail models are innovating on the front end; they look like new digital channels to reach a broad base of consumers. In essence, what supports the change in the front end is huge change in the back end: the supply chain.

There would be no Meituan without the hundreds of thousands of de-livery riders equipped with smart-route algorithms; no Hema if they hadn't built the fresh-food supply chain; no PDD if they hadn't created a link to the small factories or farmers who needed a channel to sell their excess capacities; no celebrity selling if there was no agile supply chain that the cycle from design to the market is measured in days. The new retail really goes far beyond the digital channels; it is about the integration of the full value chain from the factories to the end users. If companies want to participate in new retail, they need to rethink their whole value chain and find the courage and determination to transform their business.

### *Lesson 6: go beyond B2C*

If going beyond the front end of retail is to integrate the value chain from the front end to the back end, then to go beyond B2C is to blend B2C with C2B. We are familiar with B2C, C2C and B2B. Amazon, Tmall and JD are typical B2C businesses; Taobao and eBay are C2C businesses; and Alibaba is a B2B business. These three models have been co-existing since the very early stage of e-commerce and now, C2B has finally appeared. The core characteristic of C2B is that it is user driven. Alibaba has already started C2B practices. In 2014, Tmall's electronics channel announced the contracting of 12 production lines of ten well-known brands such as Midea, Joy-oung, Supor and Airmate. The products include kitchen appliances, vacuum cleaners, electric fans and other major categories. The analysis of the data collected from Tmall guides the research and development, design, production and pricing of these products. For example, consumer feedback on Midea's rice cooker said that it got dirty easily, so Tmall's production line improved it to an all-steel design, which not only looks tough, but is also more durable and hygienic. People liked the "luxury golden colour" of the Joyoung Soymilk machine, so the production line retained the colour and, at the same time, added a filter-free speed-grinding function that saves users time and effort. The product was positioned to target mainstream, online "lazy people" aged 25–35.

In 2018, PDD launched the "New Brand Plan", which designed to support 1,000 factory brands in various industries. In the New Brand Plan, the support that PDD provides to the manufacturers includes not only more consumer traffic but, more importantly, extracting demand information through big data on the PDD platform, and using this big data to give suggestions and directions on research and development and production design.

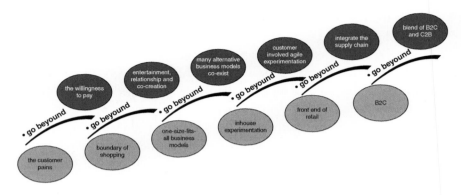

Figure 12.4 "Beyond" value chain model.

The above six lessons form the basis of the **"Beyond" value chain model.** It offers a new way of looking at your customers, your offerings, your business model, your innovation, your supply chain and your ecosystem. It is not about business as usual. What made your company successful in the past may not work in the future. The future is about transformation of the "beyond" (Figure 12.4).

## Prepare for the future: what are the important trends

**The "sinking market" has huge growth prospects.** The sinking market is a unique Chinese expression for reaching the lowest tier segment (it could refer to the mass market or the bottom of the pyramid). This Chinese concept is about sinking down, moving down and reaching down. The expression emerged from PDD and Kuaishou successfully reaching the third and below-tier cities and the vast rural areas. The typical characteristics of consumers in the sinking market are that they are not well educated, have low income and have more free time. After 20 years' development of e-commerce, the competition for the users in the first and second tiers has been fierce, and penetration has been saturated. At the same time there are more than one billion people living in third and below-tier cities who are untapped. No new retail player in China can afford to miss the sheer size of the sinking market.

**The competition for the Chinese market is becoming more intense.** In today's rapidly changing global environment and American Chinese relationship, the pace of globalisation may be hindered. One sign is that TikTok might be kicked out of the United States – and it is already banned in India. With ByteDance's global expansion stopped cold in two of its most important markets, it may refocus its resources on its home market. ByteDance's rapid growth has already challenged Alibaba and Tencent and its refocus on China may be bad news for them. This is not only about ByteDance, though. The delink between the United States and China could make Chinese firms even more determined to find new sources of growth at home.

**The rise and fast growth of local brands.** The winner of the Tmall Golden Makeup Award for 2019 was the "Perfect Diary", a new Chinese cosmetics brand that was just two years old, which beat established brands L'Oréal and Estee Lauder into second and third place. Ten years ago, many Chinese brands made an effort to look like they were a foreign product in order to attract local customers. Now things have changed, and more and more brands are moulding themselves in Chinese traditions and styles. In 2019, one of the most popular shoes, by Chinese shoe company Li-Ning, was the "Wu Dao" (悟道), which was launched at New York Fashion Week. The concept of Wu Dao is deeply rooted in Chinese Daoism. Besides these examples, new retail platforms such as PDD have begun to collaborate with local manufacturers to improve the "made in China" mark.

**More craftsmen like Li Ziqi will emerge.** The rise of social media platforms such as Weibo and Xiaohongshu, and the rise of short video platforms such as Douyin and Kuiashou, provides opportunities for artisans like Li Ziqi. Grandpa Amu, a 63-year-old carpenter, became famous via Toutiao and Xigua Video. His popularity is starting to gain traction on YouTube. He has been dubbed a "21st century Lu Ban" – a legendary wood handyman (considered a bit of a magician) in ancient China, who today is regarded as the god of builders. Grandpa Anu employs an ancient Chinese mortise and tenon technique to create structures and craft furniture: no nails or glue are used in the entire process. There are many talents living among us yet to be discovered. There will be more Li Ziqi's in the future.

**Food security becomes more and more important**. The outbreak of Covid-19 in 2020 has attracted unparalleled attention to food safety in China. The whole country has strengthened the traceability management of food. Food safety issues have been around in China for a long time. Before the Covid epidemic, there were episodes of avian influenza, aftosa and other livestock and poultry diseases, as well as food poisoning caused by pesticide residues. Nowadays, the maturity of IOT technology makes a food traceability system possible and one was launched in June 2020: Ali Health's "Mashangfangxin 码上放心". Using technologies such as IoT and cloud computing, it marks fresh food with a unique "ID card" (barcodes or QR codes).

**Surplus food stores will be one of the fastest-growing businesses in the next decade.** Surplus food stores sell goods that are nearing their "best before" date. The goods are still edible and safe to consume but regular supermarkets are not willing to risk storing them so close to their expiration date. The price advantage of surplus food stores is obvious. In a discount store that sells imported goods in Beijing, customers can buy two boxes of imported mineral water, priced at RMB169 (US$25) per box in regular stores, for just RMB99 (US$15). In recent years, although bricks-and-mortar retail stores have been experiencing stagnation, surplus food stores have become popular not only in China but also worldwide. In 2016, Dollar General, a discount community supermarket chain in the United States, acquired 41 community supermarkets from Walmart.[15] In China, physical surplus food stores are popping up like mushrooms. In parallel, many mobile apps and Taobao online stores also sell surplus goods. Interestingly, customers who shop at surplus food stores are not just the older generations wanting to save money, there are also young customers looking for branded surplus goods, especially foreign brands. They view surplus stores as a new way of reducing food waste and contributing to a low-carbon and environmentally friendly society. It was estimated that food wastage in circulation in China is as much as tens of billions of US dollars a year. Surplus stores will be another new retailing venue for branded manufacturers to consider when facing an overstock of the goods near to their expiration date.

**New retail is smart retail.** Big data, machine learning, and sophisticated algorithms are playing a critical role in the new retail. The killer algorithms that push "relevant" news and short videos to unsuspected users are largely responsible for the success of Toutiao, PDD, Douyin and Kuaishou. Recommendation algorithms help people make better decisions minimising the searching time. With more data and more understanding of user preferences, more accurate recommendations can be employed in turn, to create more stickiness.

**Autonomous delivery to support various models of new retail.** The Covid-19 pandemic in early 2020 has accelerated the development of autonomous delivery. During the epidemic, autonomous delivery vehicles, drones and robots became solutions for contactless delivery, providing services in Beijing, Wuhan, Changsha, Sichuan and other cities. When a driverless vehicle sets out to make a delivery, a message is sent to the consignee. When the vehicle arrives at the delivery location, the consignee receives a voice call or a text message. All they need to do is enter the order number on the vehicle screen and the corresponding container door will open. Once the consignee has closed the door, the vehicle leaves and continues to its next stop. Alibaba, JD, SF express and Meituan are all deploying autonomous delivery vehicles to solve the "last-mile" delivery issue. Autonomous delivery vehicles have a much larger capacity and can deliver more orders in one go. They will also do a better job in keeping food fresh and warm. It is expected in the next three to five years, autonomous delivery will become widely used.

Many of these new retail models have sprung up on Chinese soil and could not have developed without China's unique conditions and culture. If the application of a model is thus limited, is it still worth studying? When your company has a business in China and when the revenue from China is significant, the answer is an affirmative yes. What if your company has no business in China? We still believe the answer is yes. We think China is leading the pack in the practice of new retail. The evolution of new retail and the multi-levels and complexity of the Chinese consumer market are relevant to its development in other parts of the world.

## Notes

1   https://v.qq.com/x/page/00799iae4n8.html.
2   http://www.360doc.com/content/19/0714/09/55092353_848589102. shtml.
3   http://finance.ifeng.com/c/7ubV7aoplYj.
4   http://www.chinairn.com/hyzx/20190713/100414260.shtml.
5   https://zhuanlan.zhihu.com/p/150490724?from_voters_page=true.
6   https://www.sohu.com/a/297678193_260616.
7   https://www.sohu.com/a/297678193_260616.
8   http://www.100ec.cn/detail--6071538.html.

9   https://baijiahao.baidu.com/s?id=168311930967083689&wfr=spider&-
    for=pc.
10  https://dy.163.com/article/FR8LTN5J0518L346.html.
11  https://dy.163.com/article/FRA8FME205373KVM.html.
12  https://dy.163.com/article/FR8LTN5J0518L346.html.
13  https://dy.163.com/article/FR8LTN5J0518L346.html.
14  http://www.pinguan.com/article/content/17355.
15  https://mp.weixin.qq.com/s/EK2CynZ-Vl3MSiWmNyGAXw.

# INDEX

Locators in **bold** refer to tables and those in *italics* to figures.